Decolonizing the Republic

Ruth Simms Hamilton
AFRICAN DIASPORA SERIES

The Ruth Simms Hamilton African Diaspora series at Michigan State University Press presents the past and contemporary experiences of African people throughout the world, written by emerging and established scholars in various fields in the social sciences and humanities in pursuit of a reconceptualization of the historical global movements of African peoples. This series pays tribute to the life and legacy of Dr. Ruth Simms Hamilton, a pioneer in African Diaspora Studies, and builds on her seminal work and conceptualization of the African diaspora.

The series editors are particularly interested in innovative book length manuscripts grounded in scholarly research and inquiry that challenge both pre-existing and established notions of the African diaspora by engaging new regions, conceptualizations, and articulations of diaspora that move the field forward. In underscoring new frontiers and frameworks in the study of African descendants' lived experiences, the series presents new approaches to the production of knowledge on African diasporas. In keeping with the tradition of the field, the series is an interdisciplinary undertaking devoted to scholarship on the histories, political movements, institutions, cultures, intellectual discourse, ways of knowing, and identities of African and African descended peoples. Since the diaspora is based largely on movement, the transnational migrations of Africans throughout history and in contemporary times have complicated what it means to be black and or African depending on the political, economic, religious, geographical, and cultural context Africans find themselves. As a result, scholars are forced to confront the evolving realities and constructions of blackness and Africanness in a changing world. While much of the scholarship in the diaspora continues to focus on the Americas due to the enduring legacy of the middle passage and trans-Atlantic slave trade, in addition to these areas the editors encourage manuscript submissions that bring greater visibility to less studied but nonetheless critical areas of the Africana world. This includes internal diasporas within the African continent and African diasporas of the Indian Ocean, Pacific and European regions.

The series highlights the global experiences and dynamic dimensions of peoples of African descent. It maps their historical and contemporary movements, speaks from their radical (unique) narratives and explores their critical relationships with one another. By exploring Afrodescendents within their particular and broader sociocultural, historical, political, and economic contexts, it contemplates similarities, difference, continuity and transformation.

CO-EDITORS
Glenn Chambers, *Michigan State University*
Quito Swan, *Howard University*

EDITORIAL BOARD
Afua Cooper, *Dalhousie University*
Gerald Horne, *University of Houston*
Franklin W. Knight, *Johns Hopkins University*
Besi Muhonja, *James Madison University*
Cheikh Thiam, *The Ohio State University*
Robert Trent Vinson, *The College of William and Mary*

Decolonizing the Republic

AFRICAN AND CARIBBEAN MIGRANTS IN POSTWAR PARIS, 1946–1974

Félix F. Germain

Michigan State University Press • *East Lansing*

Copyright © 2016 by Félix F. Germain

♾ The paper used in this publication meets the minimum requirements of
ANSI/NISO Z39.48-1992 (R 1997) (Permanence of Paper).

Michigan State University Press
East Lansing, Michigan 48823-5245

Printed and bound in the United States of America.

22 21 20 19 18 17 16   1 2 3 4 5 6 7 8 9 10

LIBRARY OF CONGRESS CATALOGING-IN-PUBLICATION DATA
Germain, Félix F., author.
Decolonizing the republic : African and Caribbean migrants in postwar Paris (1946-1974)
/ Félix F. Germain.
pages cm—(Ruth Simms Hamilton African diaspora series)
ISBN 978-1-61186-204-1 (pbk. : alk. paper)—ISBN 978-1-60917-489-7 (pdf)—
ISBN 978-1-62895-263-6 (epub)—ISBN 978-1-62896-263-5 (kindle) 1. Africans—France—
Paris. 2. West Indians—France—Paris. 3. Paris (France)—Emigration and immigration—
History—20th century. 4. Paris (France)—Ethnic relations—History—20th century.
5. Immigrants—France—Paris—History—20th century. I. Title. II. Series: Ruth Simms
Hamilton African diaspora series.
DC718.A34G47 2016
944.36108996—dc23
2015033652

Book design by Charlie Sharp, Sharp Des!gns, Lansing, Michigan
Cover design by Erin Kirk New
Cover image is of the funeral of African workers who died at Aubervilliers, 1970.
Photo by E. Lamy, agence de diffusion nouvelle photographique, used with permission of
Archives CFDT (Confederation Française Democratique Du Travail), 6E/1970/8439.

Michigan State University Press is a member of the Green Press Initiative and is
committed to developing and encouraging ecologically responsible publishing
practices. For more information about the Green Press Initiative and the use of
recycled paper in book publishing, please visit *www.greenpressinitiative.org*.

Visit Michigan State University Press at *www.msupress.org*

To my mother and father
To Ama, Felix, and Fernando

Contents

FOREWORD, *Patrick Manning* ix
PREFACE xi
INTRODUCTION xv

CHAPTER ONE. Black Internationalism and Student Activism in Paris
    of the Fifties.. 1
CHAPTER TWO. African Migration to Paris of the Sixties 21
CHAPTER THREE. French Documentaries and the Representation
    of African Experiences 41
CHAPTER FOUR. Work, Housing, Colonial Relations, and the Formation
    of Oppositional Identities among Working-Class African Workers 57
CHAPTER FIVE. Caribbean Women in Postwar France, 1946–1974 75
CHAPTER SIX. Henri Salvador's Music and Working-Class Caribbean
    Males in Paris of the Sixties 93
CHAPTER SEVEN. French Labor Unions, Black Community and Political
    Activism, and Decolonization in Postcolonial Paris, 1960–1974 117
CHAPTER EIGHT. May '68 in Black 141
CHAPTER NINE. Music, Le Pen, and "New" Black Activism in Contemporary
    France, 1974–2005 159
CONCLUSION 177

NOTES... 181
BIBLIOGRAPHY 213
INDEX 229

Foreword

Patrick Manning

Félix Germain's history of Caribbean and African workers in Paris addresses one of the most important questions in historical studies today—to what extent did common people challenge colonialism and cut back racial discrimination? As he shows, black Parisians—in their daily labors, weekend celebrations, and periodic protests—opened the way to "decolonizing the Republic," advancing the respect for their rights as citizens.

Postwar Paris, liberated from Nazi occupation, became the home of steadily growing numbers of settlers from the Caribbean territories and from West Africa. The students were first, attending lycées and then universities; workers came later to labor in the automobile factories of Renault and as domestics. Previously, Africans and Caribbeans had each lived as subjects of the French Empire. Then their legal status changed: the Caribbeans became formal French citizens beginning in 1946; the Africans were colonial subjects before 1960 and foreign nationals from 1960 as their lands became independent. The Caribbeans were brought to France by the government migration agency, BUMIDOM; the Africans, arriving on their own, often found housing in government-owned *foyers*.

They were well established in France by the time of the great student-worker uprising of May 1968. They joined the national uprising, especially the Caribbean settlers, who occupied BUMIDOM during May and June, forcing it to recognize the skills and aspirations of those moving from Guadeloupe, Martinique, and Guyane to France. Gradually, Paris became cosmopolitan in a new way: as a center of global black culture.

Foreword

Still, discrimination did not disappear, and in 2005 young urbanites, born in France or Africa, rose up in protest against the police surveillance under which they lived in overcrowded public housing. Yet by then, the black population of France had grown to nearly four million, proud at once of their national and racial identity. This book presents fascinating individual stories and an overall narrative of this important transformation in France.

Preface

In the late forties, Alioune Diop, a Senegalese intellectual, founded *Présence Africaine*, Europe's first black-owned publishing house and academic journal. With *Présence Africaine*, he offered black intellectuals a much-needed forum to publish their political essays and poems. In 1956, he also organized the First Congress of Black Writers and Artists, an international conference that brought famous writers from the Americas, France, and Africa to Paris, where they debated about black cultures and the sociopolitical conditions of people of African descent throughout the globe. In the process, Diop revived the black internationalist tradition of the interwar period, which had been disrupted by the carnage of World War II. Simultaneously, using the pen and student organizations as weapons, just like their counterparts of the interwar period, Caribbean and African students transformed the beautiful and romantic City of Light into an anticolonial battleground.

Ultimately, this thriving black internationalism and student activism subsided. The transition from French colonies to sovereign sub-Saharan African nation-states; departmentalization in Martinique, Guadeloupe, and French Guiana; and the civil rights movement in the United States quelled black social movements and encouraged many black intellectuals to return to their respective homelands. This unforeseen change, however, did not mean that black France would only exist in the pages of history books on negritude and the Jazz Age of the interwar era. Au contraire! Paris, which had been a hub for black internationalism, became a magnet for Caribbean and African people from the lower classes; black Paris flourished, and the fight for equality

Preface

continued to thrive. But unlike the intellectuals, the vast majority of the migrants would fight for bread-and-butter issues. In the process, their community activism imparted other visions of African and Caribbean identities to many French people.

African and Caribbean community activism emerged during the late fifties' and sixties' labor migration. This was a new genre of black activism in the French Republic, one where Caribbean and African migrants created dozens of community and workers' organizations to address their material needs and provide support to otherwise isolated members of their community. These organizations also served as cultural and psychological sanctuaries, allowing the migrants to cope with their new and sometimes hostile environment. This was especially true for African migrants, who unlike their Caribbean counterparts did not have French citizenship. In hindsight, community activism rooted black identities within the fabric of French society. Equally important, community activism engendered new forms of relations between certain French citizens and African and Caribbean people. By refusing to be treated like colonial subjects and protesting for better living and working conditions, African and Caribbean migrants from the lower classes encouraged certain French individuals to reflect on their conception of Caribbean and African identity, and to some extent, acknowledge the changing characteristics of their own national identity.

Decolonizing the Republic suggests that colonial relations persisted in the postcolonial era. The book paints Caribbean and African labor migrants and political and community activists of the sixties as agents of decolonization. In fact, it aims to center black migrants as the primary agents of social change in black France of the postwar period. Indeed, the scholarship on black France has minimized this important social phenomenon. All too often, the experiences of the lower classes in France are overshadowed by the contributions of black intellectuals, particularly Frantz Fanon and the negritude writers. But we should remember that from a local perspective—Fanon wrote his first book in France and negritude flourished in Paris—these black francophone intellectuals shared a very small audience. From a transnational perspective, however, Fanon and the negritude writers were acclaimed in the Americas, Africa, and Asia; they inspired social movements and generations of intellectuals. Who can deny that during the tumultuous sixties African Americans were more likely to be familiar with Fanon than French people?

Thus, in writing about black France we must question if we have privileged black intellectuals at the expense of humble black migrants and black French people. Is our scholarship biased and full of double standards? Are we, as chapter five illustrates, embracing the works of intellectuals like Fanon while ignoring their inhuman acts and personal shortcomings, which sometimes contradict the very essence of their ideas? By the same token, are we guilty of oversimplifying the achievements of the lower classes, because unlike the intellectuals we accept, in fact, we expect their humanity to be imperfect? Indeed, we are not surprised when black peasants drink rum and hit their wives, and we often presume that prominent black male intellectuals respect their wives and enjoy expensive wine.

I began research for this book more than ten years ago. The John L. Simpson Memorial Research Fellowship in International and Comparative Studies that I received in 2003 from the University of California at Berkeley allowed me to live in France for twelve months. During that time I interviewed participants and explored numerous archives. In 2008, I also received a generous summer research grant from St. John's University that allowed me to continue archival research. Many people have read parts of the manuscript with a critical eye. Faculty members from the department of history at the University of North Carolina at Charlotte, particularly Gregory Mixon, Karen Flint, and Christine Haynes, provided substantive comments on specific chapters. Tyler Stovall, my advisor from graduate school, has been extremely supportive since I started the project. Branda Berrian, Rahsaan Maxwell, and Carol Boyce Davis also offered constructive criticism. Finally, Brett Berliner and Jennifer Boittin's close reading of the manuscript has been priceless. I am deeply grateful for their support.

Introduction

We've arrived and others will come. We must tell what brought us here because besides the truth, there are only lies. Senegal is very far. We did not come here to stay and settle down; we came for work; we'll return home. Some will stay because they are happy here; others may just encounter death . . . if people want to help us, then that's fine. If they don't want to help us, then they should leave us alone. After all, each individual carries his own burden.

—A Senegalese migrant speaks in a French documentary,
Travailleurs Africains (1962)

From 1946 to the mid-seventies, the world's geopolitical landscape changed drastically. Two superpowers surfaced, waging a Cold War that has left indelible marks throughout the five continents. But most importantly, dozens of countries gained their independence from European colonizers. Although these sweeping changes have been well documented, questions about the implications of decolonization still remain unanswered. These questions are not necessarily about the history of decolonization in the former British, Belgian, Portuguese, or French colonies. As recent studies on contemporary France indicate, they also try to address how decolonization affected the colonizing nations.[1] My study is situated within this latest round of research. Specifically, it examines the connections between colonial continuities, resistance, decolonization, and the migration of

Introduction

French Caribbean and sub-Saharan African people to the Parisian region from 1946 to 1974, a period that French historians identify as the *Trente Glorieuses* (the Glorious Thirty) to mark the economic growth and prosperity that France experienced.[2] The study tells another story that unfolded during the Glorious Thirty. By reflecting on African and Caribbean political and community activism and exploring the experiences of black migrants in the housing and labor markets, it sheds light on the formation of the black working class in France, illustrating how seemingly docile individuals played an important role in eradicating certain colonial continuities in the French Republic.[3] Unlike recent collaborative studies that examine the intersection between black identities and the construction of the French nation across time and space, my work focuses on black experiences during a relatively short period to discuss the complexities of a major theme, namely, decolonization in the postcolonial period.[4]

But before analyzing the connections between decolonization and the lived experiences of black labor migrants, allow me to discuss the theory that has helped me substantiate my claims. In other words, how are the concepts of colonization and decolonization deployed in this book about black experiences in postwar France (1946–1974), a period during which the political status of French Caribbean and sub-Saharan African people evolved from colonial subjects to French citizens and citizens of independent nation-states respectively? I believe this is an important question because, after 1960, matters of colonization or decolonization supposedly became paramount to blacks in France.

From a theoretical perspective, the book draws from Ramon Grosfoguel's scholarship on subaltern experiences in the West to investigate the formation of the black working class in France and its connections to decolonization. Grosfoguel utilizes colonialism to refer to the period of "classical colonialism," or more specifically, when European nations administered their colonies across the globe. Simultaneously, he argues that "colonial situations," which he defines as "the cultural, political, economic and sexual oppression/exploitation of subordinate racialized/ethnic groups by dominant ethnic/racial groups with or without the existence of colonial administrations," persist in the present.[5] For him, decolonization did not usher in an era of social equality between the French and their former colonial subjects, and by association this means that struggles for equality, struggles that this book explores, continued after formal decolonization. Indeed, migrants from sub-Saharan Africa and the Caribbean, people who were allegedly seen and treated as inferior colonial subjects, did not merely accept being dominated and oppressed by the French institutions and individuals with whom they interacted. Following a long tradition of resistance, they sought to improve their working and living environment, and to some extent, French perceptions of black identity. Thus, with a particular emphasis on student activism, and especially on Caribbean and African experiences in the labor and housing markets, my book demonstrates how these racialized migrants negotiated what Grosfoguel calls "colonial situations." By bringing these experiences into the light, I invite readers to see these negotiations as an integral part of the decolonization process.

Many anecdotal references to "colonial situations" could anchor this manuscript; however, in the next paragraphs, I have chosen three stories that truly encapsulate the larger story that I tell. The first story is about a Senegalese man who worked in a retirement home; the second revisits the experiences of a Caribbean woman during her first day at work; and the last story focuses on a group of French Caribbean men dining in a Parisian bistro. These experiences, which have fallen under the scholarly radar, illustrate how Caribbean and African subjects negotiated "colonial situations." More importantly, they underscore the connections between black resistance and the decolonization of Franco-Caribbean or Franco-African relations.

In story one, Oumar Dia, a migrant from Senegal, arrived in Paris in 1970, searching for work.[6] After a couple of door-knocking months, he found a labor-intensive, low-paying job allowing him to send money back to his village. Mr. Dia's first months in Paris proved very difficult. He experienced isolation; his workload was excruciating. But for Mr. Dia, a young and energetic man, the hard work was not the toughest challenge. Paradoxically, it was living in the beautiful City of Light that offered the most challenges. He was constantly aware of the French gaze; he often felt intimidated and uncomfortable. When he walked into certain cafés or bakeries, he sensed that his blackness disturbed people. Worse, when he overstayed his visa, he feared being deported back to Senegal. Police officers could check his papers in the metro, and at the drop of a hat, his hope of earning a living in France for a better future in Senegal would vanish.

After a few stressful and isolated months in Paris, he met other Senegalese migrants who invited him to join a Senegalese community organization. This was a turning point in his life. Happy to confront his problems with members of his community, he regularly attended meetings and ultimately started developing a new consciousness about immigrants' rights in France.[7] As someone from rural Africa unfamiliar with the intricacies of labor relations in urban France, he found that the organization played a central role in his life. It was, so to say, his first educational experience in France.

Approximately three years after his arrival in Paris, Mr. Dia legalized his residential status. It allowed him to find a position as *homme de service* (an attendant) in a retirement home, where he was responsible for preparing food and cleaning the residents' rooms. Yet, he was not satisfied. He was longing for better living and working conditions. But most importantly, he was homesick. Although he was physically in

France, his mind and "spirit" had remained in his beloved Senegal. Like many of his contemporaries hoping to return home, ambitious and idealistic, Mr. Dia decided to learn a trade that he could use in Senegal. For practical and obvious reasons, he chose the medical field.

He relentlessly pursued a nurse's aide diploma while working full-time at the retirement home.[8] For him, it was an exciting and intellectually stimulating adventure. Not only did he appreciate studying, but he also understood that attending school in France was an opportunity that very few Senegalese people from his area, much less from his village, enjoyed. However, attending school while working offered new challenges. Despite his enthusiasm and ambition, his colleagues still refused to relinquish their colonial notions of African identity. They doubted Mr. Dia's ability to learn; they ridiculed him, calling him "a stubborn, rude, bad-mannered, or disgusting child."[9] But Mr. Dia remained strong. With a large dose of self-confidence, he usually brushed off his colleagues' derogatory comments, replying religiously, "I don't really care about what you say because I know who I am."[10] Only after he had spent three years at the retirement home did his colleagues finally change their behavior. By keeping his *sang-froid* (cool), contesting the demeaning comments, and displaying a strong work ethic, Mr. Dia had successfully decolonized social relations at his job. Indeed, who, after observing the man work and interacting with him, could dare call him a stubborn, rude, bad-mannered, or disgusting child?

In story two, Jacqueline Ansel, a woman from the small town of Carbet, Martinique, arrived in Paris in 1967. In those days she clearly figured in the French colonial imaginary; she incarnated difference. Her identity was "island-bound," apparently incompatible with urban France and modernity. Like her "sisters" from the French Caribbean, she embodied the exotic other or a nonintellectual, hypersexual individual. But in truth, Mrs. Ansel was a highly motivated young woman. She was one of the few French Caribbean women who had received her high school degree prior to migrating to France; she was more educated than the average French woman. So, naturally, when she arrived in Paris she looked tirelessly for administrative positions. Yet despite her credentials, French employers kept on offering her janitorial positions. Only after a few months of door-knocking did she finally land a job as a payroll clerk in a mutual fund. Her workplace, however, became a site of colonial encounters and negotiations. It became a site where Mrs. Ansel encouraged her French colleagues to treat her with dignity and reconceptualize their understanding of French Caribbean identity.

Mrs. Ansel's struggle began the first day she went to work. That day, she walked into a noisy room where about twenty French employees performed various tasks. But to her surprise, all the employees became very quiet, staring at her indiscreetly, as if she did not belong there. No one came to introduce him/herself, a customary practice in France. So she broke the silence, loudly introducing herself: "Bonjour! I am from Martinique, I have a high school degree, and I'm here to work!" With much discomfort, one after the other, her colleagues uttered their names.[11] Her audacity and courage reflect the experiences of many young Caribbean and African men and women, people who battled to obtain positions matching their skill sets and encouraged French people doubting their professional integrity to accept them as equal human beings and colleagues. These seemingly irrelevant or mundane interactions were truly "colonial situations" during which Caribbean and African subjects altered patterns of social relations established in the colonial period.

The last story illustrating this "invisible struggle" to decolonize French society and mentality is about a group of French Caribbean men attempting to enjoy their meals at Parisian bistros. In the early sixties, Caribbean migrants had problems eating in some of these venues because a few managers refused to serve the African migrants who had recently surfaced in their neighborhoods. Lumping all blacks together in the same bag, they also turned away French citizens from Martinique, Guadeloupe, and French Guiana. It took the collaboration of a group of Caribbean activists with the Mouvement Contre le Racisme et pour l'Amitié entre les Peuples (MRAP), a civil rights organization, to bring this anachronistic practice into the public eye. Georges Lassare Michalon, a political and community activist who served as president of a Caribbean student organization in the 1950s, remembers how they tackled this issue:

> We knew that certain places refused to serve black people and we wanted to expose this problem. Our strategy was simple. We located the business, usually a café or bistro, and during lunch or dinner three or four of us would try to get a table. Then we waited to be served. If they refused to serve us, we walked away. But the owner did not know that we had asked a member of the MRAP[12]—a white man—to sit at another table and observe our interaction with the staff. He witnessed everything and exposed it to the public. This is how we stopped this problem.[13]

Blame it on amnesia or government officials who never addressed or publicized such problems, this battle to end "colonial situations" in Parisian bistros has fallen through the cracks of French history. As illustrated by police reports, the French painted this accomplishment as a trivial incident. Referring to this historical fight to end discrimination in restaurants, bistros, and cafés, the Parisian police claimed, "The few aggressions against blacks, which occurred throughout the Parisian region, were isolated incidents, the doings of a minority that remains fundamentally racist. The manager of a café-brasserie next to the Gare de Lyon who refused to serve five Martinicans because of the color of their skin exemplifies those rare cases."[14] In hindsight, these instances of aggression and discrimination were not isolated incidents. They occurred frequently and in different forms. Arguably, physical aggression against blacks still persists in the twenty-first century, but thanks to the intervention of Caribbean activists, restaurant discrimination has officially disappeared from the Parisian landscape. Indeed, it is safe to credit Mr. Michalon and his fellow French Caribbean activists with helping abolish this colonial practice.

The above struggle to eradicate colonial relations between the French and people from the former colonies was certainly not new. In previous decades, to use Jennifer Boittin's expression, Paris had been "a colonial metropolis" where people of African descent experienced various forms of marginalization.[15] Boittin contends that this very suffocating colonial climate brewed resistance within the African diaspora in Paris. As they developed a new appreciation for black cultures, during the interwar period, black intellectuals criticized the French tradition of republican universalism and began a quest to reconfigure the political relationship between France and her "black colonies." Thus, building on her scholarship, my book suggests that Paris continued to be a colonial metropolis after the independence of the sub-Saharan African French colonies in 1960 and the departmentalization of Martinique, Guadeloupe, and French Guiana in 1946. But unlike any other books on the African diaspora in France, it illustrates how black community activism and encounters between French people and African and Caribbean migrants from the lower classes[16] changed the colonial climate still reigning over the city.

The book has two goals. First, it explores the connections between the experiences of humble African and Caribbean migrants in the labor and housing markets and certain French people and institutions, suggesting that the former actually encouraged the latter to reform their beliefs and behaviors. Indeed, I had initially begun this project to merely historicize the formation of the African diaspora in postwar Paris and map the ways in which black activism contradicted the very essence of the French Republic—the notion that liberty, equality, and fraternity applies to everyone in France. But my training in French history and African diaspora studies invited me to expand the scope of the research. More precisely, pondering the ways in which African American social movements, music, and arts have shaped the contours of American society encouraged me to reflect on how sub-Saharan African and Caribbean labor migrants from the lower classes also influenced French society. By listening to black migrants' testimonies and reexamining the historical record, I concluded that humble African and Caribbean people have been more influential than given credit for. I effectively reached the same conclusion as French philosopher Michel Foucault, who reminds us that "The exercise of power is not simply a relationship between partners, individual or collective; it is a way in which certain actions modify others."[17] In other words, I realized that black migrants from the lower classes were playing an important role in eradicating the colonial relations between them and the French that persisted in the postcolonial era.

In many ways, the book begins to put into words the story that Frantz Fanon (1925-1961), the Martinican psychiatrist who analyzed how French people, institutions, and culture brutalized colonized peoples, did not live to tell. In other words, it outlines the ways in which people of African descent in France encouraged many white French individuals to reconceptualize their notions of Caribbean and African identity and therefore reevaluate how ethnocentrism and cultural racism—the pillars of French colonialism—were still playing a prominent role in their lives. In focusing on the intersection between migration and activism in the Caribbean and sub-Saharan African migrant communities of the sixties and early seventies, it becomes obvious that the reconfiguration of colonial relations—or better yet, the decolonization of social relations between the French, and French Caribbean and sub-Saharan African migrants—is not the byproduct of French intellectuals or government policies. Indeed, while the French government supported the transition of Martinique, Guadeloupe, and French Guiana from colonies to the Overseas French Departments, and the transition of the sub-Saharan African colonies to sovereign nation-states, it never pronounced anything against the discourse that had justified colonization. As a result, in the French imaginary, African and Caribbean individuals still embodied the colonial other, and many French individuals still treated African and Caribbean migrants as lazy, passive, or uneducated individuals only capable of performing menial tasks or sexual acts.[18]

Thus, in France of the sixties and early seventies, the decolonization of social relations—in other words, the process by which white French individuals reconceptualized their colonial notions of black identities—stemmed from below. Arguably, negritude intellectuals had already begun this process.[19] But even if black intellectuals of the negritude movement had been preaching the gospel of decolonization, they only reached Caribbean, African, Afro-South American, and African American audiences. French audiences remained far from their realm of influence; great thinkers like Aimé Césaire, Léopold Senghor, Léon Damas, Jean-Paul Sartre, and Frantz Fanon could not have eradicated "colonial situations" in mainland France because few French people of the interwar and postwar period had ever read their writings.[20] While black students and professionals respected the works of black intellectuals, French intellectuals, the potential conduit between French citizens and black intellectuals, rarely cited Caribbean and African authors. Only Jean-Paul Sartre left strong evidence of collaboration with African and Caribbean authors. Michel Foucault, Jacques Lacan, Jacques Derrida, and Pierre Bourdieu, the French intellectuals who gained notoriety

Introduction

during the postwar era, developed hardly any connections with their counterparts from the South.

How, then, did French citizens unlearn to treat sub-Saharan African and Caribbean people like colonial subjects when they ignored the labor of black intellectuals and could rarely find unbiased information about people of African descent in the writings of most French intellectuals? Could it be that the sixties generation, which had not experienced colonialism and had developed "Third-Worldist" sensitivities, suddenly perceived and related to blacks in a much more equitable manner than previous generations? Was there a major state program focusing on educating French citizens about people from the former colonies? Or, did the French change some of their colonial behaviors, such as greeting African and Caribbean people with a "Salut négro" (good day, nigger) as a result of social encounters and negotiations with sub-Saharan African and Caribbean migrants of the postwar period?

In truth, the twentieth century never witnessed the implementation of state-sponsored programs dedicated to helping the French value the cultures and identities of people from the former colonies. Additionally, concerns about the plight of the Third World, which had fueled protests during May '68, quickly faded as French citizens increasingly worried about the impact of the global economic crisis (1973-1974) on their own welfare. Moreover, most French scholars waited well into the nineties to show serious interest in the condition of black people in contemporary France.[21] Hence, it becomes evident that the decolonization of relations between black individuals from the former French colonies and white French people who endorsed colonial notions of black identities resulted from the encounters between these groups throughout the various spheres of French society. It is a process that stemmed from the former colonial subjects' efforts to transcend colonial notions of blackness and secure the basic necessities of life in the French Republic.

In exploring this phenomenon, the book also addresses a second topic, namely, the evolution of Caribbean and African relations since the interwar period. Indeed, despite major differences among black intellectuals, Paris of the interwar period had been a hub for black political activism.[22] African, Caribbean, and African American intellectuals and political activists developed friendships and feuds. They created political organizations and journals. The extent to which black authors of the interwar period influenced each other's work has been particularly well documented in Brent Hayes Edwards's award-winning book *The Practice of Diaspora: Literature, Translation, and the Rise of Black Internationalism*. However, few scholars have examined how black subjects in France cooperated across class, ethnic, and national lines beyond the 1950s.

Hoping to fill this gap, the book builds on the scholarship of Philippe Dewitte and Jennifer Boittin, two scholars who discuss Caribbean and African anticolonial activism and highlight the sociocultural and political fragmentation of the African diaspora in France of the interwar period, to suggest that black Paris of the postwar period remained politically engaged yet socially and culturally fragmented along class and national lines.[23] In many ways, the manuscript is indebted to scholars of the African diaspora who study black subjects from different spatial, ethnic, cultural, or national origins simultaneously.[24] Having spent graduate school in the hallways of African Diaspora Studies programs analyzing, among other things, the intersection between identity construction, race, class, marginality, and territoriality, I believe there are benefits to examining African and Caribbean experiences simultaneously.[25]

My study uses a distinctive methodological approach. On the one hand, it is conventional; it relies on archival materials from the National Archives at Fontainebleau; the Bureau pour le Développement des Migrations Intéressant les Départements d'Outre-Mer (BUMIDOM) archives at St. Denis; the Police archives in Paris; the Aumônerie Nationale Antilles Guyane in Paris; the Confédération Française Démocratique du Travail (CFDT) and Confédération Générale du Travail (CGT) in Paris (labor-union archives); and the Bibliothèque de Documentation Internationale Contemporaine at Nanterre. On the other hand, it is nontraditional; it embraces an interdisciplinary framework that foregrounds an intersectional analytical approach that pays close attention to the interplay of colonial relations, racism, class, gender, nationality, and black activism. This aforementioned interdisciplinary approach uses film study and musical analysis, while combining archival evidence with ethnographic data obtained during one year of fieldwork in Paris.

My work is indebted to specialists of the interwar and postwar eras. These scholars, however, have embraced strikingly different methodological approaches. Specialists of the interwar period use the African diaspora as a category of analysis to construct their narrative. They highlight the subjects' efforts to improve black communities throughout the world and emphasize the connections between migration, Pan-Africanism, black internationalism, gender relations, and the heterogeneity of the black political and sociocultural landscape.[26] Specialists of the postwar and postcolonial period, including my study, tend to examine black France through the lenses of sociology of migration, critical race theory/studies, and new imperial/colonial history.[27] However, my study attempts to go a bit further. I use the African diaspora as a category of analysis to better understand the experiences of underprivileged African and Caribbean migrants in postwar France. I draw from scholars like Kim Butler and Robin D. G. Kelley, who carefully explain the relevance of looking at black subjectivities through an "African diasporic" framework. My manuscript is particularly indebted to Kim Butler, who calls for investigating "(1) the reasons for and conditions of the relocation; (2) relationships with the homeland; (3) relationships with hostlands; and

(4) interrelationships within the diasporan group."[28] In following this process, she suggests scholars can better understand the lived experiences of people of African descent across space, time, and origin. But this methodology, I confess, may not fulfill the intellectual expectations of French historians, Caribbeanists, or Africanists because their scholarship is often informed by a distinct body of knowledge. Still, it raises and answers important questions about race relations, ethnic relations, decolonization, and gender relations in postwar France.

In many ways, this manuscript chronicles one of the most important demographic changes in the history of black France. In the period under investigation, France gradually became the European country with the largest black population.[29] Admittedly, up to the mid-fifties only 50,000 blacks, most of whom were professionals and students, lived in France.[30] However, by 1975 the number had soared to a quarter-million people. Three-quarters of the black population lived in the Parisian region alone, making it Europe's largest "chocolate region."[31] Allison Blakely, an expert on black Europe, and a recent study conducted by the *New York Times* confirm that with a population of about 3 to 5 million people, France is now the European nation with the highest number of blacks, surpassing the United Kingdom by nearly 2 million.[32] In fact, it is likely that more black people live in the Parisian region alone than in the entire United Kingdom. Thus, by focusing on the integration of black labor migrants into the fabric of Parisian society and discussing the nature of their sociopolitical activism in the fifties and sixties, the book offers an important contribution to research examining the complex process of African diasporic formation in contemporary France, and for that matter, Europe.

Chapter 1

Black Internationalism and Student Activism in Paris of the Fifties

> What is serious is that "Europe" is morally, spiritually indefensible. And today the indictment is brought against it not by the European masses alone, but on a world scale, by tens and tens of millions of men who, from the depths of slavery, set themselves up as judges.
>
> —Aimé Césaire, *Discourse on Colonialism* (1955)

After World War II, many black students and intellectuals from the former colonies converged on Paris. As the seeds of negritude continued to grow, Aimé Césaire, Léon Damas, and Léopold Senghor became the most popular figures of the black Francophone world. New writers and intellectuals also appeared on the stage. In 1950, Joseph Zobel published *Sugar Cane Alley*, an autobiographical novel that won the Prix des Lecteurs. The following year Frantz Fanon came out with *Black Skin, White Masks*, one of the most influential books of the twentieth century by a black writer. A few years later, Edouard Glissant followed the path of his compatriots, publishing *La Lézarde*, now a classic in Caribbean literature. Not only were black intellectuals prolific, but they also maintained politically active lives. As the above epigraph from Césaire's *Discourse on Colonialism* demonstrates, they had grown more radical, questioning the foundation and integrity of Western societies. The challenge, however, was finding a space to voice criticism and outline new visions of a free and decolonized world. This endeavor proved difficult because few French presses would dare publish anticolonial manifestos such as *Discourse on Colonialism*.[1] In general, French presses still craved exotic literature flattering the French civilizing mission. But thanks to efforts by Alioune Diop, new avenues for publication were opening for prospective writers.

Diop, a devout anticolonialist, built an amazing intellectual infrastructure allowing people from Africa and the African diaspora to express their political views and discuss a variety of social and cultural issues. Living in an era when blacks still figured as Europe's "objects" of study, Diop sought to valorize their humanity by creating a publishing house and a rigorous interdisciplinary journal focusing on the black condition from a black perspective. Moreover, he also organized major international conferences, bringing to Paris the most influential black intellectuals of his era. In many ways, Diop was building on the legacy of his predecessors, who during the interwar period convened literary salons and created similar but short-lived journals.[2]

As Alioune Diop's initiatives reinvigorated the black intellectual landscape, the number of African and Caribbean students in Paris was increasing steadily. This new generation of Caribbean and African students—avid consumers of negritude—often lived in *foyers d'étudiants des colonies* (dormitories for students from the colonies). These dormitories, which were usually divided along national lines—African and Caribbean students lived in different dormitories—also functioned as cultural sanctuaries. Surely, certain African students disliked the paternalism of Frenchmen who managed their foyers, but overall, they felt comfortable and shielded from common displays of ethnocentrism and anti-black racism, which they encountered at school and throughout Paris.

Eventually, the political climate altered the basic function of the foyers for African students. By living in a group setting during these intensely political moments, African students gained a sense of confidence and strength; they transformed these "sanctuaries," supposedly sites of rest and peace, into anticolonial battlefields where they fought for reforming Franco-African political relations or for radical decolonization. These *foyers d'étudiants* became a terrain fertile for protest against French colonization and led to the creation of new student organizations with far-reaching influence.

In hindsight, two different yet connected stories were unfolding simultaneously in Paris of the fifties. On the one hand, Alioune Diop was revitalizing black internationalism; on the other influential African and Caribbean student organizations were flourishing. This phenomenon raises the questions of whether these student organizations were following a Pan-African agenda; if they endorsed decolonization in Africa and the Overseas French Departments; and what sort of relationship they maintained with Caribbean and African intellectuals like Diop.

Alioune Diop and Black Internationalism in Paris of the Fifties

Like many Francophone colonial subjects, in the late thirties Diop had migrated from Senegal to study in Paris. But to his surprise, after the war broke out he found himself stuck in a Nazi-occupied city. This must have been a difficult and dangerous period for him, as many black men, including African American expatriates, were also sent to concentration camps.[3] But Diop remained unharmed. Despite the German occupation and the vanishing of Jewish and black bodies, he remained active in various social circles of foreign students from the former French colonies. There, according to V. Y. Mudimbe, colonial students constantly questioned their relationship with a suffering and diminished France still pretending to be a powerful empire.[4] It is during this period of "French decline" that the idea of founding a quarterly journal germinated in Diop's mind. It was not an entirely new idea. Many black journals had already seen the light of day in Paris.[5] Yet by 1939 they had disappeared, as many Caribbean and African students and prominent intellectuals like Césaire and the Nardal sisters returned to their native lands. In any case, barely two years after the armistice, in 1947, Diop created *Présence Africaine*, the first black interdisciplinary quarterly journal in Europe, which from its inception challenged Eurocentric theories of Africa and its diaspora and pledged to examine black subjectivities from the perspective of black people.

In 1949, Diop, ambitious and politically engaged, developed a full-fledged publishing house. Also named Présence Africaine, his publishing house welcomed authors who were inspired and devoted to studying and writing critically about Africa and its diaspora. This was a major contribution to the black intellectual landscape in France because many "politically conscious" authors had limited publishing opportunities. French publishing houses still preferred authors with a penchant for exoticism, something that black academics, writers, and students had grown to despise.[6] For that reason, black intellectuals fell in love with both the journal and the publishing house. Moreover, with Richard Wright and Aimé Césaire serving as editors, the journal was a magnet for aspiring young intellectuals seeking recognition from these notorious figures.

Présence Africaine's success was immediate, and in many ways, long-lasting. At the turn of the twenty-first century, the publishing house and the journal are still important mouthpieces for authors who are either from the "African world" or interested in writing about "Afro-issues." Likewise, in terms of the quality and quantity of articles, essays, poems, and short stories written by accomplished writers, *Présence Africaine* has very few equals; some of the contributors include legendary figures such as W.

E. B. Dubois, Aimé Césaire, Maryse Condé, Kwame Nkrumah, Melville Herskovits, Basil Davidson, Immanuel Wallerstein, John Henrik Clark, Cheik Anta Diop, George Padmore, and St. Claire Drake. But the question is, what motivated these scholars and writers, who came from different countries and shared different political/ideological perspectives, to contribute to the journal?

Presumably, in the fifties, *Présence Africaine*'s inclusive philosophy, non-ideological alignment, anticolonial position, Pan-African orientation, and commitment to rigorous scholarship acted as a magnet for intellectuals from Africa, the African diaspora, and beyond.[7] In the first issue, Diop outlined his vision for the journal in "Niam n'goura ou les raisons d'être de *Présence Africaine*." He emphasized abstaining from subscribing to any philosophical or political ideology, claiming that the journal aimed to facilitate "the collaboration of all men of good will (white, yellow, or black) capable of helping us to define African originality and to hasten its insertion into the modern world.... [*Présence Africaine*] will publish studies by Africanists on African culture and civilization... [and] examines the ways and means by which to integrate the black man into Western civilization."[8] Thus for Diop, modernity and tradition were mutually inclusive. The need to reclaim and rewrite Africa's silenced history was equally important as "catching up" with the scientific, medical, and technological accomplishments of the Western world. However, throughout the fifties, the colonial situation in Africa prompted *Présence Africaine* to publish anticolonial essays, poems, and articles that allegedly depicted African history and societies with authenticity. Diop's emphasis on inserting Africa within Western modernity took a backseat to "reclaiming history" and the "anti-colonial struggle" mission of the journal.[9] Yet, even though it fell short of reaching its goal, the journal was a major accomplishment in black intellectual history, as it created a space for Afrocentric and politically engaged scholarship while reinvigorating the black internationalism that had flourished in the twenties and thirties.

Jacques Howlett, a French philosopher and close friend of Diop who participated in the numerous meetings he organized to publicize *Présence Africaine*, suggests that Diop cherished black internationalism because he believed that collaboration across cultures and nationality enhanced the living conditions of black people throughout the globe. His appreciation for cross-cultural collaboration was clearly reflected in the journal, as Howlett notes: "[It was] the first time Black Africa was finding expression in a magazine of wide circulation, not only [in] Africa but [throughout] the entire Negro World." According to the French philosopher, by 1949 "Richard Wright, Gwendolyn Brooks, Horace R. Cayton, Peter Abrahams, E. F. Frazier, C. L. R. James, S. W. Allen, Frank Marshall Davis, and Vera Bush had had an opportunity in the periodical to reveal various aspects of the great common phenomenon—the Negro in the world—which white history, alas, considers an insoluble problem."[10] But Diop's contribution to black internationalism, or as the intellectuals of the fifties would commonly say, *le monde noir* (the black world), extended far beyond *Présence Africaine*. Inspired by the negritude writers, Diop wanted to create a space wherein black intellectuals would meet and discuss the cultural aesthetics of blackness and the sociopolitical conditions of people of African descent throughout the world. To implement this Pan-African agenda, or what one may call "applied negritude," Alioune Diop organized the First International Congress of Black Writers and Artists.

Supposedly, it took eighteen months of careful planning to stage this event.[11] The toughest challenge had been finding organizing money. But here again, Diop, ambitious and calculating, found ways to make it happen. He secured a space at the Sorbonne, France's most prestigious institution of higher learning. Evidently a strategic move, Diop realized that hosting the event at the Sorbonne justified its intellectual significance to the global community and offered free advertising.

The congress began on September 19, 1956. For three days, writers and artists from the Caribbean, North America, and Africa presented papers and shared their ideas. Diop had invited established writers like Richard Wright, Aimé Césaire, Léopold Senghor, and Jean Price-Mars, who was to be honored during the congress for his intellectual accomplishments. As an "intellectual entrepreneur" investing in the future, Diop did not shun the younger generation. Hence, he also invited rising stars like Edouard Glissant and George Lamming to present their work.

The congress was truly Diop's intellectual offspring. As Howlett cleverly observes, "[He] invited Negro authors, artists, and intellectuals to revive, rehabilitate, and develop those cultures so as to favor their integration into the general stream of human culture," a move that mirrored his beliefs in the importance of black intellectuals for uplifting both Europe and the '*monde noir*.'"[12] Like Damas, Senghor, the Nardal sisters, and other black Francophone writers, Diop believed the black intellectuals' immersion into the "white world," a world of "reason,"[13] as well as their immersion into the "black world," a world of "feelings" and neglected philosophies, gave them a mission to not only help their brothers and sisters on the margins, but also Europeans still mired in colonial superiority complexes. Indeed, Diop had also organized the conference to allow black intellectuals to address the colonial question, what he considered one of the greatest problems of the time.[14] And surely, anticolonial discourses constantly surfaced in the participants' presentations.

Despite promoting social justice, freedom, and equality, Diop's First International Congress of Black Writers and Artists had a major problem: it had aimed to represent the voice of the oppressed, yet a seemingly patriarchal and elitist cloud loomed large over the event. Even if black women authors like Ann Petry (USA), Dorothy West (USA),

Marie Chauvet (Haiti), Suzanne Césaire (Martinique), and Paulette Nardal (Martinique) had already left a vivid intellectual legacy, no women figured on the invitation card. Moreover, by catering exclusively to accomplished writers, Diop insinuated that other social actors could not map the contours of black culture and contribute to liberating black populations. Ironically, by privileging writers and framing them as catalyzers of social change, Diop demonstrated the extent to which black intellectuals had internalized French values. As Niilo Kaupi demonstrates, spanning from the *ancien régime* (fifteenth to eighteenth centuries) to the postwar era, the French have always portrayed writers as "noble" and gifted individuals who retain the answer to social problems.[15] Furthermore, in addition to the obvious patriarchal and elitist dimension of the congress, it appears that Diop did not solicit the participation of black students. Maryse Condé, the most prolific Caribbean female writer, who migrated from Guadeloupe to Paris in the early fifties to complete her high school degree and attend university, recalls that most black students did not even know that such an important event was occurring only a metro ride away from their dormitories.[16] This was particularly surprising because the students were extremely politically active and constituted the largest group of black people in Paris.

Despite the glaring absence of students and black women, the First International Congress of Black Writers and Artists was successful. Much of the success was the product of Mrs. Diop's labor. Nicol Davidson, the famous Sierra Leonean writer who attended the congress, noted her central role in the event, asserting, "[She] worked quietly and with great effectiveness behind the scene. She performed all the necessary work to secure the success of the international conference, including displaying Présence Africaine's journals and books, taking orders, and making arrangements for translation and publication of manuscripts writers had brought with them."[17] The event was so professional, well-organized, and attended by so many important black intellectuals that even the French press hailed it as an important forum for understanding the complexities of "black culture."[18] But for Diop and the participants, the conference represented much more than an opportunity to discuss black cultures. The colonial question seemed to impose its presence; most of the participants offered papers expressing their opinions on the "colonial" and "race problem," which, as expected, generated reflections, applause, and criticism.

The First International Congress of Black Writers and Artists exceeded expectations. Not only was the event well attended, but the French press also acknowledged its significance for the African diaspora. This success encouraged Diop to organize a sequel in Rome. But to his surprise, the second congress was not as well attended. Many important black intellectuals sent letters apologizing for their absence due to professional responsibilities. Nonetheless, the second congress bore fruit: the arts commission suggested that African governments sponsor a Festival of Black Arts and Culture, an idea that eventually materialized in 1966, in Dakar, Senegal.

Nicol Davidson, who once again attended the festival, was amazed by the music and the sight of youthful black bodies in motion. Like most of the participants, he had been hypnotized by Catherine Dunham's sizzling performances, which illustrated how African cultural expressions had traveled, survived, evolved, and thrived across the Atlantic.[19] Yet as an intellectual and social commentator, Davidson could not refrain from comparing the festival to the previous gatherings in Rome and Paris. Interestingly, he was struck by the number of black professionals, intellectuals, and artists who had moved from Paris to the United States, the Caribbean, or more frequently, the African continent. For Davidson, "The difference between Paris 1956 and Dakar 1966 was striking. Intellectuals had either become Cabinet Ministers or were being jailed by their fellow Africans instead of the British or the French. . . . [They] were by then men and women chastened by national and civic responsibility."[20] Thus, the civil rights movement in the United States, departmentalization in the French Caribbean, and the new independent and sovereign political status that most African countries enjoyed had reconfigured the Black Atlantic. *Au lieu de Paris*, urban America, the French Caribbean, and the former sub-Saharan African colonies became the black intellectuals' and aspiring politicians' center of gravity.

In the fifties, however, Alioune Diop played a critical role in black France. He revived the black internationalism of the interwar period, creating a journal and a publishing house, and inviting many authors to the First International Congress of Black Writers and Artists. Only black students left trails of activism as significant as Diop's. As a general rule, sensing that independence was within their grasp, most of the African students who arrived in France after the war had grown more radical than the older generation of African intellectuals in Paris. In fact, Salah Hassan contends that the students actually radicalized *Présence Africaine*, pushing it to prioritize the struggle against colonialism over any other political issue.[21]

Nevertheless, student activism in black Paris of the fifties was hardly a homogeneous affair. Differences in citizenship and national origin encouraged African and Caribbean students to deploy different kinds of political activism. Although they experienced common challenges in the host country—both groups faced discrimination in the housing and educational sectors—their political interests took them along different paths. Yet, despite a growing sociopolitical cleavage between African and Caribbean students, both groups, in their own ways, were deeply involved in searching for and constructing new identities for their respective homelands.

Chapter One

BLACK STUDENTS' ACTIVISM IN PARIS OF THE FIFTIES

Very few African and Caribbean individuals studied in Paris during the interwar period; only privileged or intellectually gifted people like Senghor and Césaire enjoyed this rare opportunity. However, after World War II, due to increased access to education in the French Caribbean and a growing class of French-educated Africans, thousands of students left their homelands for French universities, usually in the Parisian region. By 1952 between four thousand and six thousand African students and about ten thousand Caribbean students lived in France.[22] Though more numerous than the previous generation, many of these Caribbean and African students felt quite isolated. Paris was different from their societies, which commonly placed a strong emphasis on familial and communal life, so much so that many Caribbean and African writers emphasize this dilemma in their novels.[23] Moreover, in addition to living in a more individualistic urban environment, they often tasted the bitterness of xenophobia and racism. Maryse Condé, the celebrated Guadeloupean author who lived in France during the fifties, illustrates this point when she recalls how French teachers mistreated her and Marguerite Senghor, a classmate from Senegal:

> In 2010, when we talk about racism we forget or we ignore the characteristics of racism in the fifties. When I attended the lycée [high school], Marguerite Senghor and I were the only two black students in the class. People compared us shamelessly, saying Maryse is like that . . . Marguerite is like this. You see, they treated us just like objects; they did not acknowledge our individuality; they often compared us negatively, mocked us, and hardly took what we said seriously. We were strangers to the lycée. Those were very difficult days. Fortunately, there were other black students in Paris and we could meet on weekends to talk about Africa and other things.[24]

Similar to other Caribbean and African students, Condé drew comfort from living in a dormitory for Caribbean students. There, she did not have to deal with anti-black racism and xenophobia. The dormitory was like a sanctuary, a place where she could find common cultural markers and talk about home. Nonetheless, class differences often structured relationships among the residents. For instance, Condé, who comes from a privileged family in Guadeloupe, reminds us that she mostly socialized with other Caribbean students who shared her class affiliation. In hindsight, she admits, "I was a *petite bourgeoise* who only socialized with other *petits bourgeois*. We went to concerts and movies together, but we had no contact with the rest of the Antillean community. So yes, class was a factor that structured social relations."[25] The cleavage along national lines was even deeper. Few Caribbean students interacted with their African counterparts. Yet, because Condé discovered the poetry of negritude writers, she successfully transcended national boundaries and forged relationships with black students from diverse backgrounds, particularly from the African continent. Condé admits:

> I had a different relationship with Africans than most Antilleans. I came to France without any knowledge of Africa, my roots. I wanted to find out more about Africa, especially after reading Césaire's *Notebook of a Return to a Native Land*, since in many ways, he paints us as Africans. However, there were other Antillean bourgeois, who had a deep-seated complex of superiority vis-à-vis Africans. In fact, these bourgeois called themselves "les Grands Nègres." I did not share their sentiments because in Césaire's poem I discovered a beautiful, powerful, and noble Africa. It is only when I went to Africa that I was able to discern between the real Africa and Césaire's mythical Africa.[26]

Thus, like Condé, certain Caribbean students, especially those who had been transformed by "conscious" literature, interacted with other students from the colonies. Many of these students also participated in the Association des Etudiants de la Martinique (Association of Martinican Students—AMS) and the Association Générale des Etudiants Guadeloupéens (General Association of Guadeloupean Students—AGEG), which had been created in the late forties. However, by no means did these Caribbean student organizations sponsor political or cultural events with African student organizations. They merely expressed some interest in African affairs and supported, from a distance, the decolonization of French colonies in both North and sub-Saharan Africa.

In truth, the generation of Caribbean students who migrated to France after the war only developed an interest in African and Caribbean politics toward the mid-fifties. Initially, these students, usually members of AMS and AGEG, did not express much interest in Caribbean or African political issues. Sentiments of nostalgia for Martinique and Guadeloupe had led to the creation of AMS and AGEG, and as a result, during the first couple of years members usually preferred organizing cultural activities. They invited speakers from Guadeloupe or Martinique, scheduled outings in the French countryside, and threw lively parties where they danced the night away to the rhythms of biguine, mazurka, and jazz.[27] In sum, for most Caribbean students the late forties and early fifties symbolized good times. The students felt confident about departmentalization, thinking that the new political status would end the long colonial chapter of exploitation; for sure, they anticipated returning to prosperous Caribbean islands offering many professional opportunities.[28]

While they anticipated a better future, certain Caribbean students in France still had their share of personal problems. Georges Lassare Michalon, the activist

Chapter One

who migrated to Paris after the war and served as AMS's president from 1953 to 1954, remembers that the biggest challenge came after summer break, when school started but students had not received their fellowships. Although many students came from a middle-class background and could manage the wait, a few of them were dirt poor, and logically, as people living below the threshold of poverty they depended on reliable and punctual financial help from their local government and the Ministry of Education.[29] Yet, this financial support—*le complément* (complementary funding from Martinique, Guadeloupe, or French Guiana's Conseil Général)—which the poorest students received to pay for housing and food, almost never arrived on time. For this reason, it was not unusual for disadvantaged students to rely on AMS and AGEG to lobby Caribbean and French institutions on their behalf and provide them with much-needed financial assistance from revenues generated during the hot beguine and jazz parties.

Eventually, after ten years of departmentalization without much improvement in Martinique and Guadeloupe's economy, the concerns of Caribbean students grew beyond issues of personal finance and fellowships. Impatient for change, they began asking about the rationale for receiving higher education in France when their homelands only offered menial and agricultural jobs. Furthermore, as evidenced by their refusal to idolize Victor Schoelcher, a French abolitionist who has perhaps received too much credit for the emancipation of slavery in the old colonies, they began to develop an appreciation for French Caribbean culture and historical figures. By the mid-fifties, a major political and intellectual shift was occurring within the community of Caribbean students in Paris. In many ways, the Journée Delgrès (Delgrès Day), a day commemorating the achievements of a Martinican officer, embodies this radical change.

In the mid-fifties, Caribbean students organized Delgrès Day to recognize the man's accomplishments. The event, however, had a double meaning. Under the veneer of celebration lay the students' defiance and resentment towards French policies affecting Guadeloupe, Martinique, and French Guiana.[30] Indeed, Delgrès (1766–1802), a Martinican colonel stationed in Guadeloupe in 1802, was protecting the island against British invasions. Slavery had been abolished in the French colonies since 1794, and he had recruited hundreds of black men into the French military. He had become quite an important leader in the island. Under his leadership, the men fought to keep Guadeloupe within a French empire guaranteeing freedom for all. This was a major accomplishment, since England, which possessed the most powerful navy, had defeated the French and taken over Martinique, the sister island.[31] However, by 1802, the French Republic had grown more conservative and authoritarian in style, and Napoleon, who proclaimed himself "consul à vie" (head of the government for life), decided to reestablish slavery throughout the colonies. After sending a letter outlining the impending change, he sent an armada of fourteen ships to implement his goal. At the sight of the armada, Delgrès deserted the French army and quickly organized a resistance movement. In a heroic battle, with a few hundred men and a handful of male and female civilians, he fought against a better armed and numerically superior French army. But after two days of bloodshed, he retreated to Fort Matouba, where he and his three hundred men chose to commit suicide rather than experience torture, imprisonment, and enslavement. In a final gesture, Delgrès acted upon what he had previously called for—live free or die.[32]

Thus, the celebration of Delgrès Day indicated that Caribbean students in Paris had changed their center of gravity. No longer did they merely seek to emulate "great" French men; they were now giving proper respect to their own heroes, a movement that also exacerbated nationalistic sentiments and oppositional thinking against a previously irreproachable French Republic. Illustrating their growing distrust in the republic, during the Delgrès celebration of February 25, 1957, the Caribbean students' organizations demanded that France end the Algerian War. In the process, they displayed a soupçon of Pan-Africanism, as they condemned colonialism in all shapes and forms. But the students' Pan-African gesture did not go beyond extending moral support to their "brothers and sisters" from the African continent—who, after all, seemed on their way to having free nations.

Essentially, by the late fifties Caribbean students were calling for upgrading Guadeloupe, French Guiana, and Martinique's political status into one that would provide them with more agency in managing their own affairs.[33] However, for the most part, the students did not ask for full-fledged independence. In reality, throughout the postwar period most students constantly asked France to invest more thoroughly in their homelands; they were merely yearning for the attributes of French citizenship, apparently a fleeting illusion forcing them to reconsider their relationship with the "motherland." Frustrated with the stagnant economy and influenced by the wave of independence in Africa, they asked for political autonomy, a status whose definition varied significantly from one individual to another. Illustrating this point, in 1965 *Alizé*, a Catholic newsletter published by Caribbean students, printed a short essay indicating the varied meanings of "autonomy" among Caribbean students in Paris. According to *Alizé*, 13.8 percent of the student population in Paris wanted a gradual assimilation into France, 10.2 percent wanted immediate independence, 15 percent were undecided, and 61 percent preferred an unspecified intermediate solution.[34]

Thus, throughout the postwar period, especially from the mid-fifties onward, Caribbean students pondered the meaning of their postcolonial identity. In the process, they reflected on issues of French cultural hegemony in their societies, leading them to organize Delgrès Day. Their general disappointment with Martinique and Guadeloupe's socioeconomic conditions planted seeds of doubt about departmentalization, which eventually grew into protest. Many students protested with the pen, sending letters to both French officials and Caribbean politicians. For example, on August 1, 1958, they sent the following letter to Aimé Césaire, who had been elected Fort-de-France's mayor and Martinique's deputy to the French National Assembly:

> Mr. Césaire, this is a moment when Antillean intellectuals must assume their responsibility to lead their homeland. As students we proudly pledge to defend our *Antillo-Guyanais* homelands. We reject the integrationist strategies that certain of our predecessors adopted. Despite our inexperience, we are aware that we share an important mission, which is why we ask you for an explanation. Mr. Aimé Césaire, your prestige and intellectual capabilities are precious and must serve the French Antilles' interest. You must be their messenger and help fulfill their most profound desire.... Mr. Aimé Césaire, time is of the essence, you must choose now; either you will help unleash the forces that will break our shackles, or you will be among those responsible for a second assimilation, and no one will forgive you for that tragedy.[35]

By the late sixties and early seventies, influenced by burgeoning nationalist organizations, the students veered to the left. It was common to find Caribbean students in Paris flirting with the idea of an independent Martinique, Guadeloupe, or French Guiana. Decolonization was a word constantly seeping through their daily conversation, and they even tried to "decolonize" certain French administrative offices dealing with Caribbean migrants in Paris.

While Caribbean students began drawing parallels between departmentalization and colonial continuities around the mid-fifties, African students who arrived in Paris after the war immediately started crusading against French colonialism. The spectacle of World War II had shown them a vulnerable France pretending to be a powerful empire, and nationalist movements in Asia invited them to reflect on the possibility of independence for Africa. Additionally, negritude writers had crafted intellectual tools allowing them to reinvent their identities from colonial subjects to proud and free individuals. For these reasons, African students challenged the very foundation of French colonialism, notably the idea that changing Africans into "black Frenchmen" or what was commonly referred to as "l'assimilation," translated into improving African societies and cultures.

By 1953, Alioune Diop had recognized the growing presence of African students in Paris. Not only had they become an essential component of the African diaspora in France, but they played an important role in transnational politics, prompting Diop to solicit their opinions on African and French affairs in a special issue of *Présence Africaine*. Prefacing the issue, he outlined the triple burden of African students; namely, the poor educational infrastructure in Africa forced the youth to leave their beloved countries for France, and when they returned home, not only did they face a hostile environment, but African societies also expected them to initiate development projects and assume leadership positions.[36] Thus, the students' essays built on his insightful introduction, thoroughly examining the impact of colonization on the African youth in both Africa and France.

Focusing on their role in Africa, the students echoed what Frantz Fanon would later outline in *The Wretched of the Earth*. They called for changing a colonial system manufacturing elites serving as intermediaries between the French colonial government and the majority of African people. Instead, they wanted the educated youth to emerge as a politically engaged group of people that would eventually represent the interests of most Africans. Their political discourse differed drastically from that of the previous generation of African students in Paris, who generally equated assimilation with "depersonalization." Pragmatic in scope, African students of the fifties advocated for independence, yet simultaneously they suggested that Africa's success rested on combining traditional African cultures with the Latin heritage. In other words, they rejected the notion that France had a mission to civilize "inferior" peoples, but they approved importing and adapting European "modernity" to the realities of the African continent. After all, they were longing for a free, modern, and culturally vibrant Africa offering educational opportunities, jobs, and health care to all Africans.

The students also devoted a large part of the special issue to the challenges they encountered in France. They used *Présence Africaine* to highlight the double standard that constantly hammered them. For instance, despite above-and-beyond school performances—African students graduated at a rate hovering around 100 percent—their academic accomplishments went unpraised; worse, they frequently received criticism for partying too much at bebop bars.[37] Clearly feeling as if their colonial origins tarnished their intellectual integrity, the students utilized *Présence Africaine* as a space where they could, without fear of reprisal, express anger against a French society that all too frequently painted them as uneducated colonial subjects. Using the journal, they voiced feelings of resentment against certain French individuals who always reduced them to being *Tirailleurs Sénégalais*, the African soldiers who fought bravely for France during World Wars I and II. While they drew pride from the soldiers' heroic accomplishments, they truly lamented this constant stereotyping.

The students also used *Présence Africaine* to express their distaste for primitivism and exoticism.[38] For them, primitivism was a plague permeating French society and corrupting African writers. Writing about this phenomenon, they claimed:

Even if the author had no talent, the French would enjoy reading about his childhood. They would gladly imagine him living in a hut with a leaky roof; they would feel his torrid romantic relationships and witness his circumcision at the hands of the witch doctor; they would run with him in the muddy streets and laugh at the ignorant and superstitious black instructor teaching him the alphabet. Finally, they would appreciate the devotion of a bearded European missionary dressed in a long black robe, for only he can supposedly teach us.[39]

Through *Présence Africaine*, the students hoped to convince Africans aspiring to become administrators, teachers, or writers to resist the temptation of portraying their societies based on French colonial paradigms. For them, depictions of African societies and peoples should stem from "real" African experiences and desires, not French understanding of Africa. In *Présence Africaine*, they also found a space to talk about their living conditions, particularly in Paris where most of them resided. Based on their writings, it seems as if these students lived as black pioneers in urban France. They had left nurturing homes to live in a city where they worried about affording the basic necessities of life, sometimes sleeping under the stars. In fact, it was not uncommon that the least privileged students would live with a French family in exchange for domestic services.[40]

Housing was an important issue for many African students. In one of the most interesting articles, "Le paternalisme contre l'étudiant africain" (paternalism toward African students), Albert Franklin, a Togolese student who played an important role in African student organizations, explains how the politics of housing permeated their lives. According to Franklin, the majority of African students lived in *foyers d'étudiants des colonies* (housing for students from the colonies), but unfortunately tense relations with French managers overshadowed the comfort of living in a community setting. The situation between African students and French foyer managers was so unbearable that the former opted for self-management, a quest that the French ministry in charge of foreign students opposed.

But denying the students the opportunity to have a say in their own affairs only created rebellious residents. By 1951, tired of French paternalism in the foyers, African student organizations had already staged a number of protests.[41] Unsurprisingly, officials from the Ministry of Education in charge of colonial students' affairs in France reacted swiftly, as Franklin notes:

In 1951 the F.O.M. Ministry denied their request. Officials from the Ministry even threatened to permanently close the *foyer* of African students in Bordeaux, which as we know, is extremely well kept. Thankfully, our comrades defended their home. But a few months later, in retaliation against our comrades in Paris who protested for the same right, the services of rue Oudinot closed down the *foyer* located on boulevard Saint-Germain. It was the only place where colonial students could gather without spending much money. Regardless of the explanation provided, it is clear that they closed the *foyer* to prevent the students from managing it.[42]

In an era when African students were growing increasingly radical, they viewed the foyer as a refuge where they could also organize political meetings, colloquiums, and symposiums focusing on decolonizing their homelands.[43] In hindsight, something bigger was happening at the foyers for students from the colonies. For all intents and purposes, these foyers, some of the very few African spaces in Paris, became anticolonial battlegrounds. Not only was the students' quest for managing the foyers an explicit rejection of French paternalism painting them as *grand enfants* (big children), but it also asserted their capability to manage their own affairs, a euphemism for nations. In other words, the struggle in the foyers became a proxy for the anticolonial struggle.

Ironically, while the first foyers of colonial students had been created during the interwar period to control and suppress their activities, by the postwar era they became breeding grounds for student activism.[44] As early as June 1946, African students residing in foyers were already networking and organizing political meetings, which ultimately led to the creation of the Association Générale des Etudiants Africains de Paris (African Student Organization of Paris or ASOP). ASOP was Pan-African at heart; its primary goal consisted of fostering unity among African students to improve the colonial condition in Africa.[45] In the same year, African students also founded Etudiants RDA (Student RDA), literally the student version of the Rassemblement Démocratique Africain (RDA), a Pan-African organization created by elected African officials who rejected French colonialism and favored political union with France. RDA brought new political agendas to the table. Its discourse centered on the promotion of African development and unity, which at the time meant improving the health-care and educational systems, developing internal trade within the French colonies, and promoting African cultures and values.[46]

Following RDA's lead, Etudiants RDA emerged as a politically engaged student organization in the Parisian landscape. However, ideological and political differences among the adherents soon cropped up within the organization. Seduced by Marxism, certain students joined the French Communist Party, thinking it offered a quicker road to social equality across the globe. Like many individuals from Africa and the African diaspora, they saw the European bourgeoisie as the culprit oppressing both the African and European proletariat. But many members of Etudiants RDA did not identify with the tenets of Marxism, much less the French Communist Party, claiming that French Marxists and communists also endorsed racist visions of Africa.⁴⁷ Moreover, under the influence of young and charismatic intellectuals like Cheikh Anta Diop, certain students strongly aspired to having African nations be free from any political attachments with France; these nations, they believed, should be entitled to develop their own political culture and philosophy. Consequently, as a result of strong ideological differences among the members, Etudiants RDA's influence on the community of African students in Paris faded rapidly. Within two years the organization collapsed. However, the students' quest for free and independent African nations did not die with Etudiants RDA.⁴⁸

By 1950, after many meetings in Lyon and Bordeaux, African students created the Fédération des Etudiants d'Afrique noire en France (Federation of Students from Black Africa in France or FEANF). As the name indicates, FEANF was a federation of all African student organizations in France. Under the leadership of Solange Faladé, a young woman from Benin, FEANF had both pragmatic and lofty goals. On the more practical side, FEANF sought to protect the students' moral and material interests. It advocated on behalf of its members at French institutions, including the Ministère de la France d'Outre-Mer and l'Office des Etudiants d'Outre-Mer, the agencies responsible for allocating fellowships to students from the colonies. On the more ambitious side, reflecting its youthful membership, FEANF wanted to be an educational outlet for both French people and African students; the former would learn about African societies and Africa's potential, and the latter about opportunities for African students in Europe. Finally, reflecting its members' discontentment with French colonialism, FEANF wanted to reconfigure the African colonies' relationship with France.⁴⁹

Amady Aly Dieng, a member of FEANF in the fifties, who also headed the organization from 1961 to 1962, wrote a fascinating monograph chronicling the activities and legacy of the organization. According to Mr. Dieng, from 1950 to 1955, FEANF primarily focused on protecting the moral and material conditions of African students in Paris. The organization's leadership only made humble appearances at the multiple conferences organized by Third World students and political organizations. Dieng contends that only after 1955, when it joined l'Union Internationale des Etudiants, did FEANF's politics become more transnational in character. Indeed, the same year, the organization had sent representatives to the Afro-Asian conference held in Bandoung, Indonesia, which aimed to assess the consequences of the War in Indochina (1946–1954) and foster unity among colonized countries. The following year, FEANF also sent representatives to a student-sponsored Afro-Asian conference in Indonesia, which further galvanized African students in France to fight for the independence of the "Third World."⁵⁰ In other words, FEANF always embraced decolonization, but its fight for freedom intensified after 1955, when the participants rubbed shoulders with their counterparts from Asia and Africa. Moreover, Césaire's *Discourse on Colonialism*, by far the most radical and influential work of the negritude writers, was also published in 1955. *Discourse on Colonialism* attacked the foundation of colonialism, blaming the agents, as well as the "unwilling" participants, of a capitalist system allegedly oppressing people from the Global South. To be sure, Césaire's *Discourse on Colonialism* was the intellectual force behind FEANF's relentless fight against French colonialism.

But as a radical student group, FEANF had to walk a very fine line. When they protested at French ministries or government agencies, they often faced the wrath of the police. For instance, in 1959 they had organized a rally in front of Hotel Matignon, the prime minister's official residence. The students wanted to protest against a pending nuclear test in the Sahara desert. Why, they asked, couldn't the French do this at home? Nearly five hundred students had answered FEANF's call. But the police had anticipated their move, and within an hour, the students crowded Parisian prisons.[51] This sort of police intimidation forced African students to protest cautiously, or as FEANF illustrates, with the pen.

The students' protest essays constantly called for political change in sub-Saharan Africa. They even voiced their opinions on Algeria, religiously criticizing the French occupation. In the midst of the Algerian War, FEANF dared to publish *Le sang de Bandoung*, a manuscript that denounced French war crimes and called for Algeria's freedom.[52] In many ways, *L'Etudiant d'Afrique Noire* (Students from Black Africa), FEANF's journal, became the students' most powerful weapon in the fight for independence. From 1956 to 1960, *L'Etudiant d'Afrique Noire* published a number of anticolonial essays describing French abuses in the colonies and reaffirming the colonies' capabilities to govern themselves. In fact, due to the incendiary nature of certain articles, the French government forbade the circulation of issue 28, which came out in June 1958.[53] *L'Etudiant d'Afrique Noire* incarnated the Pan-African spirit that consumed African students in Paris of the fifties. The journal's logo, black hands keeping a broken African jar together, was a metaphor suggesting that Africans should unite to obtain freedom and thrive. But this Pan-Africanism rested on the quest for political independence. It differed drastically from its counterpart of the interwar period, which emphasized cultural unity among all people of African descent. Perhaps for this reason, African and Caribbean students' activism rarely intersected. Would this phenomenon change in the following decade, when Africa finally broke the shackles of colonization?

In 1961, after the long fight for independence, Schofield Coryell, a journalist traveling to France, observed that most of the 8,000 African students in France were still affiliated with FEANF. Coryell was highly impressed by the ways in which *L'Etudiant d'Afrique Noire* engaged in African politics, claiming that "[the journal] takes a bold stand on every political and economic question relating to Africa, without pretending to confine itself to purely student affairs."[54] Coryell's assessment truly captured the commitment to uplifting Africa that most African students still shared. Nonetheless, a wind of change was blowing through the air. As the bells of independence rang, African student activism hit a turning point. In the fifties, the students had been meeting, organizing, writing, and protesting for national sovereignty; however, in gaining independence they lost the impetus for working across national boundaries to achieve sociopolitical change. France, the "colonial dragon," had been slain and the "anticolonial knights" scattered back to their kingdoms.

Moreover, in 1961, the students faced a major setback. When news of Patrice Lumumba's death arrived in Paris, they organized a large-scale protest in front of the Belgian embassy. Once again, in a Pan-African gesture of solidarity, hundreds of African students responded to the call, denouncing the U.S., French, and Belgian participation in killing the Congo's independence leader and prime minister. But to their surprise, the French government reacted swiftly. With the blessing of the Ministry of the Interior, the French police arrested and deported many students back to their homelands.[55] In a clear message, French officials warned the students not to protest against the new and all-too-often repressive African regimes, which for all intents and purposes supported France's interests. These suppressive methods forced African student activists to operate even more carefully than in previous years. In fact, despite a few sporadic protests, it seems as if radical student activism went on a hiatus for a few years. Only after May 1968, when French students took over the Sorbonne and Université Paris X Nanterre, did radical protests among African students resurface, as they fearlessly took over certain African embassies, which they deemed puppets of France and representatives of reactionary governments. By the late sixties, student activism in the Caribbean and African communities of the Parisian region had changed drastically.

A New Black France in the Horizon

The independence of the sub-Saharan African colonies marked a turning point in Alioune Diop's political activism. No longer could he use colonization to solicit the participation of black intellectuals in his grandiose Pan-African events. After 1960, Diop's leadership was mostly confined to the literary and publishing world—a world that actually mirrored the political changes that had occurred globally. Authors publishing with Présence Africaine were now addressing issues related to neocolonialism, underdevelopment, governance, and postcolonial black migrations. This visible change in Diop's Présence Africaine was also noticeable in the communities of black students who lived in Paris. Much had changed since the first wave of African and Caribbean students arrived after the armistice of May 8, 1945.

Indeed, in 1946, the year marking Martinique, Guadeloupe, and French Guiana's transition from French colonies into Overseas French Departments, French Caribbean people began migrating to France at a much higher rate. This increasing migration was first noticeable among the student population, which slowly became politically active. Likewise, the number of African students in France also increased drastically after World War II. But unlike most of their Caribbean counterparts, they arrived in France with a new political consciousness. The war experience had changed their perspective of France and generated visions of a free Africa. Consequently, African students started creating organizations aiming to reconfigure Africa's political relationship with France, effectively becoming important actors of the independence movement. Jean Pierre N'Diaye and Charles Diané, two scholars who wrote extensively about African students in Paris of the fifties, frame this era as their decade of fame, glory, and success.[56]

That said, by the turn of the sixties, black Paris seemed drastically different from previous decades. Many Caribbean, African, and African American intellectuals had returned to their native lands. Due to the departmentalization of the French Caribbean and the independence of former African colonies, the relationship that Caribbean and African students had developed during the interwar period deteriorated. When African students founded oppositional organizations like Etudiants RDA or FEANF, they did not invite French Caribbean students to participate in their affairs. After all, their "brothers and sisters" from the Americas recently earned French citizenship, which had been a fleeting illusion for the former sub-Saharan African French colonies.

The political dissonance between Caribbean and African students was obvious. The gap only widened with the independence of the sub-Saharan African colonies in 1960, because ironically, as African students fulfilled their wishes for independence, Caribbean students began advocating for their own. This increasing political fragmentation among black students, coupled with the black intellectuals' flight to Africa, the United States, or the French Caribbean, represents a major change in black France. But, as the book suggests, this change pales in comparison to what happened throughout the sixties and seventies, the decades that witnessed the emergence of a black working class in France.

Sociologists have written much about why migration from the Global South to the West occurs. They contend that warfare, poor governance, labor recruitment, and the international division of labor foster migration. They also suggest that cultural, linguistic, and socioeconomic connections created during the colonial period encourage people from former colonies to migrate to the former colonizing countries.[57] Their findings explain why many sub-Saharan African people first migrated to France. That being said, the question is how did the French welcome these people?

Chapter 2

African Migration to Paris of the Sixties

Let us clarify what we mean by moralité publique: We believe the spectacle of African misery in France is an affront to both their and our dignity. The lack of respectable housing and the abuses committed by landlords is another affront to our dignity. The rise of racism in France is a serious danger. It is looming large over us. So far, aside from a few exceptions, the French are proud of not being racist against Africans. They sympathize with Africans, who are very quiet and still remain objects of curiosity. But all of this can change if the press publishes articles about cases of contamination, if the public finds out about the fires in African quarters, or if they begin competing against the French for jobs.

—M. Jourdan, an official from the Direction des Affaires Sociales at the Préfecture of the Seine, Paris

In 1949, as Africans intensified their demands for independence, a national poll indicated that 85 percent of French high school seniors still believed colonialism was beneficial to the colonies.[1] When asked about professional goals, 30 percent of students declared they wanted to work in Africa.[2] In other words, after the war, dreams of prosperity in Africa still haunted the French. Most French citizens did not challenge the moral integrity of the civilizing mission. They believed the north to south migration offered benefits to both France and her former sub-Saharan African colonies. Reflecting this phenomenon, in 1958, at the dawn of independence, without accounting for North and Central Africa, about 90,000 French people still lived in West Africa.[3] But the independence of the sub-Saharan African French colonies changed the pattern of migration established during the colonial era. The scarcity of economic opportunities in the former colonies, improvement in transportation services, and new immigration agreements between France and her former sub-Saharan African colonies led to a burgeoning migration of Africans from the lower echelon of the colonial hierarchy. Usually urban dwellers or residents of rural villages, the French considered these people to be *indigènes*. They were supposedly inferior to the évolués, French-speaking Africans who held positions in the colonial administration.[4]

These new African migrants made their way to France when many government officials favored a European migration. Indeed, after the war, Michel Debré, the Fifth Republic's first prime minister, and Alfred Sauvy, the father of postwar French demography, designed discriminatory immigration policies.[5] Debré and Sauvy argued that 50 percent of the migrants should be Belgian, Danish, Scandinavian, German, Irish, British, and Canadian; 30 percent should be Spanish, Portuguese, and Italian; and the remaining 20 percent Polish, Czechoslovakian, and Yugoslavian.[6] Thus, by the sixties, French officials grew weary of black African bodies migrating to their beloved capital. They began policing their borders more rigorously, and the airport, which was truly the nation's new revolving door, became hostile to African travelers. Africans had to be deported. However, immigration agreements promoting freedom of movement between France and her former sub-Saharan African colonies complicated the issue. Deportation alone could not solve the "problem." French officials from the Ministry of the Interior realized they had to reform the immigration agreements signed during the decolonization process.

Interestingly, the Ministry of the Interior decided to use findings from public health institutions that depicted African migrants as physically weak and intellectually backward individuals to justify implementing new anti-African immigration policies. But these new immigration policies were not blatantly racist or xenophobic. In a seemingly counterintuitive strategy, government officials offered their support to non-governmental organizations (NGOs) that educated and trained African migrants in Paris. Similar to the organizations, they believed educating Africans would reduce emigration from Africa, because, upon returning home, the migrants would put their newly acquired skills at the service of their nation. This process allegedly fostered development and job creation in the former colonies, and to the delight of French officials, it encouraged Africans to earn their livelihood at home, not in France. However, behind this immigration-control strategy dressed in self-flattering Third-Worldist rhetoric lay a strong connection with France's colonial past. Similar to the *mission civilisatrice* of the colonial period, in what I call a postcolonial civilizing mission, French officials apparently sought to "improve" African migrants; they merely wanted to guide culturally and socially "inferior" individuals onto the path of modernity. In sum, the French welcomed Africans ambivalently. They viewed Africans as a problem for France and therefore attempted to keep them outside the boundaries of the nation. For the French, former African colonial subjects—healthy people who French employers utilized as disposable objects—became the gangrene of postcolonial Parisian society. Simultaneously, they believed the new African migration represented an opportunity to continue "civilizing" African subjects.

How Africans Became a Postcolonial Immigration "Problem"

After World War II, France was facing a severe shortage of workers. Not only had the country been suffering from a low birth rate, but hundreds of thousands of men and women had died during the war. At a time of high demand, the scarcity of workers encouraged both the public and private sectors to consider recruiting foreign labor. They recruited thousands of Southern and Eastern European workers through the Office National d'Immigration (ONI), a national organization in charge of recruiting labor migrants. Though the French government did not endorse recruiting laborers below the Sahara desert, the private sector, particularly French factories, dared to hire "uncivilized" West African workers. From their capitalist perspective, African colonial subjects made excellent temporary workers. French factories viewed them as affordable workers capable of quickly replacing French employees on vacation or striking for higher wages.[7]

Typically, factory representatives traveled to the African continent and hired a few men, who would work until they were sent back home. Sometimes African men found *soutiers* (coal room workers) and *manœuvres* (manual laborers) positions with French naval companies transporting finished goods to the African continent and raw materials back to France. These poorly remunerated and physically excruciating positions were plentiful, but for obvious reasons they kept Frenchmen at bay, leaving a plethora of menial jobs for African workers.[8] When these hard-working African seamen found more lucrative employment opportunities in Marseilles, the port city where cargo boats departed for Africa, they settled down and slowly made up a distinct community. In his classic novel *Black Docker*, Ousmane Sembène, the famous Senegalese writer, filmmaker, and former dockworker in Marseilles, eloquently depicts the burgeoning of this small, heterogeneous, yet vibrant African enclave:

> Black people poured in from all sides. . . . United by a community spirit and mutual support, they formed this village. Most of them experienced seamen, each one having sailed round the world at least twice. In this little Africa in the south of France, all the countries, all the different ethnic groups were represented.[9]

Up until the late fifties, most French citizens believed that black people only lived in Paris. They imagined the black community as a group of African American artists who lived in the flamboyant St.-Germain-des-Prés neighborhood where, outside of the United States, the jazz scene was nothing less than sensational. As a general rule, the African community of Marseilles did not attract much scrutiny from the press and government agencies. However, the situation changed drastically when the African colonies gained their independence.

Indeed, after three years of independence, the new nations' economies had been at a standstill. In countries like Senegal, where the economy rested on the export of one cash crop (peanuts), social conditions had actually worsened. This phenomenon forced thousands of men to look for wages in France—particularly in Paris, where small African social networks already existed and low-skilled jobs were plentiful. These men, usually unemployed city dwellers, peasants, fishermen, or sometimes manual laborers, were desperate for work, even if it meant earning a modest salary. African women, though in smaller numbers, also looked for jobs in France.

From 1959 to 1962, due to liberal immigration policies, most African men and women migrated to France fairly easily. They only needed a tourist visa. The border had remained porous because French companies still owned large operations in Africa and the French business class could not be bothered with obtaining visas to travel. Moreover, the French government sought to maintain its influence over its former colonies.[10] But French government officials had made some fundamental miscalculations. Thinking about their own interest in Africa, they actually underestimated the number of Africans who would migrate to France. Indeed, the African population in Paris went from 13,517 in 1946 to 15,220 in 1962 to 27,540 in 1968. By 1968, the number of Africans in France, a number that typically hovered around 15,000, exceeded 40,000.[11] In a period during which the state preferred recruiting white migrants via the Office National d'Immigration (ONI), the state agency responsible for supervising labor migration to France, they began to view the "uncontrolled" African migration as a new social problem (see table 1).[12]

In the midst of unprecedented economic growth, this new "African immigration problem" stood as a great irony in French society because not only was France considered an immigrant-friendly country—a *terre d'acceuil*—but it was also in desperate need of workers. After all, this was the *Trente Glorieuses* (the glorious thirty, 1946–1974).

Table 1. Labor migrants sponsored by the Office National d'Immigration, Year 1947, 1963, and 1968

	ITALIANS	GERMANS	SPANISH	MOROCCANS	YUGOSLAVIANS	PORTUGUESE
1947	51,339	3,416	0	2,258	0	0
1963	21,516	1,585	63,535	8,626	490	12,916
1968	5,860	1,421	19,332	13,339	7,953	30,868

Source: *Journal Officiel de la République,* March 27, 1969.

France had evolved from an industrial to a full-fledged consumer society that was experiencing a period of near full employment.[13] There were too many jobs and not enough French people. But, for reasons related to colonial understanding of Africans, the French did not welcome the black labor migrants.

Many French officials from the Ministry of the Interior misunderstood the nature of the African migration. They merely viewed sub-Saharan African migrants as permanent settlers. In truth, unlike their European counterparts, these Africans—young Mauritanians, Senegalese, Ivorian, and Malian people—were actually transnational labor migrants who obtained a three-month tourist visa hoping to work in France for a few years and send remittances to their families.[14] They most certainly did not want to settle in France permanently. Illustrating this vibrant transnational migration, records from the Ministry of the Interior indicate that in 1969, some 6,873 Africans entered as tourists and 3,503 returned to Africa.[15] Like most transnational labor migrants, these predominately young African people hoped to return home to build new lives. But the French chose to ignore this postcolonial narrative. In their eyes, African migrants were permanent settlers, people who like the thousands of Portuguese, Italians, Spaniards, and Yugoslavians hoped to start a new life in France.[16] *Des Africains en France! Pas possible!* (Africans in France! No way!) Such was the French reaction. For French officials, this new postcolonial African migration was an unconceivable phenomenon, because after all, in French logic, migration occurred from France to the uncivilized parts of the Southern Hemisphere, not vice versa.

Thus, by 1963, hoping to stop what they considered a new immigration problem, French officials turned to the airport. When flights from the former African colonies landed at Orly Airport, with the Ministry of the Interior's blessing, customs officers religiously stopped African passengers. It seems as if the men and women's skin color signaled a condition of illegality. Even when they possessed proper documentation, French customs officers treated them like fake tourists seeking a better life in France. In *Ouvriers noirs de Paris*, a documentary about African workers in the Parisian region, one can truly see the role that skin complexion and origin played at the airport; it reveals how French customs officers routinely pulled African travelers aside to interrogate them in the most humiliating manner, as if they were still children.[17]

In some instances, the French deported African travelers for failing to provide a proof of address in Paris, because by law, Africans needed a proof of address in France to enter the country. Although African travelers usually possessed an address, customs officers determined its credibility—if they deemed the address fake, they deported travelers back to their point of departure. That said, according to the French government, throughout the sixties, each month between 5 and 8 percent of African travelers were deported back to their homelands.[18] This was clearly an act of blatant discrimination since most Italians, Portuguese, and Spanish labor migrants usually arrived in France without proper documentation, yet they remained and lived in France as quasi-French citizens.[19] In fact, Victor Pereira, a scholar specializing in Portuguese migration, argues that between 1959 and 1971 the French government actually encouraged a clandestine Portuguese migration by legalizing hundreds of thousands of illegal migrants. Echoing Patrick Weil, the renowned French expert on contemporary migration, he notes that the French adopted a laissez-faire policy vis-à-vis the Portuguese migration because they wanted cheap laborers who shared a similar cultural background. Additionally, illegal Portuguese workers cost the state little money; they relied on their own community and networks for a variety of social services and rarely protested against unfair working conditions—a combination that made them all the more attractive to the public and the private sectors.[20]

While French officials closed their eyes to the illegal migration from neighboring countries—presumably because of the migrants' whiteness—they worked hard to reduce the African migratory rate to Paris. Since policing African bodies at the airport was fruitless, they went to the heart of the problem, namely, the bilateral agreements with Senegal, Mali, and Mauritania, the countries sending the most migrants. French officials tried tirelessly to renegotiate the agreements. By 1964, after barely a few months of negotiation, France had signed new immigration agreements with these countries that outlined new requirements for working and living in France. In short, these requirements stipulated that Malian, Senegalese, Ivorian, and Mauritanian citizens were not ipso facto entitled to a *carte de séjour* (a long-term visa). To obtain the highly coveted visa and *carte de travail* (work permit), they needed a labor contract, proof of residence, and an up-to-date medical exam.[21] In other words, the agreements made it practically impossible for Africans to work in France legally, because few French corporations recruited in Africa, and the Office National d'Immigration did not have any offices south of the Sahara. The question is why such an anti-African social climate structured French immigration policies.

Although this may come as a surprise, there were clear connections between the anti-African immigration policies and the public health sector. As early as 1963, the discourse of public health officials already hinted that African migrants represented a threat to public safety. Many French administrators and medical practitioners—people who worked under the auspices of the Public Health Ministry—shared colonial notions of African identities, and unfortunately for African migrants, these individuals' opinions weighed heavily in French society. Indeed, founded in 1930, the Public Health Ministry had an immediate impact on France. Not only did the ministry's surrogates, the various *grands docteurs* and health practitioners, play an important role in their own cities and villages, but they also influenced the national political landscape, as politicians routinely courted them for votes.[22] Moreover, after World War II, embarrassed by the Vichy regime, Frenchmen sought to build a stronger France and redeem their honor—France, so to say, had to be cleansed from the Nazi occupation. This quest for a pure and healthy nation magnified French public health officials' role in society.

After the war, many public health officials became obsessed with French women; they believed women, supposedly the roots of good and evil, had to be controlled and properly educated in order to prevent societal decay. Initially, concerned with women's "evil" side, in a sad episode known as "the purge," public health officials sought to rid the nation of the specter of Nazi occupation, an endeavor that translated into punishing women who had romantic relationships with German soldiers. Angry mobs publicly humiliated hundreds of women at various *places publiques*, spitting in their faces, cursing, and shaving their hair.[23] Though weighing heavily on the French consciousness, this episode in modern French history was brief. By the beginning of the fifties, public health officials focused on the "good" characteristics of French women, a new perspective entangled with rising nationalist sentiments. In a nutshell, they believed that if women ran their households efficiently—and after all, it was supposed to be their role—then France would have stronger, smarter, and healthier citizens. However, if women could not fulfill their task efficiently—if, for example, they did not feed their children properly and kept a "dirty" household—French officials worried that France could not become a strong, well-organized, and healthy nation.[24] Thus by the start of the sixties, amid this national obsession about proper hygiene and health, the arrival of black bodies, which still embodied the quintessential dirty and uneducated colonial subjects, raised the alarm of public health officials invested in making France a "stronger" nation.

French public health workers had a long and complicated relationship with people from sub-Saharan Africa. During the colonial period, French doctors believed colonial administrators and soldiers should serve as examples for Africans, who allegedly suffered from moral/intellectual deficiency and lacked basic nutritional/hygiene skills. Throughout their reports, French doctors argued that the entire African ecosystem, including the people's cultures, customs, habits, and behaviors, promoted the spread of diseases. As a result, improving African health was an integral part of the civilizing mission, even though colonial funding was usually allocated for caring for French patients at the expense of Africans' health needs.[25] Thus, in the postcolonial era, young African migrants allegedly infected by a number of potentially contagious tropical diseases, who tirelessly knocked at France's door, caused quite a stir in the public health community.[26]

But, as the complicated historical relationship between French public health workers and the former sub-Saharan African colonies reveals, these fears were not grounded in rational thinking. To be sure, a few African migrants had been diagnosed with tuberculosis. But this handful of contaminated workers hardly posed a threat to France. In truth, colonial ideas of African identities still structured the health practitioners' thought process. Moreover, racial eugenics—the belief that proximity to certain "races" contributed to the biological degeneration of the nation—had been highly popularized during the interwar period. In fact, William Schneider notes a strong connection between the interwar eugenics movement, the Vichy regime, and the postcolonial African migrations, claiming, "Only in the case of anti-Semitism had activities in the Vichy era discredited racial eugenics to the point of being unthinkable in the postwar era. But even here, the persistence of colonial and postcolonial independence migration to France eventually resurrected the biological eugenic racism of the 1930s."[27] Consequently, it is important to examine the extent to which public health officials under the spell of colonial thinking and racial eugenics fostered an anti-African social climate in Paris and the development of anti-African immigration policies.

The public health sector, which at the time focused on preventing the spread of diseases and improving the national health, sheltered many government officials who opposed African migration. Those individuals considered Africans to be an inferior, disease-ridden race incapable of adapting to French society and its climate. They effectively published a number of reports that not only reflected this belief, but also suggested that Africans actually posed a threat to the public's health. *Les travailleurs noirs dans la région parisienne* (Black workers in the Parisian region), a study featuring articles by prominent individuals from the medical field, confirms this phenomenon. Published just a few months after the participants presented their papers at a conference organized by the Préfecture de Paris in 1963, the study shows strong connections between the research of certain public health officials, racial eugenics, and the development of anti-African immigration policies, which appeared in the *Journal Officiel de la République Française* in 1964.[28]

First, *Les travailleurs noirs dans la région parisienne* suggests that the French climate is unsuitable to Africans because "They are accustomed to wearing practically nothing in Africa where the temperature ranges from 90 to 100 degrees, and when they arrive in Paris, especially during the cold winter, they are highly prone to catching diseases like tuberculosis."[29] Such statements indicate that many public health officials still ignored the characteristics of African geography and societies, and viewed race as a biological rather than a social construct. Accordingly, they believed that each "race" evolves best in its respective climate, an idea that emerged with the French naturalists of the eighteenth century and flourished throughout the nineteenth and early twentieth centuries, when Frenchmen dared to face the "dangers" of the African climate to export civilization.[30] But in the sixties, the conditions were very different. Frenchmen no longer risked their health to bring civilization to the "uncivilized" people of the South; rather, unwelcomed tropical bodies incapable of tolerating the cold allegedly carried tropical diseases to France.

Second, the study on Africans in Paris stresses the primitive aspect of their diet. In an ethnocentric fashion, public health officials criticized the seemingly healthy meals that African migrants ate communally, arguing that they would perish in France if they continued eating "frugal meals comprised of rice and beans." Such meals, they claimed, "are not appropriate for the cold climate and cannot help workers sustain a heavy workload, particularly in France where it is much heavier than in the former African colonies."[31] Yet these Africans, who often abstained from drinking alcohol because of their Muslim faith, ate well. Their diet was comprised of rice, beans, fish, lamb, vegetables, bread, and dairy products, evidently proper meals to remain fit and healthy. Third, the report also discussed the topic worrying all public health officials, namely, the possibility that Africans could spread diseases in France. For example, echoing his colleagues, who feared that African migrants suffered from dangerous gastrointestinal viruses and tropical venereal diseases, Lucien Petit, the head of the Préfecture of the Seine Research Services, cautioned, "Although the etiologies of these tropical diseases are well known, in light of the lifestyle that Africans lead in France we wonder about the behavior of these viruses and their capabilities of spreading in France."[32]

In March 1963, another study by Mr. Lépine, an eminent doctor, stressed the importance of assessing the health of African migrants prior to their departure to France. During a conference held at Paris's Académie de Médecine, Lépine affirmed that many African migrants carried contagious diseases such as leprosy, syphilis, tuberculosis, and other chronic diseases that could easily spread in France, and as a result, he proposed performing mandatory medical exams in their respective countries.[33] The exam, apparently a highly elaborate affair designed to successfully detect "African diseases," consisted of seven distinctive steps:

1. A complete clinical exam to detect "leprosy, the *hépatomégalies*, or the *splénomégalies*"
2. An eye exam
3. A thorax x-ray
4. Administering the BCG vaccine
5. A complete serological exam to detect syphilis
6. A urinary exam
7. An exam to detect intestinal parasites

The reports published by Parisian public health officials such as Lucien Petit and Lépine, which described Africans as unfit for the cold climate, lacking proper hygienic and dietary habits, disease-ridden, and illiterate people, clearly influenced officials from the Ministry of the Interior. This connection is evidenced by the July 1964 issue of the *Journal Officiel de la République Française*, in which officials from the Ministry of the Interior argued against the African migration based on evidence from the medical community. Similar to their public health colleagues, they contended that Africans were unskilled, illiterate, unable to speak French (at least 40 percent of the migrants), in poor physical and psychological health, and incapable of adapting to the French climate. Citing another study on West Africans in Paris completed by public health workers, the *Journal Officiel de la République Française* stated, "They have poor eating habits and their diet is extremely precarious . . . in a small room many men eat rice mixed with carrots, peppers, and raw fish from the same bowl."[34] In sum, using evidence from public health workers, officials from the Ministry of the Interior argued that Africans were still too primitive to migrate and live in modern France.

By 1965, after the French government renegotiated immigration agreements with the four African countries sending the most migrants to France, certain public health officials were still arguing for controlling the migration based on the possibility of contamination and their lack of intellectual integrity. A team of researchers headed by M. Jourdan, an official from the Direction des Affaires Sociales at the Préfecture of the Seine, used the findings of Professor Boyer, the head of the Seine Department's Council for Public Hygiene, to suggest that the lifestyle of Africans in Paris could spur the comeback of leprosy. They noted that Saint Louis Hospital had treated eleven African workers for leprosy, three of whom left for their country and eventually returned to Paris.[35]

The following year, in 1966, Dr. Robin, the director of public health in France, still maintained that African migrants posed a threat to France. Citing another report by Dr. Henri Brocard, he signaled that many Africans suffered from tuberculosis and should only be allowed into France if they passed a medical exam and possessed a job

CARNET de SANTÉ AFRICAIN

Last Name:	First Name:	Immunization:
Weight:	Height:	Antivariolique:
Birthplace:	Place of Origin:	B.C.G.:
Ethnicity:	Family Status:	T.A.B.:
Identity Card Number:	Address:	Anti-Polio:
Profession:	Employer:	Diphtheria:
		Tetanus:
		Antimalarial:
		Other:
General Condition:	Genital and Urinary System:	Nervous System:
Respiratory System:	Urine:	Lungs:
Pulse:	Sugar:	Serological Exam:
Digestive System:	Albumin:	Bowel Exam:
Chewing Coefficient:		
Teeth Condition:		
Conclusion:		
General assessment:		
Professional Aptitude:		
Recommendation:		

Source: Direction Générale de la Santé Publique, "Travailleurs Noirs: Carnet de santé," Centre des Archives Contemporaines, Fontainebleau, Box 19780262, art. 11.

contract.³⁶ Mr. Robin also suggested that each African carry a special *carnet de santé* (a small booklet that contains the individual's medical records). However, there was a striking difference between the *carnet de santé* designed for sub-Saharan African migrants and the one allocated to every French citizen. The French citizens' *carnet de santé* merely included the names of one's mother and father, one's date of birth, height, and immunology record. But Mr. Robin's *carnet de santé* for African migrants covered a wide range of bodily functions. Designed to monitor health deficiencies of African people, Mr. Robin's *carnet de santé* demonstrated that colonial perception of African identities and racial eugenics thinking still plagued the public health community well into the sixties.³⁷

Finally, certain public health officials also called for scrutinizing and stopping the African migration out of pure racism. They hid behind academic credentials to produce dubious research inferring that Africans were not sufficiently intelligent to meaningfully contribute to French society. For instance, in describing the Sarakolés, the largest African ethnic group in Paris, Jourdan's report painted them as backward people who had primitive eating habits and practiced consanguineous marriages, ironically a tradition of the French nobility.³⁸ The study even insinuated that Sarakolé people suffered from nihilistic impulses.³⁹ Based on informants' testimonies, one of the researchers concluded that many Sarakolés migrated to France despite knowing that it actually compromised their health. With a hint of sarcasm, the French researcher asked:

> Is the Sarakolé an inherently backward ethnicity? Medical exams indicate that many Africans are weak and sick when they arrive in France. Are the transplantation effects so rapid? Many claim they do not understand why they are healthy in Africa but become ill when they arrive in France. Some who have successfully adapted to France become ill when they return to Africa. The mortality rate is high. Using his African notion of numbers, one man told us that half of the migrants died upon returning to their village. Because we were surprised, we asked "why you are still coming?" With a smile, he answered, "Death is always for the other."⁴⁰

Not only did the researchers from the public health community mentioned above influence officials from the city of Paris and the Ministry of the Interior, but they also affected the press and various non-governmental organizations involved in the African community. However, these sectors of French society did not necessarily react like government officials. Most government officials used data from the public health sector to voice opposition to the African migration. But certain NGOs and French newspapers viewed the migration as an opportunity to educate African subjects. As in the colonial era, they hoped these French-educated Africans would return home and help "civilize" their brothers and sisters still living primitively.[41] In fact, certain NGOs were so sure that educating Africans translated into improving African societies and reducing emigration to France, that they successfully convinced government officials to endorse their plans.

The Press and the Postcolonial Civilizing Mission

During the interwar period, most newspapers endorsed the civilizing mission. Columnists and cartoonists routinely paraded Africans as uncivilized and inferior to the French. By the mid-fifties, in light of the First International Congress of Black Writers and Artists organized by Alioune Diop and looming independence agreements, the press adopted a more respectful tone vis-à-vis Africa and her diaspora. But in the following decade, representations of African identities actually worsened. Newspapers became obsessed with the poor living conditions of Africans in Paris, so much so that many French people believed all Africans were illiterate people burdening their overly hospitable country.[42] Most articles about African migrants published between 1960 and 1965 by prominent newspapers like *Le Monde*, *Le Figaro*, *La Croix*, or *L'Humanité* sensationalized the African presence in the City of Light, framing Africans as victims of modernity.[43] For instance, in a shocking title, "40,000 Voluntary Slaves in France," *Le Monde* suggested that African migrants represented a new problem for the city. Echoing public health officials, it affirmed that unlike the Portuguese and other European squatters of Nanterre (a commune in the western suburbs of Paris), the "exploited" and "sick" African workers lived in close proximity to French citizens, which could lead to widespread contamination.[44] For *Le Monde*, the solution to this so-called modern slave trade was keeping the "slaves" at home. Interestingly, even though African migrants in Paris lived in similar (or sometimes better) conditions than the thousands of Portuguese and Spanish migrants who squatted in dilapidated factories or abandoned parks, *Le Monde* emphasized how they "threatened" the ecology of Paris.

La Croix, the most popular Catholic newspaper, was equally alarmed by the African presence in Paris. In an article entitled "1,000 New Ones per Month," Noel Copin described Africans as great workers capable of earning a job promotion. Yet, he also shared the concerns of French xenophobes, stating, "They have an insurmountable imperfection, which is that too many of them are coming to France. This is increasingly problematic because throughout 1963 Africans migrated at the rate of 1,000 per month, but for the past five months, the Algerian population, which was supposed to return home, has actually increased by 25,000." This situation, he observed, "worries French officials, who apparently wonder whether France will be colonized by people from the former colonies."[45]

Le Figaro, one of the most popular conservative newspapers, maintained a similar discourse. However, while it empathized with the difficult living and working conditions of sub-Saharan African workers in France, *Le Figaro* also expressed xenophobic sentiments against them. The newspaper even manifested desires for a racially homogeneous nation by pointing out how Africans could not integrate into French society—they were truly social misfits. In an article entitled "One exit for 50,000 trafficked and uprooted bodies living in hell: Hard work," it cautioned that African labor migrants actually "migrated their lives away." Satirizing Africans, the article tells the story of Gamba Camara, an African man working for Paris's sanitation department. Probably a fictive character, Mr. Camara conveys the idea that Africans are essentially good-hearted individuals, but unfortunately too good-hearted and primitive to function in Paris, the urban jungle:

> Night had fallen a long time ago. A black man bigger than the devil was sweeping the Place de la Concorde impassively, gathering in small piles the dead leaves which the autumn wind had blown upon the sidewalk. Surprised by the sight of this man working beyond regular hours, a policeman called him over for questioning. But the worker, Gamba Camara, a twenty-year-old man from Mauritania, did not know more than ten French words. Not without much effort, the agent finally understood that Gamba Camara, who was hired the same morning by the Department of Sanitation, had lost his crew. Paid to work, he refused to stop, and marching straightforward with his broom, he continued cleaning the capital's sidewalks throughout the night.[46]

For *Le Figaro*, Mr. Camara, who is later identified as a member of the Sarakolé "tribe," embodies the uncivilized African colonial subject, the *indigène* par excellence, who is clearly out of place in France. Yet, in the tradition of French colonial paternalism, *Le Figaro* advocated for helping Africans. Using a study published by l'Institut Français d'Opinion Publique, the newspaper highlighted seven reasons why France should not "abandon" Africans:

> One, it is our duty to help because they helped us during the previous wars. Two, supporting African countries guarantees an outlet for France's products and access to raw materials. Three, helping them also allows France to maintain her cultural influence in the world. Four, it is the duty of industrialized countries to support poor countries. Five, France began civilizing Africa and should continue the job. Six, France

should help African nations to secure their allegiance and to make sure that they finally become adult nations. Seven, chaos will reign in Africa if France neglects Africans.[47]

Thus, promoting civilizing Africans, *Le Figaro* still saw Africa in Europe's past. However, in the early postcolonial period, *Le Figaro*'s notion of the civilizing mission translated into helping the new African nations become "adult nations." In other words, it seems as if the conservative newspaper's discourse had shifted from uplifting the individuals—the big children—to uplifting the "infant nations." In sum, *Le Figaro* believed that France still had the moral responsibility to help African nations, an endeavor that ultimately offered financial benefits to France and her former colonies.

Like *Le Figaro*, other newspapers believed that France still had the responsibility to "modernize" African subjects. For instance, *La Croix* argued that France should view the African migration as an opportunity to teach the migrants how to properly manage their lives. In that spirit, it published a story praising l'Association Accueil et Promotion, an organization established at the start of the sixties that launched programs offering literacy and hygiene classes, judicial and housing assistance, and a beginner's class on using the Parisian transportation system. L'Association Accueil et Promotion also oriented African migrants towards the Bureau de Placement de la Main d'Oeuvre (Office for Manual Workers' jobs), an organization channeling them towards employment opportunities.[48] Likewise, *L'Humanité*, the communist newspaper, endorsed initiatives aimed to "uplift" Africans in Paris. It praised Auguste Guillot, the communist mayor of Saint-Denis, for offering literacy classes to poor African migrants at certain city venues. For the leftist newspaper, the solution to Africa's underdevelopment lay in teaching Africans a trade, and of course, introducing them to the wonders of trade unionism.[49] One should note, however, that *L'Humanité* portrayed Africans more respectfully than conservative and religious newspapers, and invited French workers to unite with their struggling African comrades. For *L'Humanité*, capitalism was the mutual foe. Still, despite its good intentions, *L'Humanité* offered controversial solutions to solving "underdevelopment" in the former African colonies; it prescribed French remedies to address African ailments, thereby perpetuating the long tradition of French ethnocentrism towards people of African descent.[50]

In retrospect, the press maintained a discourse emphasizing compassion for exploited African workers. The religious and left-leaning newspapers argued that France should take this opportunity to improve the African condition by getting the migrants acquainted with trade unionism, and most importantly, by teaching them a trade that they could use to develop Africa. However, aside from the communist newspaper, the press maintained that Africans could not adapt to the French lifestyle. The conservative press, usually the mouthpiece of ultranationalist individuals, openly voiced opposition to any sort of African migration. Ultimately, irrespective of their ideological inclination, the press suggested Africans needed a stronger dose of modernization to reach acceptable standards of humanity; in the sixties, for French individuals involved in NGOs, the press, or the public health sector, modernizing African people translated into offering literacy and hygiene classes, as well as job training in trades such as bricklaying or painting. In other words, it meant offering the migrants vocational training. That said, in 1960s parlance and thinking, the line between modernizing and civilizing people from sub-Saharan Africa was very blurred.

NGOs and the Postcolonial Civilizing Mission in Paris

Like the Association Accueil et Promotion, most NGOs catering to Africans in Paris offered literacy and hygiene classes, as well as housing assistance. Certain organizations acted as informal "temp agencies," orienting migrants towards potential jobs in factories or construction sites. However, one NGO, the Association pour la Formation Technique de Base des Africains et Malgaches Résidant en France (AFTAM) played a key role in the lives of most African labor migrants in Paris.[51] Inaugurated in February 1962, AFTAM, the largest NGO servicing the community of African workers, was born out of the concern that a sharp increase in African migration would create what it termed "a black proletariat in Paris."[52] Its first president, Stéphane Hessel, a hero of the French Resistance dedicated to public service who actually became popular across the globe in 2010,[53] feared the formation of black ghettos in Paris and thus pledged to improve the living conditions of African migrants in the City of Light.

But AFTAM was also cognizant of its limitations. It saw itself as the Band-Aid of a bleeding wound—Africa—which was literally losing its blood to France. Hence, hoping to be the cure for a long-term problem—underdevelopment—AFTAM also wished to impart to the migrants the necessary skills to develop their own nation, a strategy that they also argued would decrease the African migratory rate to France. In a report published just days after its inauguration, AFTAM asserted:

> The best remedy against the proliferation of an "under-proletariat" in France is preparing African migrants for a successful return to their country by offering them professional training. This strategy will transform the chaotic and uncontrolled African migration into a tool for development. Indeed, thus far, we have observed that efficient development programs cannot survive if uncontrolled emigration persists.[54]

In accordance with what it preached—educating the migrants as a development strategy—AFTAM was among the first organizations offering literacy classes to African labor migrants. It had solicited help from the Ministry of National Education, which agreed to offer night classes throughout certain schools of the Parisian region. After seeing the enthusiasm of African students and the overall positive results of the literacy programs, AFTAM's employees were convinced that African migrants could receive professional training, even in the most rudimentary form. In a communiqué outlining the success of the first classes, the organization asserted with much exhilaration:

> The teaching was done based on a method established by the Centre de Recherche et d'Etude pour la Diffusion du Français. The results were marvelous because many of the illiterate students learned how to read and write within three months. Moreover, the program directors and the teachers discovered that some students had a lot of potential, albeit in a purely raw form. Thus, we are confident they can obtain a basic professional formation. Essentially, our goal is to educate them, even if they just learn about hygiene.[55]

Similar to public health officials, AFTAM questioned the migrants' capability to follow proper hygiene rules. The organization did not challenge French stereotypical notions of African identities. However, since its mission entailed uplifting the African community in Paris, AFTAM quickly became aware of the major challenges plaguing the black migrants. Its conclusion was straightforward: Africans needed access to affordable and clean housing. Pragmatic in scope, AFTAM realized that many migrants had been victimized by slumlords renting substandard dwellings; some landlords even converted damp and dark underground wine cellars into "apartments." Consequently, by the mid-sixties, AFTAM decided to open foyers for African labor migrants.[56] Opening the foyers—establishments offering a bed and basic services—proved to be a rewarding initiative for both the migrants and the NGO, as it provided the migrants with a decent living environment and allowed AFTAM workers to interact with hundreds of African workers who otherwise would have been scattered throughout the Parisian region. After all, if AFTAM intended to successfully implement the "education for development" strategy, it had to reach as many migrants as possible.[57]

Although AFTAM recognized that investing in housing development for the black migrants was mutually beneficial, it still proceeded with much caution. The organization did not want Africans to view the foyers as an open invitation to migrate to France; the foyers, it argued, "should only offer basic comfort and accommodate the African communitarian lifestyle. In no way should they be luxurious because it would prevent the migrants from returning to their society, which too often lacked the amenities of

Western societies."[58] In sum, for AFTAM the foyers were both temporary housing and a social laboratory, where the staff could identify the migrants deemed most entrepreneurial and worthy of learning a trade useful to developing Africa.

Although AFTAM viewed the foyers as an opportunity to achieve sustainable development in Africa, certain government officials who interacted with the agency remained skeptical. They agreed that having hundreds of African migrants living in one building was cost-effective and facilitated "civilizing" them, but they still questioned the efficacy of education as a development strategy. In short, these government officials appreciated the foyers for containing potentially sick individuals in a controlled and managed location where French administrators could select African workers with a "sufficient level of instruction to attend professional formation centers."[59] However, they expressed skepticism about the raison d'être of the foyers, particularly with regard to educating the supposedly least "évolués" migrants (literally the less evolved); first and foremost, French officials working with AFTAM believed the least "évolués" needed to improve their hygiene culture and dietary habits before receiving any sort of "high knowledge." Furthermore, they doubted if the skills, which the most "évolués" would acquire in France, corresponded with the skills needed to develop the "Third World."[60] Nonetheless, despite their reservations, throughout the sixties, French officials continued to subsidize AFTAM and similar organizations professing that education led to economic development in Africa and reduced the African migratory rate to France.

Le Secours Catholique, the largest Catholic organization in France, was one of these organizations advocating educating Africans in Paris to foster development in Africa and reduce emigration to France.[61] It offered hygiene and literacy classes to African migrants. Unlike AFTAM, the Catholic organizations did not create African foyers. In its early days, AFTAM was partly subsidized by the state, allowing it to extend housing services to African migrants. Le Secours Catholique, on the other hand, generated its own revenue, making it more difficult to offer housing services. However, Le Secours Catholique did receive state subsidies indirectly for its work in the African community. For instance, the Assistance publique–Hôpitaux de Paris (AP-HP), Paris's public hospital system, lent the organization classroom space, where volunteers—usually African or French students—taught reading, writing, and hygiene skills to convalescing African migrants.

The organization, which embraced humanist and Christian principles, devoted much effort to helping Africans in Paris. However, despite its good intentions, Le Secours Catholique still viewed Africans through ethnocentric lenses. Simone Bière, the leading administrator in Paris, openly believed that Africans came from inferior societies, which supposedly hindered them from thriving in France. Like many public health officials, she seemed to be under the spell of racial eugenics—fearing, for example, that "Certain African ethnic groups suffered from a number of diseases which could have devastating consequences for France."[62] In other words, just like government officials and the press, members of Catholic organizations who interacted with postcolonial African migrants did not come to terms with their preconceived notions of African identity. For them, Africans still remained the quintessential colonial subjects in desperate need of a helping hand.

Essentially, this amalgam of reactionary thoughts and good-hearted initiatives coming from the press, the NGOs, and the city officials, which intended to improve Africa and the lives of Africans in Paris, is what constitutes the "postcolonial civilizing mission." But unlike the *mission civilisatrice* of the Third Republic (1870-1940), "the postcolonial civilizing mission" of the sixties did not invest in large "civilizing projects" such as building schools and other civic organizations. French officials did not emphasize converting African subjects to Christianity and spreading French culture; transmitting the French language and culture was important insofar as it allowed African migrants to learn a trade that they could use to develop Africa. Neither the French government nor associations like AFTAM or Le Secours Catholique wanted to turn African migrants from the lower classes into Frenchmen. The civilizing mission of the sixties focused on providing Africans with the tools to catch up to modernity and potentially achieve greater socioeconomic growth in Africa. Simultaneously, as a product of ethnocentrism, xenophobia, and anti-black racism, the postcolonial civilizing mission aimed to keep Africans at bay. Most French public officials, medical practitioners, journalists, and NGO workers did not display blatant forms of anti-black racism, yet in their eyes all African workers embodied the quintessential unproductive migrant, almost a parasite of the state, who still needed a strong dose of civilization to improve their own affairs and stay home.

To be sure, as soon as a few thousand sub-Saharan African migrants arrived in Paris, they became the elephant in the room—undesired people causing a strange feeling of discomfort. For that reason, scholars should reevaluate the historiography of the African migration, which suggests that France closed its doors on the migrants after 1974, when it implemented a policy of family reunification.[63] In truth, France never opened its doors to African migrants. Since the early sixties, government officials have tirelessly tried to send Africans back and keep them at home. Reflecting this trend, many French citizens also displayed skepticism or even hostility towards the African migration. Influenced by the media, particularly documentaries about African migrants that reinforced certain colonial stereotypes, the French had very few reasons to welcome African students and "disease-ridden," "uncivilized" labor migrants.

For contemporary scholars, many of these documentaries, which have been relegated to the land of the forgotten, represent an invaluable treasure. Not only do they provide important data for research, but they also open a window onto the field of social encounters between Africans and French people. These documentaries can help answer important questions—namely, how most French people viewed working-class African migrants; how the migrants adapted to Parisian society; if they developed close relations with certain French people or other European migrants; how African labor migrants found employment, and if they were well treated at work.

Chapter 3

French Documentaries and the Representation of African Experiences

You know, I saw the France of yesterday, and she looked quite different from the France of today. I was in France in 1944, then in Tunisia. I participated in the construction of St. Tropez. I saw what happened when the young adults of today were just babies. I lived through it all. France was like the Senegal of today. There were no jobs in France and French people migrated to Senegal. Today, the Senegalese are in France, and such is life ... but one should know that foreigners always welcome a helping hand. Whoever leaves abroad without help and without knowing people cannot be happy; that's our problem.

—A Senegalese migrant speaks in a French documentary, *Travailleurs Africains* (1962)

In the fifties, the French fell in love with television. *Les rateaux* (the rakes), the pseudonym used to describe the thousands of antennas conquering the roofs of their homes, symbolized the growing popularity of television during that era.[1] Most of the shows stressed the importance of family, religious, and moral values, and in retaliation against Hollywood, which successfully promoted American culture, they celebrated French culture.[2] By the beginning of the sixties, television was a source of entertainment and an educational outlet, a combination paving the way for new genres of programs, namely the *reportages* (documentaries). The first *reportage*—*Cinq Colonnes à la Une*, which aired in 1959—was an immediate success. According to Jean-Noel Jeanneney and Monique Sauvage, movie theaters, the usual destination for leisure, were deserted when the *reportage* was broadcast on the first Fridays of the month.[3] The amalgamation of well-planned presentations and carefully chosen images and comments from experts made *Cinq Colonnes à la Une* irresistible. It quenched the curiosity of viewers interested in learning about space exploration or discovering the latest technological innovations, such as the first U.S. nuclear submarine and the "exotic" cultures of African, South American, or Asian societies.[4] By the mid-sixties, *Zoom*, a more intellectually oriented *reportage*, appeared on the air. Its topics, more local in scope, focused mostly on controversial issues like divorce, racism, euthanasia, sexual freedom, drugs, prison, and prostitution. *Zoom* was truly a product of the French sixties. It effectively used jazz and rock-and-roll for sound effects. Using audiovisual techniques and a mise-en-scène influenced by the groundbreaking filmmaker Jean-Luc Godard, it denounced the rhythm and logic of the industrial world and the growing gap between the North and the Global South.[5] Thus, it is in the context of film innovation and new discourses on social inequality that the documentaries about African migrants in Paris emerged.[6]

The documentaries about African migrants represent a huge break from the ways in which the French—or for that matter, the Americans—had traditionally portrayed Africans on the screen. They were no Tarzan movies. They described the heterogeneous characteristics of the African community, stressing the differences between the labor migrants and the professionals and students. Indeed, born in the wee hours of the postcolonial era, these documentaries do not paint a simplistic picture of the African community in Paris. They highlight the importance of class differences. One can easily see how students and professionals led much different lifestyles than the workers, who usually toiled in factories, shops, restaurants, or at construction sites. The lives of these two groups rarely intersected. As the documentaries reveal, African students and professionals shared more connections with their French counterparts than African workers. In fact, it was not uncommon for African students to develop friendships or romantic relationships across the color line. In contrast, most African workers, usually men, longed to return home and rejoin their families or future wives.

By exploring themes such as the migrants' communal and transnational lifestyle, as well as their "proletarian pleasures" and experiences in the labor and housing markets, the documentaries truly give a sense of the sort of challenges African migrants encountered in postcolonial Paris. Yet despite their relevance, they have certain limitations. For one, while they tried depicting the African community "objectively," the French documentaries still reinforced the évolué/*indigène* colonial dichotomy that separated Africans into two distinct classes—one French-educated, and the other illiterate with basic knowledge of French. In reproducing this paradigmatic approach, the documentaries ignored two important characteristics of the "Paris Africain." First, despite the presence of thousands of African women in France, the camera did not capture their stories, which are often very different than their male counterparts'. Second, the documentary makers could not fathom the idea that African migrants from both the lower and upper classes could actually influence the French. When they depicted postcolonial encounters between French citizens and African migrants, the former were usually in a position of power; the French always exploited or minimized Africans, who were generally uneducated and unable to function in France. But in reality, these encounters also bore new revelations for the French.

Indeed, not only did Africans challenge the concept of *indigènes*, but they also invited the French to reflect on the construction of their own identity. To highlight this point, I use data from my fieldwork, particularly interviews that I conducted with Mrs. Christiane Diop, the wife of the late Alioune Diop, and Madame Dacosta, a community activist in Paris. Madame Dacosta's testimonies are particularly relevant, as she played an important role in her community during the late sixties. Moreover, her personal stories—stories that can serve as epigraphs for the lived experiences of many African women—help to explain the connections between migration, decolonization, and the insertion of African migrants into the fabric of French society.

France Learns about Migration and Class Differences in African Communities

In the first scene of *Ouvriers noirs de Paris*, a documentary about the "adventure" of an African man from Orly (a major airport) to his new life in Paris, one notes how customs officers scrutinize the man as soon as he steps off the plane. As he moves forward and slowly merges in a line of white passengers, the color of his skin apparently disturbs his surroundings. It represents a violation; it embodies a physiological condition that foreshadows the man's goals—namely, to settle in France. For this reason, customs officers take him into custody.

The African passenger has a tourist visa. If he possesses an address and has no illicit items, he should, by rights, proceed to cross the border legally. Yet that is not the case. Despite having a tourist visa, he is presumed to be an illegal immigrant. In the early 1960s almost all Africans were stereotyped as illegal labor migrants escaping a life of poverty in the savannah. Most French officials could not fathom the idea that they could be transnational labor migrants, visitors, students, diplomatic attachés, artists, or scholars. Thus, even if he is within his rights and has done nothing wrong, the passenger is searched. His belongings are put on display and the customs officers assault him with a series of questions.

Wearing a suit and tie, the young African passenger is dressed professionally. Yet despite his attire signaling adulthood and commanding respect, the customs officers speak to him like a child. They disregard French social norms for talking to adults and strangers, addressing him with the "tu" personal pronoun as opposed to the more respectful "vous," which is typically utilized in formal settings. Interestingly, within the first couple of verbal exchanges, one notices that issues of public safety and legality are seemingly trivial to the French customs officers; for all intents and purposes, this ritual conveys the message that he does not belong in the French Republic. Nonetheless, apparently against the customs officers' wish, the young man successfully crosses the border. He has a tourist visa and a valid address in Paris, the necessary weapons to protect him against deportation.

As the man leaves the airport, the documentary makers follow him, clearly wanting to share this man's experience with the French nation. When the young man boards the train to Paris, the cameraman does a close-up of his face, hoping to capture his first impression of "modern" life. Of course, like anyone visiting a new country, the African passenger gazes through the windows, exited to discover a new environment. Suddenly, interrupting his first acquaintance with suburban Paris, the narrator asks him in a cold but curious tone, "How do you find Paris?" "Different," the passenger answers dismissively. "Different than what?" the narrator insists. "Just different," he replies. Then, apparently influenced by the idea that Africans are best suited for a tropical climate, the narrator wonders if the passenger is already adapting to his new environment. Out of sympathy, he asks if he is cold. But intoxicated by the view, the African man dismisses the question. Still, the narrator persists. Again, he asks the young man if he is cold, graciously offering a jacket as he states compellingly, "We have an extra jacket; take it, please, take it." But dressed like most passengers, the African man kindly rejects the offer: "Non merci Monsieur."[7] An awkward moment ensues; the narrator seems to wonder why the man refused his help.

However, the documentary, which literally delivered the lives of African migrants into the living rooms of French audiences, becomes more interesting when the subject under the lens arrives at his final destination: a small, poorly lit apartment shared among a few other migrants. One observes how these black city dwellers live humbly, without much electricity or the other amenities commonly enjoyed by Westerners. In contrast to the French, who would probably not tolerate such living conditions, they seem happy, which gives the impression that all African migrants feel at ease with practically nothing. But the documentary is not condescending towards the migrants.

It tries to keep its promise of showing the public "du réel," a supposedly "objective" representation of the world. Thus, it proceeds to explain in greater detail why the African migration occurs and how the migrants fare in France.

By and large, *Ouvriers noirs de Paris* and other documentaries on working-class African migrants in Paris suggest that migration results from Africa's poor economic conditions. Postcolonial African migrants are victims of history, allegedly unable to control their continent's fate. Hence, like NGOs such as AFTAM and Le Secours Catholique, the documentaries suggest that it is France's duty to help Africa and African migrants facing a harsh life in Paris. Yet beneath this veneer of pity and compassion also lay sentiments of admiration, particularly in regard to the mechanics of the migration. Africans impressed the French filmmakers because they developed a complex system of transnational migration, which among other things helped them find housing and employment in Paris. Their web of solidarity defied the individualism that reigned in the modern city. For that reason, the more "primitive" and interdependent African workers in Paris, who successfully reconstituted an organic community and ostensibly filled their lives with the proper dosage of proletarian pleasures, could apparently teach the French how to enjoy the simple pleasures of life. This sort of primitivism was prevalent during the interwar period, when, healing from the trauma of World War I, the French sought to escape the monotony of modernity by embracing black arts and music. They literally danced their problems away.[8]

But primitivism was subtler in the documentaries of the sixties. French filmmakers paid closer attention to the migrants' communal lifestyle; only occasionally did they focus on African arts and dance. For example, in *L'Afrique des banlieues*, a documentary by Jean Schmidt, one sees a group of young men dancing frantically to the rhythm of drums and chants at an African cultural event unfolding in the streets of Paris. In accordance with the tradition of French primitivism, it seems as if Schmidt filmed the performances to promote the idea that "primitive" dances are Africa's gift to an overly intellectual, mechanic, and industrialized Europe. Accordingly, the twisting and twirling black bodies of the poor and exploited African male migrants should inspire French society to relinquish its countless social inhibitions.

Indeed, as the men danced uninhibitedly without the company of women, an act that defied conventional boundaries of masculinity, which in the postwar period was characterized by physical toughness and hypervirility, they inspired Frenchmen to rethink French notions of masculinity.[9] In other words, by highlighting how the rules of gender relations and masculinity are allegedly irrelevant to "primitive" people, the documentary expressed the views of French citizens who understood identity formation more broadly and believed that French modernity was both oppressive and suppressive, leading the French to live unnatural and unhealthy lives. Ultimately,

L'Afrique des banlieues and *Ouvriers noirs* reflect the views of French leftists who shared an affinity for African "communalism." Indeed, not only did these French leftists deplore materialism and equate French modernity with a loss of human values, but they also romanticized the past.

Unlike the majority of government officials, who generally saw African migrants through xenophobic and racist lenses, the documentary makers did not challenge their right to live in Paris. However, by suggesting that Africans survived Paris because their "primitive" culture helped them cope with the insanity of modernity, the documentaries still perpetuated colonial stereotypes of Africans. In hindsight, they depicted working-class African migrants as *indigènes* in the City of Light. By contrast, they painted an entirely different picture of the African middle class. Following a colonial paradigm, their cameras framed the African middle class as évolués in the City of Light.

For French documentary makers, there were two distinct groups of Africans in Paris: the largest one was comprised of low-skilled workers, while the other, smaller in character, included intellectuals, students, and professionals—a group of people that resembled W. E. B. Dubois's talented tenth (the educated class of African Americans who supposedly would lead the race out of its pains and tribulations). These educated Africans, who often came from a privileged background, constantly crossed cultural and racial boundaries. As Mr. Gissoko, an African worker who migrated to Paris in the early sixties, mentioned, they did not lead a life of *boulot, metro, dodo* (traveling to work by the metro, working hard, and crashing onto their beds after a long, exhausting workday).[10] This class distinction is clearly visible in *L'Afrique des banlieues*, which interviews a well-dressed African student at an upscale Parisian nightclub where whites and blacks mingle on the dance floor. The documentary emphasizes his comfort with the French language and the ease with which he moves within French society. Apparently, this man does not deal with poor living and working conditions, problems that many African workers confronted in Paris. Like most graduate students, he has his sights set on a lucrative career.

In many ways, despite perpetuating colonial notions of African identities, *L'Afrique des banlieues* did portray the distinction between the workers and the students and professionals accurately; throughout my interviews, many African students and professionals of the fifties and sixties agreed that class division played an important role in their "community." In fact, when I interviewed Paulin Joachim, a journalist from Benin who not only migrated to France at the turn of the fifties and published many political essays, but also attended the First Congress of Black Writers in Paris in 1956, as well as Yandé Christiane Diop, the director of Présence Africaine, the famous black publishing house founded by her late husband Alioune Diop in 1954, both admitted that class was an important factor structuring relationships within the Continental African diaspora. For Mrs. Diop and Mr. Joachim, the Continental African diaspora of Paris was divided into two distinct groups; they claimed that "On the one hand stood the exploited laborers, who lived in the *foyers*, and on the other the professionals, usually educated and financially comfortable people from the upper classes of African societies."[11]

The professionals shared radically different experiences than the workers, and the students, for sure, shared different goals. Determined to complete their studies, they longed to return home and swell the ranks of the new postcolonial elite. They also led a much different lifestyle than the workers. Many students resided at the Cité universitaire (university housing) or paid for room and board in a French family. As described in *Jeunes Africains à Paris* (Young Africans in Paris), a documentary produced by ORTF, the national television station, most students depended on scholarships to survive. But it was not unusual that a few students worked part-time to supplement their scholarships, which all too often did not cover most of their living expenses. The least privileged students who did not find part-time employment often struggled to make ends meet. For that reason, they found roommates and rented cheap rooms in generally undesirable hotels. But as one student recalls, many of these small hotels were extremely prejudiced towards Africans, frequently refusing to rent to any blacks, even when most of the rooms were vacant.[12]

In spite of these kinds of discrimination, most African students and professionals frequently crossed the color line, and as could be expected, forged friendships with French people. Occasionally, these friendships evolved into intimate relationships and partnerships—usually between African men and French women because the African male-to-female ratio was much higher for the men. But even here, the situation was more complex than the documentaries suggest. *L'Afrique des banlieues* and *Jeunes Africains à Paris* imply that African students easily forged romantic unions with their white counterparts, yet a number of studies surfacing in the sixties reveal that many French people viewed these relationships with contempt; they warned of their "unnatural" characteristics, stressing the couples' cultural incompatibility.[13] Interestingly, while Frenchmen have historically praised *métissage*, a euphemism for the spread of French sociocultural values, they seemed uncomfortable with *métissage* at home, especially when it involved a white woman and an African man.[14] In 1963, a study found that 68 percent of French people were willing to work with sub-Saharan African migrants, and an astounding 63 percent opposed the idea of interracial marriage. Reflecting the post–Algerian War climate, the French attitude toward North Africans tended to be even grimmer.[15] In other words, whether Africans were educated or not, most French people sought to distance themselves from them, especially when it came to love across the color line.

Chapter Three

However, many Africans dismissed this behavior. As agents of their destiny, who viewed the world through their own intellectual, cultural, ethnic, racial, and class lenses, they also formulated their own opinions of French people and interracial relationships. Many did not mind having meaningful relations with progressive French people; not without reason, they preferred open-minded and formally educated French people, but remained suspicious of the *petit Français* (French people from the lower classes). African parents also encouraged their children to search for partners in circles of well-to-do African families with whom they shared cultural similarities. As Mrs. Diop remembers, "We knew our roots and we were proud of our heritage. Some white families worried that our children would develop romantic relationships with their children . . . well, they probably would be surprised to know that we frequently found their children unworthy of our own children."[16]

In retrospect, during the late postwar period, most African students and professionals remained within their respective social class and interacted with French people. Only a few African students, usually those who taught literacy classes with AFTAM and Le Secours Catholique, maintained regular contact with African workers.[17] Reflecting upon the roots of this phenomenon, in 2004 Mr. Lafon, a retired Cameroonian professional, remembered that he used to look down upon "lesser"-educated African migrants, particularly Malian, Senegalese, Mauritanian, and Ivorian workers. Though he was living in France and the French no longer colonized Cameroon, he maintained that the colonial ideology, which accentuated differences between non-French and French-educated Africans, strongly affected him.[18] Thus, for this man, distancing himself from African laborers in Paris was merely an attempt to validate his place in French society as a productive, intelligent, and honorable individual—in sum, a member of the French middle class.

But in 2004, when I first interviewed Mr. Lafon, the tide had turned; illustrating the intellectual evolution that has occurred since independence and the declining significance of class among the African diaspora in France, the retired Cameroonian professional held different views of Malian, Senegalese, Mauritanian, or Ivorian workers. He no longer saw a major class and intellectual divide between African workers and professionals. He now gravitates toward spaces frequented by all kinds of African people, usually markets where he buys African food, spices, and vegetables, or the African foyers near the Chevaleret metro station, where he can eat a sumptuous and affordable West African meal at the cafeteria. The social context is entirely different. Whereas forty years ago he avoided the foyers, supposedly populated by "lower-class" African migrants, in the post-2000 era they have become his preferred location to socialize and dine. In many ways, the foyer of the Chevaleret metro station, which among other things offers barber services, African products, food, and entertainment, has become his Africa in Paris.

Without a doubt, this man's testimony corroborates with the documentaries, which highlight the importance of class division within the Continental African diaspora during the postwar period. Still, my Cameroonian informant and the documentaries failed to discuss a major component of the African community in Paris, namely, women. Indeed, African women migrated to France as wives, students, professionals, and even as migrant workers, usually domestics sponsored by French families returning from the former colonies. After all, the services they provided—cooking, cleaning, and babysitting—were highly desirable in the context of urban France. *Black Girl*, Ousmane Sembène's classic film about a Senegalese woman who works as a live-in maid/cook/babysitter, both captures and dramatizes this postcolonial phenomenon, as Diouana, the main character, commits suicide after suffering from isolation and labor exploitation.[19] But aside from Ousmane Sembène's film, African women are invisible in French scholarship and media. Yet, the archives, and especially my fieldwork, suggest otherwise.

Although more African males migrated to Paris, a small number of women also journeyed and lived in the City of Light throughout the sixties. In 1962 the Ministry of the Interior found that 3,820 African women lived in France, and by 1968, the number had modestly increased to 4,460.[20] Moreover, as Mrs. Diop and Mr. Joachim stated, they shared a circle of friends, which included many women from the middle class, although the majority worked in the domestic sphere.[21] Naturally, during my fieldwork I tried to know more about the lives of these women—who they were, what kind of lifestyle they led, and what challenges they faced. When I interviewed Mrs. Diop and Mr. Joachim, I attempted to develop a conversation with Mrs. Diop about the condition of women in Paris, asking her about her own experiences as a young Senegalese woman; however, she politely indicated that she mainly took care of her family. I felt that she did not want to delve into the past, so I continued my conversation with Mr. Joachim as she listened, nodded, and looked at documents on her desk, sometimes interrupting Mr. Joachim to add a few comments.

A couple of weeks later, as I was heading to the Bibliothèque François Mitterrand for research, by sheer luck I stumbled upon a small, not-for-profit organization catering to African women in Paris. Curious about the organization, and searching for potential leads, I walked in, thirsty for information. At the same time, the director, Mrs. Dacosta, a Senegalese woman who had been in France since the late sixties, arrived. We met and I introduced her to my research, which she found interesting. I subsequently asked her for an interview, and despite her busy schedule, she kindly agreed to give me a few minutes. As soon as we began our discussion, I knew that her educational background, commitment to helping African women, and wealth of experiences in Paris would enrich my study. Neither the archives nor the documentaries have documented the lives of African women who, like Mrs. Dacosta, lived in or migrated to Paris during that era. As you shall see in the following paragraphs, not only do Mrs. Dacosta's experiences shed much light on the condition of African women from the upper classes in Paris of the sixties, but her testimonies also open a window onto the challenges that are unique to women across all classes. Though I only begin to scratch the surface of African women's history in postcolonial Paris, Mrs. Dacosta's testimony reveals much about the ways in which certain African individuals influenced the French, as well as the complex process of African community formation.

Originally from Guinea-Bissau, Mrs. Dacosta grew up in Senegal. In 1967, she migrated to Paris with her late husband, who had been recruited by a renowned international company.[22] She had already passed her *baccalauréat* and intended to continue studying at a French university, but an unexpected pregnancy forced her to reconsider her plans. As we began our discussion, I clearly realized that African women shared different experiences than the men. I first asked Madame Dacosta if she had been lonely when she initially arrived in the French capital. After all, if one thing distinguished Paris from urban and rural sub-Saharan Africa, and for that matter, the Caribbean, it was social interaction. Unlike the beautiful City of Light, where like most Western cities one can live in total anonymity, in the former colonies people, especially women, are always surrounded by family members or friends; solitude is almost a curse.

To my surprise, Mrs. Dacosta did not feel isolated or alone when she arrived in Paris. She and her husband successfully reconstructed their Senegalese community in France, as she claims:

> We integrated Paris fairly easily. We rented a large house and often organized small social gatherings. Once a month we had a huge party, during which I asked for small contributions. I used the money to cover the expenses for the party and help someone in need. Most of our friends were young professionals, students, or people that we knew from Senegal. Our house was alive. We usually had a guest or two—a family member visiting France, someone in transition who needed temporary housing—people needed help for various reasons. I also met another Senegalese woman and we developed a strong friendship. I think our friendship helped both of us cope with our new environment.[23]

Mrs. Dacosta suggested that her life was rather pleasant. In fact, due to her social status, she was able to raise money at parties she organized at her house. She helped needy students, or sometimes families struggling to make ends meet, which suggests that many African migrants depended on their community of friends and family to function. However, she noted that certain women, particularly single women, shared harsh experiences. For one, despite having small social networks and limited funds, these young women had to secure housing in an expensive city. Like the men, women students did not always secure a room at the Cité universitaire (university housing), which forced them to look for roommates; certain female students even took live-in domestic jobs while attending school.

Above all, single women who became pregnant faced the toughest ordeal. As Mrs. Dacosta recalls, "They had to care for themselves and their newborn. It was a financially, psychologically, and emotionally draining experience. They needed help from French social agencies; however, during that time only one organization assisted foreign women in this predicament."[24] In many ways, these women had been victimized by the double-edged sword of patriarchy; their male "partner" easily avoided the weight of paternity, and French agencies assumed they depended upon a working male. On top of this marginalizing phenomenon, Parisian city officials considered the number of African women in Paris to be marginal, which according to Mrs. Dacosta created a double standard. For example, African male workers had access to foyers; African female workers did not. As a result, many single African women lived in fear of being forced onto the street, a fear that, according to Mrs. Dacosta, also concerned the males. Indeed, she remembers that during this era, African people displayed much solidarity toward each other, especially in the foyers. However, conflicts between people and groups erupted, which forced certain migrants to spend a few nights in parks or under bridges.[25]

Mrs. Dacosta also noticed that family issues concerned African women greatly. Apparently many African mothers worried that their children faced unusual circumstances at school. More precisely, they often felt as if the educational landscape was polluted by anti-black racism. As Maryse Condé reminds us, French teachers displayed much prejudice towards black students—particularly African students, whom they often considered inferior to their Caribbean counterparts.[26] However, Mrs. Dacosta believes that in those days most African mothers were on top of this situation, as their educational and socioeconomic background gave them the necessary ammunition to defend and empower their children to manage these obstacles.

In addition to the well-being of children, it seems that issues of gender relations also troubled women. Mrs. Dacosta suggests that migrating to France did not influence family and couple dynamics. She claims, "Women still maintained the same roles as in Africa; they did the household chores and took care of the children, even if they had a job." However, she observed that married couples faced new challenges; certain women wanted to play a more prominent role in managing the household, which often created clashes with their husbands. Indeed, it may have been that gender parity was more common in France than West Africa. After all, the African continent had experienced Islamization and decades of colonization, which regrettably stalled progress in this domain.[27] Consequently, as the equality of the sexes appeared more palpable in France, marital conflicts between certain African couples increased.

For Mrs. Dacosta, control over financial matters represented the principal source of contention. Certain men assumed that marriage gave them absolute power over everything and everyone in the household. So, even if their wives led professional lives, these men wanted complete control over them, including taking their monthly paychecks. Logically, in addition to the unbalanced division of labor at home, such dictatorial behavior led many women to seek a divorce—a phenomenon, Mrs. Dacosta argues, that has persisted up to the present time (2004).[28]

Madame Dacosta's testimony gives meaning to the scholarship on black women in Europe and the United States, which generally highlights how the intersection of race, class, and gender translates into exclusion, oppression, and above all, resistance.[29] In the context of Paris of the sixties, African women coped with unequal gendered relations and anti-black racism. Like the males, they embodied the uncivilized colonial subjects, but unlike them, they also negotiated the multiple dimensions of patriarchy. Thus, as expected, this injurious combination engendered resistance. Sometimes women sought to free themselves from oppressive relationships. As mothers, they also protected their children from French teachers and administrators who often viewed black students through colonial lenses. But most importantly, African women helped decolonize French notions of African identity. In fact, Mrs. Dacosta remembered an anecdote that truly speaks to the dialectics between marginalization, resistance, and the decolonization of social relations between French and African individuals in postcolonial France.

As a humble smile conquered her face, Mrs. Dacosta told me about an interesting personal encounter at a Parisian outdoor market, where the sight of fresh vegetables, meats, pastries, and cheeses typically sweeps people up into seventh heaven:

> On a Sunday, not too long after I arrived in Paris, I was shopping at a public street market when a French vendor spoke to me in *petit nègre* [broken French], probably assuming that I did not speak French. Feeling quite insulted, to his surprise, I replied in the most polite, formal, and elaborate French. He could not believe his ears, and asked where or how I learned to speak such French. I told him French was such an easy language that I learned it on the flight from Dakar to Paris![30]

The above exchange is not unlike what other African women and men routinely experienced during this era. These social encounters, although apparently insignificant, were crucially important in the scheme of French and black identity construction in postcolonial France. Indeed, by refusing to be labeled something that she is not, Mrs. Dacosta altered the vendor's conception of African identity, and in many ways, of his own French identity. Not only did her reply dethrone the French language, which was considered more complex than, and superior to, "primitive" African languages, but it also taught the Frenchman how to relate politely to someone from the former colonies. In other words, the encounter and verbal exchange between Mrs. Dacosta and the vendor is just one episode among many others that cumulatively helped decolonize social relations between African and French people.

Still, decolonizing social relations between African and French individuals in France of the sixties was a struggle, especially in regard to language, because as Mrs. Dacosta indicates, many French citizens used language to uphold colonial hierarchies. If, in the twenty-first century, France and other Western nations reward immigrants for trying to speak the host country's language, in the sixties many French citizens could not even fathom the idea that Africans, the quintessential *indigènes*, could speak, or learn how to speak, proper French; when Africans spoke or tried to speak French, it was not uncommon for certain French individuals to make fun of them. In fact, just as Mrs. Dacosta experienced, many French citizens elected to speak to Africans in *petit nègre*, a sort of broken or simplified French used in the former sub-Saharan African colonies. The term *petit nègre*, which first appeared in the *Larousse* (French dictionary) in 1927, was defined as "elementary French spoken by Negroes in the colonies." In reality, French colonial soldiers and officers probably used it more frequently to address African soldiers, domestics, and workers—in sum, the so-called *indigènes*. After all, they had invented this pseudo-language to communicate with their colonial subjects, people allegedly incapable of learning to speak proper French. In contrast, they usually spoke French to African teachers, translators, or low-ranked officers, who by virtue of their fluency in French earned the superior status of évolués. According to the historian James Genova, however, "What perhaps most distinguished the évolués from the rest of West African society was their place of residence. The French-trained elite was an urban social group . . . which occupied a separate physical space from that of the native subject, yet only part way between metropolitan and indigenous life."[31]

While scholars like Genova demonstrate how language, space, and power in colonial Africa led to the production of social inequalities, it remains unclear as to how this process persisted in the postcolonial period, particularly in the context of

Chapter Three

France. In fact, few scholars discuss the relationship between the French language, the African migration, the continuation of colonial relations, and the reproduction of social inequalities in postcolonial Paris. The documentaries on African migrants of the sixties, however, shed light on this important yet neglected phenomenon.[32] Like my ethnographic findings, they reveal that certain French people used language to reinforce the colonial dichotomy and reinvent themselves as modern "bwanas," a term that, during the colonial period, connoted the superiority of French colonizers over their African colonial subjects. In *Ouvriers noirs*, the following scene depicting an African man interviewing for a job exemplifies this phenomenon. The young man, apparently not more than twenty-five years old, walks into an office asking for work. A Frenchman, whose eyes remain glued on a pile of paper, is sitting behind a desk, seemingly hypnotized by his work. With a pen in one hand, he examines documents closely, ignoring the young man's presence. Then, abruptly, the French employer, a white male presumably in his late forties or fifties, interrupts his all-consuming office work and begins scrutinizing the applicant, apparently trying to determine his physical health. Anyone familiar with colonial relations immediately understands how, in the eyes of the French employer, the young African man represents an object of production—not a potential employee.

Subsequently, the French employer starts interviewing the worker. In a tone usually reserved for "bad-mannered" children, he addresses him in *petit nègre*, purposely shortening his sentences. "You want work?" "You use machine before?" he asks. Then, the brief interview ends on the same note as it had started; the employer dives back into his paperwork, and without looking at the applicant, shuffling papers, he dismissively offers him the position. However, what is most disheartening is what occurs after the interview. In a very nonchalant manner, stripping him of his identity, the French employer assigns the young black man a number, which he affirms will be his designated name at the workplace. Graciously, the young worker, who has become another number, exits the office with a thankful smile.

The above exchange between the employer and the African applicant mirrors the sort of dialogue between the French and people of African descent that Fanon describes in his groundbreaking monograph *Black Skin, White Masks*.[33] For Fanon, French was a tool of domination, as it perpetuated the inferiority of local languages and cultures. He believed French people utilized language to maintain their position of power vis-à-vis people of color; using *petit nègre* to address someone of Caribbean or African origin was the quintessential example of colonial domination.[34] For Fanon, speaking to black people in *petit nègre* reinforces the idea that they still have a childlike mind; it means that blacks are not civilized, and that whites must come down from their tower of knowledge to address and guide the former. In fact, according to Fanon,

"Talking to Negroes in this way gets down to their level, it puts them at ease ... it reassures them"; it expresses the thought "You'd better keep your place."[35] In other words, it is a mechanism that reinforces the colonizer/colonized dichotomy.

Reading Fanon's observation in conjunction with the documentaries demonstrates how language continuously structured social relations between the French and African migrants. Although the French did not use *petit nègre* as frequently as they did during the colonial period, certain French citizens still utilized it to reinforce colonial hierarchies. From a labor perspective, when French employers spoke *petit nègre* to African workers, not only did they assert their superiority over them, but they also implied that Africans were limited to employment that required little thinking, no reading, and intense manual labor—in other words, the lower-wage jobs that no one wanted. In hindsight, it appears that during the colonial period French people used *petit nègre* to communicate with "savages" unable to learn French. However, as *petit nègre* resurfaced in postcolonial Paris, it became entangled in a web of discrimination, and perhaps nostalgia for the "good old colonial days."

In conclusion, the documentaries about African migrants in Paris illuminate the connections between migration, colonial continuities, and social exclusion. To some extent, Max Zelenka's *Ibrahima* captures the ambivalent position of African workers in Paris, as he describes in fourteen brief and silent minutes a young man sweeping the streets and wandering throughout the capital's metro system. The young man seems invisible—an invisibility that bears many similarities to the idea of social invisibility expounded in *The Invisible Man*, Ralph Ellison's award-winning novel.[36] For Zelenka, despite their hard work and good intentions, African labor migrants cannot integrate into the fabric of Parisian society because the French choose to ignore their presence.[37]

Zelenka turned the camera into an instrument of the arts to make a social commentary on the condition of African migrants and the characteristics of French society. But aside from his contribution, French documentaries of the sixties often perpetuated preconceived notions of African identity. Even when they highlighted the importance of class differences within the Continental African diaspora, they depicted most African subjects as primitive people struggling with the French language and victimized by the modern city. In a striking fashion, not only did the documentaries fail to examine how the state apparatus influenced the migrants, but they also stripped them of any social agency in the public sphere. They avoided asking questions that would lend credence to the presence of contentious African subjects in the French Republic. For instance, they did not question the extent to which African workers tolerated or protested against certain forms of abuse at the workplace and the foyers. Or, whether African labor migrants forged connections with other migrants and French citizens striking for higher wages and demanding better working conditions. In the final analysis, the documentaries failed to give the migrants a voice. As the example of the young African worker who agreed to be called by a number suggests, Africans were seemingly acquiescent and tolerant individuals. But is that really true? Did the man portrayed in *Ouvriers noirs de Paris*—truly a symbol of African workers in France—remain just a number? Or, did he encourage his French employer to treat him respectfully and call him by his real name?

Like all migrants, Africans wanted fair pay, adequate housing, and to be treated with dignity. As proud people, they did not wish to be treated like colonial subjects. They also protested to improve their working and living conditions. Though the documentaries did not explore this theme, many Africans stood up against French employers, city officials, and foyer managers who still maintained paternalistic relations with them. Clearly, these moments and movements of resistance played an important role in rooting the African community in Paris and decolonizing social relations between African and French individuals in postcolonial France.

Chapter 4

Work, Housing, Colonial Relations, and the Formation of Oppositional Identities among Working-Class African Workers

> We must take action immediately or these protests will eventually threaten our national security. If they persist we must deport the ringleaders; they are violating our hospitality and the political accords between France and their countries.
>
> —Mr. Brassen, Le commissaire principal (police chief), Paris, 1968

In the sixties, the trope of the uncivilized African migrant victimized by modern French society regularly surfaced in government discourse and the press. In browsing through bookstores, one of the French favorite pastimes, it was not unusual to stumble upon journal articles and books depicting African migrants as "*indigènes*" incapable of living in the French Republic. In *La France étrangère*, for example, Banine satirized African workers, suggesting that migrating to France had changed them from predators of wild animals into the prey of French employers.

> One morning, at 6:00 AM, sitting peacefully on the deserted Place Victor-Hugo . . . I heard a loud noise. Suddenly a huge garbage truck appeared . . . it was a brand new model, which was followed by another, and another, and another. I alone, very attentively, witnessed this bizarre parade. While these monstrous machines swallowing our garbage soon became mundane, the two ebony lackeys standing behind the truck holding an invisible handle with one hand and swinging carelessly from left to right, quickly captured my attention. Black lackeys or monkeys holding the branch

of a tropical tree? These garbage men were tall, lean, and black as shoe polish. It was surreal; in the heart of a beautiful Parisian neighborhood, a black tribe and a horde of roaring mastodons were looking for garbage. But where are the bows and arrows, the nets and sticks, and the weapons that tame the lions and kill the antelopes? They must be rusting in the abandoned villages. In Paris, however, the tribe uses brooms, shovels, wheelbarrows, spades, and trowels. While these transplanted people no longer fear wild animals, they now have to deal with French employers who are equally tough. They cannot even consult their sorcerers who have been replaced by doctors. So how are they adapting to their new life? We can guess: poorly.[1]

Authors like Banine had a large audience of people who still believed that France had a mission to civilize its former colonies. Many Frenchmen and European migrants also treated African workers as colonial subjects. However, following a pattern that is common among migrant communities, most African workers worked hard, dismissing the demeaning comments, the misplaced sarcasm, and the other types of alienating behaviors coming from the "natives." Nonetheless, even if they kept their eyes on the prize—earning wages to send remittances home—they did not always tolerate being mistreated.

Work and the Formation of Oppositional Identities mong African Workers

Upon migrating to the Parisian region, many Africans remained on the margins of the labor market. Unlike most French workers, they rarely received a fair monthly salary, much less fringe benefits. African migrants often took jobs that repelled French workers, who generally preferred the higher paid, least physical, and more technical and administrative-oriented positions created during the economic boom.[2] In many ways, African workers shared unique experiences at the workplace. Not only did they receive the worst positions, but most of their French colleagues drew away from them.[3] In fact, a government study indicates that French workers found their African colleagues unpredictable and unapproachable—in sum, too different from them.[4] Such French perceptions of African workers relegated the latter to the bottom of the labor market.

Nonetheless, despite this uncomfortable situation, African labor migrants still had their own professional standards and desires. Above all, they disliked working for private contractors in the construction industry. These employers paid poorly and did not care if African migrants worked in unsafe conditions. Typically, when Africans worked for construction contractors, they carried heavy materials up and down small buildings, dug ditches, swept, cleaned with unhealthy chemicals, and demolished structures in good or bad weather. It was physically demanding and excruciating work. Mr. N'Diaye, a transnational Senegalese worker who ultimately settled in France, remembers that he hated working in construction when he was young. According to him, the workers were at the mercy of unreliable bosses, who gladly assigned dangerous and exhausting tasks. His comments almost paint such work environments as physically and psychologically traumatic:

> Sometimes there was a lot of tension with the other workers. The Arabs, the French, the Portuguese, and even the Spanish did not like us too much. Above all, I hated construction work. It was very difficult; in hot or cold weather, we had to dig, clean, climb, carry heavy material, push wheelbarrows, or cement foundations. We carried heavy loads up ladders, usually heavy buckets or tools. That type of work was not only draining, it was also dangerous. But we had to do it—it was that or nothing else—and as God knows, we had children to feed.[5]

The vast majority of African workers preferred working for large factories (see table 2).[6] In fact, many of these large factories, especially Renault, which competed with Peugeot, Citroën, and Simca for selling the most cars in French markets, seemed quite willing to hire African workers. In 1963, Renault was the company hiring the most workers from sub-Saharan Africa. More than a thousand men worked for the French automobile company. Traditionally, Renault was known for hiring African men as strikebreakers, but as the economy grew and the demand for labor increased, the company also turned to African workers to fill certain "permanent" positions.[7] In 1965, Renault asked the Ministère du Travail (Department of Labor) if it could hire Malian and Senegalese workers who overstayed their tourist visas. Had the Senegalese or Malian migrants been in possession of Portuguese, Italian, or Spanish passports, in accordance with the immigration policy of the postwar period, the government would have kindly granted their request. But, as institutional racism prescribed, the Ministère du Travail felt highly unsympathetic to the idea, affirming that it would stimulate the already "out of control" African migration.[8] Nonetheless, due to Renault's perseverance and appetite for cheap African workers, the Ministère caved in—at least partially—since it ruled that if the automobile factory could not find any available "legal" workers, then it could make a few exceptions and, as it commonly did for European migrants, grant Africans a job contract so they could obtain the precious *carte de travail* (a work permit).[9]

Chapter Four

Table 2. Number of Africans working in factories and small businesses (1963)

	MANŒUVRES*	OS†	OP‡
AUTOMOBILE INDUSTRY	1,350	1,080	720	0
ELECTRICAL AND MECHANICAL INDUSTRY	955	852	96	7
OTHER BUSINESSES	972	807	143	22

Source: "Enquête sur les travailleurs africains en France," Centre des Archives Contemporaines, Fontainebleau, Box 19780262, art. 11.
* A manœuvre is a manual worker who usually performs difficult physical tasks.
† Ouvrier spécialisé (specialized worker).
‡ Ouvrier professionel (professional worker).

Many Africans who received offers to work for Renault and the other large factories felt victorious. Usually, they lived in a foyer nearby the factory and rode a factory bus to work on a daily basis. Although confined to the bottom of the factory hierarchy, these men cherished the employment stability and the wages, which often surpassed what smaller French employers offered. In fact, in a very detailed study, the Préfecture de Paris highlighted the difference between the salary, the labor, and the work schedule of African migrants working for large factories and small businesses. In striking fashion, it only confirms that small businesses willingly exploited hard-working African migrants, who desperately needed an income to support their kin abroad:

> Despite having a very long work schedule, Africans are always willing to work overtime. They usually work six days a week for a total of fifty-five hours; ten hours per day from Monday to Friday, and five hours on Saturdays. When they work for large factories, they receive a salary based on their qualifications and production. In contrast, the small businesses, which were not keen to answer our questions, tend to exploit these workers. The worse cases of exploitation that we have encountered tend to be in companies where the workers are paid by the "piece," which they produce. For example, at DETHON & Cie (18th Arrondissement, Bd. de la Chapelle), a company that makes bags, an African migrant typically works eight to twelve hours a day, approximately forty-nine hours a week for a pay ranging from 70 to 90 francs per week, or 1.75 francs per hour. Their salary is much less than Africans who, as Ouvriers Spécialisés and Ouvriers Professionels in large factories, earn between 2.50 and 2.80 francs per hour.[10]

Thus, for obvious reasons, Africans preferred working for large factories. However, in no way does this signify that the work environment at the factories was African-friendly.

African workers being bused from their foyer to the Renault Factory. (Photo used with permission of the Institut CGT [Confédération Générale du Gravail] d'Histoire Sociale.)

Mr. N'Diaye, who in previous paragraphs shared his experience as a day laborer, also worked in an automobile factory. Although he earned a higher income and enjoyed better working conditions, he remembered experiencing multiple types of condescending behavior from his colleagues and managers. During our discussion, he recalled that taking breaks was usually a contested matter; his manager, a Frenchman who clearly resented African migrants, preferred seeing him mopping floors or glued to his designated workstation. The tension between certain French managers and African workers like Mr. N'Diaye was widespread. In an attempt to capture this phenomenon, jokingly, Mr. N'Diaye asserted that African workers toiling on the factory line could not even go pee. With a sense of humor, he added, "Who could have imagined that a couple of African migrants could bankrupt Renault by urinating at work?"[11] In retrospect, when thinking about his situation at the factory, Mr. N'Diaye admits to having been treated unfairly. Yet, he feels no regret. He sees this phenomenon as a reality of the sixties,

Chapter Four

when colonial paternalism truly structured Franco-African relations at the workplace. Indeed, it was not uncommon for certain African workers to conform to French notions of African identity in order to assuage or avoid tensions.

Simultaneously, and most interestingly, while the legacy of French colonialism fostered paternalism at the workplace, it also generated fears of African males. During the colonial period, Frenchmen in Africa viewed Africans as uncivilized and sometimes unpredictable and dangerous subjects.[12] These perspectives actually resurfaced in postcolonial Paris. Apparently, certain Frenchmen believed in the myth of the "passive and obedient" African subject who, unexpectedly, could change into a violent and deceptively aggressive individual. As the following anecdote from researchers affiliated with the Préfecture de Paris suggests, African subjects in the workplace were both exploited and feared:

> Totally out of breath, one afternoon an Algerian worker came running to his French manager offering his resignation. They never saw him again. He had been caught stealing 50 francs from a black African man, who took out a knife and threatened to slit his throat after work. The manager is convinced that the black man would have done it. Africans often settle their score after work. It is no secret that these meetings have turned into executions. There have been a few incidents between North and sub-Saharan Africans, but the latter usually prevail. We find that the angry black man becomes unrecognizable. He ignores all dangers and manipulates the knife with a rare dexterity. Moreover, although many blacks are mentally slow, they are very tall; some of them are particularly strong.[13]

Despite a dormant yet omnipresent fear of African labor migrants, French managers and employers still exploited and disrespected these black workers. Since most Africans could not hide behind the shield of French citizenship, they often chose not to retaliate. However, while they ignored the demeaning comments of racist coworkers, Africans surely retaliated when French managers made inappropriate physical contact. Researchers from the Préfecture de Paris observed that physical altercations between French managers and African employees were quite common, asserting, "We know that serious incidents occur frequently. Unfortunately, the physical altercations between blacks and their *chefs d'équipe* [team managers] are usually the product of misunderstandings."[14] The researchers believed the conflicts could have been avoided if French managers understood how their "primitive" colleagues functioned. Citing the testimony of a manager from DUVOISIN, a corporation located in Epinay, they argued that the solution lay in comprehending the "African mentality":

It is important that blacks are well-supervised and assigned tasks that correspond to their cognitive capabilities. French people hardly know them; they ignore their religious traditions, their acute sense of justice, their love for communal life, and how they like to learn by following examples. It is easy to deal with them. There is only one condition: one has to understand *la mentalité noire* [the black way of thinking].[15]

In retrospect, however, paternalistic managers like the one from Duvoisin seemed more successful at preventing physical altercations than blatantly racist ones, who resorted to violence. Indeed, Africans did not tolerate "corporal punishment." They associated physical abuse with colonialism and manifested their unwillingness to be treated like "disobedient children" from the former colonies.

But the most common mode of African resistance in the labor market was what I call "job flight." Due to the rapid and exponential economic growth of the "Glorious Thirty," a plethora of blue-collar and generally undesirable jobs were available. Consequently, without hesitation, when African workers found more lucrative positions, they abandoned their old jobs, leaving their responsibilities to their insensitive and/or exploitative employers. Relentlessly and without remorse, flying from one job to another, they avoided labor exploitation and increased their earnings. In fact, in the 1960s, throughout ten years of interrupted stay in France (they visited home at least once every two to three years), an African worker could have easily held five different jobs, one of which he most likely obtained "out of flight."[16] Interestingly, by changing jobs frequently, Africans influenced labor relations. They forced French employers to pay a certain amount in order to keep them on the payroll, consequently standardizing a sort of informal minimum wage, which was probably lower than the regular minimum wage. In that sense, job flight truly embodied the invisible power of dispossessed people.

African resistance in the labor market was effective yet invisible. Unlike their Caribbean counterparts, who enjoyed certain attributes of French citizenship, Africans had to walk a fine line to avoid deportation or losing their jobs. They protested with occasional fistfights, and more commonly, by flight. These fights and flights sent messages to French employers, who reluctantly or not, upgraded their colonial behavior and perception of African workers to correspond with the realities of the postcolonial era. However, the workplace is not the only site where the French encounter with Africans produced new forms of social relations. The resistance movements that unfolded throughout many African foyers from the late sixties to the mid-seventies also played a critical role in changing the colonial dimension of Franco-African relations in postcolonial Paris.

The African Foyers as Sites of Contestation and Identity Formation

The foyers emerged during the mid-nineteenth century in the context of rural-urban migration. Many young Frenchmen and women from rural areas moved to the capital seeking professional opportunities, but found themselves living in the streets, prompting French officials, who feared the youth would fall prey to moral corruption and criminals, to intervene. In that spirit, they transformed large houses and warehouses into buildings capable of accommodating dozens of young peasants unable to make their way in the city. Although the first foyers initially catered to the youth, by the turn of the twentieth century they extended their services to women, the homeless, students, and children.[17] Almost half a century later, by the 1950s, a new genre of foyers emerged in the Parisian region. Principally designed to house the increasing number of migrant workers from Algeria and the neighboring European countries, *les foyers de travailleurs migrants* (hostels for migrant workers) quickly became an integral part of the Parisian landscape. A decade later, many foyers comprised of sub-Saharan African labor migrants—what is commonly referred to as *les foyers Africains*—sprouted in Paris. French officials viewed these foyers as an opportunity to continue civilizing the "indigènes" and empower them to develop their own nation. Only a few French officials, who were profoundly plagued by anti-black racism, disapproved of this strategy, fearing that black migrants would contaminate France with their tropical diseases, or worse, create American-style black ghettos. However, unlike government officials, who from a very distant standpoint reflected on the role of African foyers in Parisian society, many white Parisians found themselves living in close proximity to the new dwellings. While certain French people accepted their new neighbors, others expressed feelings of discomfort and anger at the sight of so many black people settling in their otherwise racially homogenous community.[18]

Though violent welcomes rarely occurred, a minority of French people went to great lengths to contest the foyers' right to exist, sending letters of protest to the Préfecture de Paris and their respective city halls. The following petition, dated August 17, 1967, which was signed by seventeen people and addressed to the mayor of St. Denis, a commune located in Northern Paris, illustrates the sentiments that these angry Parisians felt towards their new African neighbors:

> Our neighborhood changed for the worse when these people moved into the *foyer*. These individuals wake up when we go to sleep. They sing, dance, and quarrel among each other beyond the wee hours of the morning. We hear the noise of water going

down the drain throughout the night. If we dare ask them to make less noise, they reply with obscenities, and sometimes, they threaten to slit our throats.... However, we know that we—the whites and the French—must respect the law. Doesn't the law apply to these people as well? Women can no longer walk alone without being harassed. Their windows face our windows, which are only standing four meters away. As you can imagine, we can no longer open our windows. Moreover, they keep the light on for the entire night, which obviously prevents us from sleeping. We want our neighborhood to be quiet again, and we want it now.[19]

But despite bothering certain white Parisians, with the support of many city officials and NGOs, the African foyers continued to sprout in the city. French officials feared that transnational African migrants living in substandard conditions would develop contagious diseases, and thus conducted a campaign to close the illegal dwellings—the basements, dilapidated warehouses, attics, and cheap hotels—which sometimes hosted twenty to thirty migrants. In fact, as early as 1964, with the support of the Ministry of the Interior and the Public Health Ministry, the Fond d'Action Social (FAS), a government agency catering to immigrants and the poor, had pledged money to build more foyers to improve the living conditions of African migrants in Paris.[20] Demonstrating its commitment to creating foyers for African migrants, the FAS proudly affirmed, "From the fall of 1964 to December 31, 1966, we have financed 31 housing operations for African migrants, which will provide 5,327 new beds upon their completion."[21]

African migrants used to dark, cold, and unhealthy basements welcomed the new foyers, which for the most part saw the light of day in the mid-sixties. However, these new dwellings engendered a more complex set of problems. For one, white French administrators and managers who had previously worked in the colonial administration usually managed the new foyers. As late as 1972, out of the 151 administrators and managers working throughout the African foyers of the Parisian region, 144 had a military background, and out of those employees, 138 had served in Africa. The civilians also had an African connection; three of the seven civilians had worked in North Africa and two others were born in Algeria.[22] Unsurprisingly, feelings of colonial nostalgia were prevalent among the foyers' staff. As the literature on the Pieds-Noirs (the French who fled the Algerian War of Independence) suggests, these feelings of nostalgia were particularly strong within this population.[23] After all, as a privileged racial minority in North Africa, they had enjoyed a lifestyle much superior to what they were experiencing in France.[24] Likewise, French people who had lived in the former sub-Saharan African colonies had many reasons to miss the colonial days. In *Black Girl*, Ousmane Sembène also demonstrates how these nostalgic sentiments infused the daily lives of French people who returned from Senegal. Thus, it would not be too far-fetched to conclude that certain foyer administrators still viewed African labor migrants as *indigènes* living in the French Republic.

Yet, these white administrators played diverse and important roles in the daily operations of the foyers. They interfaced with the main office, handled all aspects of the foyers' maintenance, and enforced the various rules and regulations; however, as former colonial administrators and settlers, they lacked professionalism and failed to serve the residents appropriately. According to Mr. Camara, a former resident, they distributed the mail inefficiently, the reception desk's attendant was generally rude, the bathrooms were insalubrious, and the sheets, which were supposed to be replaced every three weeks, remained unwashed for months.[25] Mr. Camara was not pleased with his foyer's physical condition, complaining that it was often cold, unclean, and overcrowded. Yet, he felt even more disappointed by the white concierges, who according to him, "always complicated things." For Mr. Camara, the white concierge minimized his manhood, an attitude that prevented him from inviting friends out of fear of being embarrassed.[26]

While Mr. Camara complained about the staff's attitude and his foyer's rigid rules, other foyers featured even stricter rules and regulations. On the one hand, these arbitrary rules provided guidelines for supervising and "educating" the migrants, and on the other, they made sure the foyers remained efficient, profit-generating enterprises. For example, in an effort to prevent tenants from sharing their rooms with other migrants, certain foyers forbade residents to receive guests. But these policies bore much resemblance to the colonial period, as the staff, which was supposed to cater to the residents' needs, acted as supervisors.

Yet the managers' behavioral issues were only part of the problem. The overall structural condition of the foyers also bothered the men. Many foyers had been built or fixed haphazardly; they were moldy and poorly lit, the ceilings often leaked, and the windows were too small. In many ways, they were just a step above the usual run-down apartments, basements, or wine cellars that African migrants rented from questionable landlords—the *marchands de sommeil* (literally sleep vendors)—or more precisely, the slumlords, which the press routinely described as exploiters and heartless people. A reporter from *La Vie Catholique* who described the condition of African migrants in Paris saw many similarities between the slumlords' basements and the foyers, writing in disbelief:

> Victimized by heartless slumlords, they gravitate towards *foyers*. But these dormitories are in shameful condition. I actually visited one of these so-called *foyers* in Ivry-sur-Seine. It was a former chocolate factory renovated to house Senegalese, Malian, Ivorian, and Mauritanian workers, who coexist peacefully. However, it is hard to determine

how many of them live in this *foyer*. If we count the beds and the straw mattresses, we estimate the number of men to be around 550. But the number is clearly higher than that; certain men work double or even triple shifts, and during their absence other migrants occupy their beds. Thus, about 600 or 700 hundred African migrants actually live in the disaffected chocolate factory.[27]

The above conditions angered many migrants. They felt the administration was maximizing the foyers' income at their expense. Moreover, adding insult to injury, being constantly supervised and forced to sleep on bunk beds in small, poorly lit, and moldy rooms offended the workers.

It was precisely these miserable conditions of—namely, living in unsanitary and expensive low-quality dwellings while dealing with a paternalistic staff—that brewed opposition among the residents. Unlike in the labor market, where most men confronted various forms of exploitation and colonial relations individually, and for the most part tolerated such behavior due to family, personal, or communal responsibilities, in the foyers they faced this problem as a group, a phenomenon generating a completely different reaction. The group dynamic increased self-confidence and fostered unity and strength. Many Africans began voicing their frustration about paying too much rent for such low-quality housing. As a group, the migrants felt more comfortable expressing their unwillingness to accept injustice and colonial treatment under their own roof, even if the foyer was merely a temporary home. Consequently, by the late sixties, protests against the managers' behavior and for better service had become widespread throughout many African foyers of the Parisian region.

To pay lower rent and receive better service, the majority of African residents resorted to rent strikes. They determined that rent strikes would be a successful strategy because the foyers, which were independently operated or partly subsidized by the state, depended on revenues to function and pay the staff. Thus, by the late sixties a vibrant social movement—in fact, the first black social movement in postcolonial France—emerged out of the African foyers. This movement also emerged at a time of social unrest in French society.

The trail of evidence pointing to this black social movement is extremely rich; it includes oral testimonies, newspaper articles, and precious archival documents such as leaflets and pamphlets, which were distributed to recruit disgruntled residents and advance the migrants' cause. These publications, which in the sixties were printed with much effort—one needed the services of a "dactylo" (a typist) and a professional press—outline the scope and tone of the movement. As a general rule, the protests had been carefully planned. For weeks, residents held many meetings, addressing the problems they wished to tackle. Subsequently, they chose a representative to serve

Chapter Four

as intermediary between the administration and the residents. The representative, usually an older migrant, was considered the informal ambassador of the foyers, which in many ways could be imagined as micro-level postcolonial African nations in the Parisian region. As a general rule, these older representatives encouraged residents to be patient and "tolerate" their pain; they talked about the rewards of transnational migration—namely, returning home with pockets full of money to lure young women into being their wives and build large families, a much appreciated practice during that era. But despite their discourse of appeasement, they could not tame the younger migrants, who had never imagined living in France in such deplorable conditions. Thus, as leaders and foyer ambassadors, they initiated the first contact with the administration, voicing, as the citation below indicates, the residents' demands in formal letters:

> We have the honor to ask you to fire the manager. He is untrustworthy and exploits us to the highest degree. He does not transmit phone messages, which causes many of us to miss out on job opportunities. He does not sort our mail. The manager also prevents any business representatives from visiting or interacting with the residents. He even prevents language instructors and our friends from entering the building. Yet, he sells vegetables and other items. We have been here for two years and have kept our mouths shut, but now you must hear our grievances. The meals are expensive and do not include any beverages. We are not refusing a rent increase; we are merely demanding better services.... You shall also know that upon signing the lease, each resident pays 5 francs to watch television; we are 700 people, which equals 3,500 francs.[28]

Most of the time, however, the letters fell upon deaf ears. The administration sided with the managers; after all, they hired these Frenchmen because of their experience in dealing with "colonial subjects." The complicity between the managers and the administration only amplified the residents' anger, leading them to adopt more radical alternatives—in other words, to strike for change. A pamphlet entitled "Solidarity among Malian workers in France," which police officers collected for their records during a housing strike in 1969, underscores the causes of the strikes. In a nutshell, this publication only confirms that the foyer's failure to deliver its part of the contract—namely, maintaining sanitary guidelines and providing the residents with heat, water, electricity, gas, and clean sheets on a regular basis—triggered protests. In reading the lines below, one can almost see the migrants gathered at the foyer's doorstep, chanting enthusiastically:

Pas de chauffage—pas d'argent!	No heat—no rent!
Pas d'eau—pas d'argent!	No water—no rent!

Pas de lumière—pas d'argent!	No light—no rent!
Pas de gaz—pas d'argent!	No gas—no rent!
Lavage des draps au moins 3 × par mois	Wash the sheets at least 3 × a month!
Sinon pas d'argent!	Otherwise—no rent![29]

For transnational African labor migrants, who lived in France without the protection of citizenship and a work visa, using rent strikes for self-empowerment proved to be a successful strategy. Usually, after a few weeks of ignoring their demands, without much enthusiasm, the administration, which wanted to avoid financial loss, met with the representatives at the negotiating table.[30] However, on the way to finding common ground, relations between the staff, the administration, and the residents had usually deteriorated; French administrators doubted the integrity of the African movement for better housing, thinking the migrants were merely taking advantage of the system. As Mr. Camara recalls, the managers and the administration accused African workers residing in the foyers of "coming to France to sleep for free."[31] Negotiations, thus, occurred in the midst of tensions and quarrels, a climate that the Frenchmen who worked in the former colonies did not expect.

By the late sixties, the protest for better housing had developed into a larger struggle against French hegemony over the private lives of African workers in Paris. Many African residents wanted more agency in managing their foyer; not only had they grown tired of receiving low-quality services and being subjugated to racism and paternal relations, but they also felt that members of their own community were more qualified to run these foyers. Most of the French managers, they argued, lacked professionalism yet still received handsome salaries. This situation truly angered them. Around the same time, worrying about social unrest in the foyers, the police took a greater interest in monitoring them to determine if the protests resulted from internal or external factors. After all, this was the late sixties, and French law-enforcement officials feared that radical social movements, particularly the flamboyant Black Power movement of the United States, could spill over into black France.

Hoping that Black Power movements were not sprouting among the communities of African workers, the police sent "spies" to the foyers to interview the African representatives. They truly feared that "subversive" movements like the Black Panthers and Cuban-style communism—movements that endorsed armed resistance—could infiltrate these urban dwellings.[32] They investigated the thirty-one African foyers of the Parisian region to determine if the residents posed a threat to society. The police investigation classified the foyers into four different groups, highlighting whether they were publicly or privately owned, how residents paid rent and utilities, and most importantly, if they had experienced social unrest (see table 3).

Table 3. Police investigation of African foyers in Paris of the 1960s

FOYERS' CHARACTERISTICS AND MANAGEMENT STYLE	NUMBER OF RESIDENTS
Privately owned Partly managed by Africans, who want more authority Residents only pay their water, gas, and electricity bill	998
Privately owned Residents contest the management's authority. They seek to determine which residents can pay the rent and refuse to reveal the name of illegal residents	532
Privately owned Residents recognize the management's authority but are constantly protesting and conducting rent strikes	784
State-subsidized Residents constantly challenge the management's authority and refuse to follow the rules	5,008

Source: Archive de la Préfecture de Police, Paris, "Afrique Noire: Deplacement de personnes," box GaA9.

Essentially, the police realized that the quest for self-management was the common thread uniting all the foyers.[33] Still, they worried about potential factors that could "worsen" the situation. Cross-contamination with the various French leftist groups—Trotskyites, Marxists, communists, and progressive human-rights organizations such as the MRAP (Movement Contre le Racisme et l'Antisemitisme et Pour la Paix) and l'ASTI (Aide Sociale aux Travailleurs Immigrés en France)—which wanted to restructure French society, concerned them greatly. They especially worried about cross-contamination with radical African American social movements—what they commonly referred to as *les mouvements Black Power*. In sum, they feared that these radical movements, which appealed to African students—and apparently a handful of students lived in these foyers[34]—could also attract the workers. For sure, the police did not want the housing protests to escalate into protests for racial justice.

To their satisfaction, as police officers closely monitored the foyers and the workers' interaction with African students, they concluded that unity between students and workers for a potential fight against racial inequality seemed unlikely.[35] In the final analysis, they cleverly noted that class differences trumped racial solidarity. They reaffirmed what the documentaries about Africans in Paris posited, namely, that most African professionals and students gravitated around their own social circles. However, the police saw a direct correlation between the protests and ethnic identity. They determined that African labor migrants preferred living in foyers populated with a strong contingency of residents from a similar ethnic group, and indeed, they were right. Because of transnational networks of migration, African migrants tended to live with people from the same towns or villages. They built ethnic enclaves within the foyers, a phenomenon that gave them a sense of comfort and power, and most importantly, facilitated organizing and protesting for change. But the police wanted to stop this pattern.

Noticing the connection between protest and the conglomeration of a dominant ethnic group within certain foyers, French officials decided to implement a divide-and-conquer strategy. French officials from the Préfecture de Paris decided to increase ethnic diversity within the foyers, hoping that language and cultural differences would prevent African workers from joining hands to fight against the managers and the administration. Convinced that this strategy would decrease the number of strikes and uprisings in the foyers, on October 8, 1969, in a letter from the Direction Générale de l'Action Sanitaire et Sociale of the Préfecture de Paris to the Préfet de Paris, Mr. Solminihac, a high-ranked city official, affirmed:

> With the intention to stop the uprisings, which certain African *foyers* have recently experienced, I propose that in the future all the *foyers* should be comprised of not one, but multiple ethnic groups. Perhaps we should consider mixing the Africans with other European migrants. This will reduce the temptation of creating homogeneous movements for the sole purpose of achieving self-management, a problem which occurred last June in one of the ASSOTRAF's (Association pour l'aide aux Travailleurs Africains) buildings in Saint-Denis.[36]

By the early seventies, the divide-and-conquer strategy was showing signs of success. Moreover, the campaign against French slumlords created a sort of rush to the foyers, which also contributed to increasing ethnic diversity. But ultimately, it was the changing national economy that effectively ended the African movement for better housing. Indeed, by 1974 France's economic growth had stalled dramatically, leading French officials to adopt tougher immigration policies towards all immigrants, especially migrants from sub-Saharan Africa. These restrictive immigration policies, which tamed the protests in the foyers, affected the lives of all African people in the Parisian region. Police officers, who had traditionally seen Africans as undesirable labor migrants, began to treat all Africans as illegal immigrants. This phenomenon literally became visible overnight, as the police started a tradition of arbitrary identification checks in the metro and the streets, which generated fear and discomfort within the Continental African diaspora, including the professionals and students. William N'Diaye, a biracial Senegalese man who has French citizenship and lived in Paris during the mid-seventies, shared the following anecdote, which truly captures how the police behaved towards Africans:

In those days, the days of bell-bottom pants, we dressed to impress. Few of us lived in Paris, so we were conscious of our appearance. One day, as I waited patiently in a metro station overflowing with people, two police officers looked in my direction, as if they detected an anomaly. I was wondering what was happening. Was there a sick person behind me, or worse, did someone commit a crime? I was shocked to discover that I was the problem, as the officers walked toward me, asking for my papers.[37]

Thus, all things considered, for most Africans, Paris, the beautiful City of Light, also became synonymous with the policing of their bodies. This social climate helped tame anger in the foyers, because after all, many African workers did not have documentation allowing them to stay legally in France. This new reality upset the African community, which had thus far confronted "body policing" at the airport. But it pleased the Direction Centrale des Renseignements Généraux (DCRG), the intelligence service of the French police, which operated under the Ministry of the Interior. DCRG, or, as it is often called, RG, complemented the various efforts to close the border and decrease the sub-Saharan African migration, which it argued offered no financial advantage and constituted a sanitary threat and a social burden for France. Proclaiming victory, the intelligence services noted that fewer rent strikes were occurring, and that in general, social unrest in the foyers was decreasing.[38]

But in reality, although they prevented the movement for better living conditions in the foyers from escalating into a full-fledged social movement addressing issues of flagrant racial inequality, French officials did not accomplish their ultimate goals. They failed to prevent the influx of African migrants into France, and ostensibly, to keep Paris white; on the contrary, the protests had legitimized African spaces in Paris. Thus, they had won a battle but not the war. After all, not only did African labor migrants pressure the foyers' administrators to keep the rent affordable and provide adequate services, but they also made the issue of housing for African migrants an important part of the discourse on social inequality in Paris. Moreover, as they constantly pressed administrators to keep the foyers cleaner, they forced French officials, who maintained that Africans ignored proper hygienic habits, to reflect on their conception of African identity. Indeed, as the following excerpt of the Préfecture's study on African migrants in Paris suggests, many French officials believed that Africans did not care about housing quality and hygiene; supposedly, as long as they were making enough money, Africans could live happily in any dump:

> These African city dwellers care less about cleanliness and overcrowdedness than the cost of housing. 90% of them live in insalubrious hotels and basements, which 9 out of 10 times are Algerian owned. The overcrowdedness is particularly striking. One

can find 10 bunk beds in a hotel room that typically accommodates two beds. Each set of beds is only separated by 50 lousy centimeters. In the basements, the top bed is also only 50 centimeters away from the ceiling. The lack of closets accentuates the feeling of overcrowdedness. The African, who deeply cares about his clothes, uses his suitcase as a closet and gently hangs his shirt and pants on a hanger held by a single nail. They live in a chaotic situation. When a visitor arrives black faces come out from every corner, and clearly, one notes there are more faces then beds.[39]

Thus, the movement for better housing changed the French perspective of sub-Saharan African migrants, who by virtue of demanding better services and cleaner foyers, defied the colonial stereotype of the dirty, acquiescent, and even subservient African subject. In concert with NGOs such as AFTAM, as well as African activists and associations that advocated for creating more foyers in Paris, the protests in the foyers encouraged city officials to take the matter seriously and allocate more resources to build housing for African migrant workers. This important social movement, which has fallen through the cracks of contemporary French history, stabilized rent in the foyers, forced French administrators to be more professional and improve the *maintenance des lieux*, and helped decrease the number of black tenants living in dark and cold basements. Moreover, by impressing upon the French the notion that the foyers are legitimate African spaces in Paris, where one, irrespective of his legal status, could live without being harassed by government or city officials, this unique African social movement affected both the African and French consciousness.

Ultimately, these African labor migrants strove for what black intellectuals like Fanon aspired to achieve. They did not want to be colonial subjects of the French Republic; they wanted agency in managing their affairs, respect from the French, and the opportunity to acquire capital, which for them meant having a job and paying affordable rent. As African social units in the Parisian region, the African foyers also offer stellar examples of African cooperation and success in the early postcolonial period. They defied the notion that postcolonial Africa and diasporic Africa are defined by hopelessness, corruption, and ethnic strife. Indeed, even if the foyers were ethnically diverse, the movement for better housing thrived, at least for a good five years. If it were not for tougher immigration policies and the policing of African bodies in Paris, the "fury" at the African foyers might not have been tamed, and perhaps would have evolved into a more radical social movement. Nevertheless, the residents achieved two of their goals: they successfully controlled rent inflation and decolonized the established social relations with the French managers.

Interestingly, a similar story was unfolding in the Caribbean community of Paris. At the beginning of the sixties, thousands of French Caribbean individuals from the lower classes also migrated to the Parisian region in search of work. The state had actually invited these people, promising jobs and prosperity in the beautiful City of Light. Most French Caribbean individuals felt highly enthusiastic about their professional prospects. As black French citizens, who had been inculcated with the French dream of becoming *un fonctionnaire d'état* (a well-paid white-collar worker from the public sector), they wanted to improve their social status and materialize their dreams of home ownership and discretionary income. However, upon arriving in Paris, many French Caribbean migrants felt deceived. They realized that France had broken her promise. She did not offer lucrative employment in the public sector; rather, she offered low-skilled jobs and domestic positions in the homes of the French upper classes. France seemed to treat them like second-class citizens, a rude awakening that triggered a number of reactions, including accommodation, resistance, and protest. Ultimately, similar to those of their African counterparts, these reactions changed the migrants' social conditions and affected the French perception of Caribbean identity.

Chapter 5

Caribbean Women in Postwar France, 1946–1974

The Caribbean labor migration differs drastically from the others. The number of women surpasses the men and their activity rate, which is constantly growing, stands at 80%. Today, 54% of West Indians in Paris are women and their activity rate surpasses that of men in the Parisian region. Caribbean women anticipated modernity, but they achieved this milestone with great difficulty. For Caribbean women, maternity and career have always been mutually inclusive categories, albeit by design not by choice. Caribbean women are three times more likely to be single mothers than white French women.
—Claude-Valentin Marie, Director of the Research Group against Discrimination at the Assistance Publique des Hôpitaux de Paris

Françoise Ega, a Martinican woman writer who lived in France during the postwar period, affirms that racism and discrimination form an integral part of French society. Ega feels that "the French government and society perceive all Poles as agricultural workers, all Algerians as unskilled construction workers, and all Antillean women as maids."[1] This chapter builds on the work of Françoise Ega and a few Caribbean women novelists who, pondering the themes of alienation, education, romantic relationships, work, and sexual exploitation, are among the few intellectuals manifesting a genuine interest in the lives of Caribbean women in postwar France.[2] The work of Françoise Ega and other Caribbean women novelists who explore the themes of alienation, education, labor relations, love, and sexual exploitation in the lives of Caribbean women in Paris is a source of inspiration for scholars interested in gender relations, and migration, as well as nationalism in France. Indeed, their work is particularly inspiring because representations of black women from Guadeloupe and Martinique as sexual victims and as "jezebels," sexually and morally unrestrained women became entangled with French immigration policies and French Caribbean nationalism.[3] In the postwar period, the French perceived Caribbean women as overly fertile, and therefore responsible for overpopulating the islands and creating the conditions for perpetual underdevelopment.[4] As a result, to alleviate demographic pressure, provide the women with employment, and improve their morality by inserting them into "superior" French culture, French officials affiliated with the Institut National de la Statistique et des Etudes Economiques (INSEE) suggested organizing the migration of Caribbean women to France.[5] At the same time, the women's bodies became a battlefield for Caribbean male nationalists, who appropriated their experiences in Paris to satisfy their own political agenda. For the nationalists, the organized migration, and especially the fate of Caribbean women in France, symbolized the continuation of French hegemony under the new political status of departmentalization, which Martinique, Guadeloupe, and French Guiana acquired in 1946.

As racialized working-class women migrants, Caribbean women faced the hard task of adapting to a new society with limited professional opportunities, a phenomenon that Caribbean men, particularly the nationalists, failed to evaluate objectively. Yet, Caribbean women migrants of the sixties sought to break the mold that limited their professional opportunities in France by working hard, and especially by constructing new identities that transcended the notion that they were victims, jezebels, or maids—the role government officials believed most suited their capabilities.

The Jezebel and Migration

France emerged from World War II as a devastated winner, suffering from a crippled industrial sector and the memory of the collaborationist Vichy regime. In light of the stagnating population growth, French demographers argued that additional hands, immigrants, were necessary to rebuild the country, and thus created the Office National d'Immigration (National Immigration Office), which became the organ responsible for recruiting and inserting labor migrants into France, and even repatriating them back to their homelands.[6] But not all immigrants were welcome. Only people whose culture mirrored the French—in other words, whites—were deemed desirable.[7] The demographers also suggested increasing the national birthrate, thereby giving French women a particular role in the process of national growth. This focus on women's fertility was not new to France, which had been "suffering" from low birthrates since the Franco-Prussian War (1870-1871). Stagnating population growth had often resulted in draconian measures, such as suppressing abortion and contraception, to increase the country's population.[8] In the Fourth Republic (1946-1958), the idea that French women should be good, educated mothers was widespread among many government officials; Charles de Gaulle, as early as 1945, echoed the demographers and social scientists, calling for women to bear "twelve million beautiful babies within the next ten years."[9]

But the script differed in Guadeloupe and Martinique. The idea that Guadeloupe and Martinique should invite people from neighboring islands such as St. Lucia, Dominica, or Haiti to help develop the new departments because they share a similar "Creole culture" seemed unthinkable. According to French officials, unlike the metropole, which needed more "beautiful babies," Guadeloupe and Martinique needed fewer babies because the Overseas Departments' birthrate surpassed the islands' production capabilities and contributed to chronic underdevelopment and dependency on France.[10] As in the metropole, the birthrate and women's fertility became government obsessions. But in the French Caribbean, French officials emphasized finding a way to keep women from having too many children.[11]

Such argument is entangled with the historical misrepresentation of Caribbean women as both sexually accessible and hypersexed individuals.[12] Illustrating this fact, Doris Garraway writes that in the late eighteenth century, "colonial writers sensationalized mulatto women as icons of sensual pleasure and sexual excess, figures both loved and blamed for the luxury, indebtedness and moral laxity of the colony."[13] Bernard Moitt also reveals that throughout the era of plantation slavery, enslaved women were frequently expected to extend sexual favors to both Frenchmen and men of African descent.[14] As regulations and laws limiting men's control over the black female body were enacted during the colonial era, new stereotypes hinting that black women were born to appease men's sexual desires emerged. *Négripub*, a collaborative study on the representation of black identities in French culture, shows that in the post-emancipation era, the mere sight of a Frenchman turned a seemingly docile Caribbean maid or *blanchisseuse* (laundress) into an aggressive "sexual beast."[15] Caribbean women's sexuality remained a subject of obsession during the interwar period, as movies, songs, and literature continuously depicted them as an exotic and sensuous beings. Caribbean women were not thinkers; they acted out of basic instinct and desire. As the song below illustrates, they fulfilled sexual fantasies even when they were merely maids, cleaning and cooking for French households:

Moi tout faire pour te plaire . . . toujours	Me make everything to please you . . . always
La cuisine, la vaisselle . . . l'amour	Cooking, dishes . . . love
Moi savoir repasser plein de mouchoirs	Me iron many handkerchiefs
Et chasser et pousser les idées noires	And chase away gloominess
Moi faire bons petits plats	Me make nice little dishes
Retourner matelas . . .	Turn mattress over . . .
Moi savoir taper tapis	Me know beating rugs
Moi savoir bien cracher sur chaussures	Me know spitting on shoes
Moi bien faire la tambouille	Me play fun
Les chatteries, les chatouilles	Hug and tickle
Les parquets, les bafouilles	Floors and gossip
Moi avoir petits mollets pas laids	Me has cute legs
Et beaux petits macarons tout ronds	And nice round macaroons
Moi chanter la chansonnette	Me sing *chansonette*
Souffler dans clarinette	Blow clarinet
Et claquer castagnettes	And play castanets[16]

After World War II, the French officials in charge of planning a better future for the *vieilles colonies* firmly believed that Caribbean women were jezebels overpopulating the islands, and they thus suggested developing *puericulture* programs to teach young women about domestic responsibilities and proper moral behavior.[17] These proposed programs differed sharply from those previously introduced in France, for instead of aiming to improve women's health and child-rearing practices, they intended to decrease the women's fertility rate. In a nutshell, the proposed social programs sought to promote the French nuclear family, reduce the number of children born out of wedlock, and increase awareness of the difficulties caused by rapid demographic growth in underdeveloped countries.[18] However, officials quickly found *puericulture* programs too "soft" and inefficient, consequently arguing that something more radical had to be done.

After careful planning, the Institut National de la Statistique et des Etudes Economiques (INSEE) believed that organizing a labor migration to France represented a rational plan for improving French Caribbean socioeconomic conditions.[19] Whereas most young men were destined to military service, young women would be channeled to Paris, where there was a surplus of low-skilled jobs. According to the experts, the migration would alleviate the strain on the labor market and improve Caribbean women's social behavior by exposing them to a higher French culture emphasizing marriage and domesticity. Migration was thus conceived as a form of demographic control, but also as a tool that regulated women's sexuality and fertility because it supposedly decreased women's propensity to become mothers out of wedlock.[20]

By 1962, following the recommendations of INSEE's expert, a state-sponsored agency, the Bureau pour le Développement des Migrations Intéressant les Départements d'Outre-Mer (BUMIDOM), was created to oversee the organized migration.[21] Operating under the auspices of the Ministry of the Overseas Departments and the Ministry of Finance, and chaired by Valéry Giscard d'Estaing, BUMIDOM initiated the annual migration of about five thousand young Caribbean men and women to France.[22] Considering that each island comprised about a quarter-million people, the migration was unmistakably massive, leading scholars and Caribbean migrants to refer to Paris as "La troisième île" (the third island).[23]

THE JEZEBEL IN FRANCE

While the stereotype of the Caribbean jezebel played an important role in making thousands of women cross the Atlantic, it also affected their experiences in Paris, preceding them at work, school, and throughout the streets. The stereotypes of Caribbean women as promiscuous women and good maids also influenced BUMIDOM officials in charge of inserting the women into Paris (at least throughout the fifties and sixties). Nearly a dozen white French administrators without much academic credentials (in the 1960s only the director and the vice director *may* have had the *baccalauréat*), but with substantial experience as colonial administrators in sub-Saharan Africa managed BUMIDOM.[24] These workers played a pivotal role in the women's lives: they connected them to diverse social and educational institutions, conveyed important information about life in Paris, and sometimes offered women in distress a place to sleep in a foyer of thirty-two beds that catered exclusively to Caribbean women.[25] But for the most part, BUMIDOM officials guided the migrants towards potential jobs, and as a general rule, they believed that domestic labor was most appropriate for the women. Claiming that the Parisian domestic industry was in "crisis," BUMIDOM argued that Caribbean women represented a perfect substitute for the Portuguese and Spanish women increasingly deserting these low-wage positions.[26] Although it cautioned that French families were willing to pay only according to the migrant's skill level, the agency was under the firm conviction that the *métropolitains* "wish[ed] to hire young and qualified women" and that they preferred "young French candidates, particularly Caribbean women."[27]

Thus, acting as a placement agency, BUMIDOM screened the women to place them into French households seeking live-in domestics. It quickly established a reputation as a provider of trained and reliable workers, and similar to contemporary domestic agencies, manufactured greater demand for household workers by impressing on potential clients the need for professional screening.[28] As it channeled the women into live-in domestic positions, BUMIDOM also avoided finding housing for the migrants, a daunting task due to the repatriation of hundreds of thousands of Pieds-Noirs, which created a housing shortage throughout the largest cities (this held particularly true for Marseilles, but Paris also felt the impact of the "return migration").[29]

Thus, working-class Caribbean women migrants were a hit in postwar Paris. Their arrival in Paris coincided with the increasing number of middle- and upper-class French women in the labor market—women who needed another female body to run their household.[30] As French citizens from the former colonies with a reputation as natural domestics and mothers, Caribbean women represented the ideal candidates. According to Bridget Anderson, it is likely that "privileged" Parisian women placed a premium on having a Caribbean maid, for "the domestic worker, whether 'cleaner,' 'nanny,' or 'servant,' is fulfilling a role, and crucial to that role is her reproduction of the female employer's status (middle-class, non-laborer, clean) in contrast to herself (worker, degraded, dirty)." Indeed, Anderson maintains that "it is the worker's 'personhood' rather than her labor power that the employer buys, which helps explain why domestic work is so often undertaken by racialized groups, whether they are citizens or immigrant workers."[31]

As the employment agency, BUMIDOM outlined the rules and regulations determining the workers' and employers' rights. For the sake of formality and to avoid judicial pitfalls, the agency provided a labor contract, which stated that the workers were "responsible for fulfilling all of the wife's household tasks, including shopping, washing the children, making the beds, cleaning and maintaining the house, cooking, serving dinner to the family, washing the dishes, doing the laundry, etc."[32] The contract also highlighted that workers should accomplish their duties with impeccable moral integrity and should "at all times, remain clean, discreet, good, willing, honest, and constantly display an air of happiness."[33] Thus, not only was the contract harsh and partial to the employers, but it also reinforced the patriarchal characteristics of household labor and dismissed the psychological challenge of living in someone else's space. Indeed, as Françoise Ega notes, "the odor of other people's lives is perhaps the most difficult part of the job."[34]

While offering a "good and stable" job with a housing bonus seemed like a great idea to the BUMIDOM officials, for Caribbean women, it was a setback. The women equated migration with social uplift, intending to stay away from this type of work, which their mothers, grandmothers, and aunts had often performed for the islands' privileged mulattos and *békés* (white Creoles).³⁵ Consequently, the immigration officials who invited them to France under the pretense that they could find a brighter future faced a quandary: how could they possibly promote domestic work to these young women who clearly aspired to do something else?

As a response to the migrants' lack of enthusiasm, in March 1965 French officials created a professional school for Caribbean women migrants, whose main goal consisted of promoting domestic work as an honorable and financially rewarding profession. In the spirit of Napoleon, who used medals and ribbons to attract soldiers into the ranks of his army, French officials believed that granting a certificate upon completion of a two- to five-weeks-long program would both generate the desire to become domestics and secure competent candidates for the potential employers.³⁶

The school was established in Crouy-sur-Ourcq, a small village located two hours away from Paris. Crouyciens conceivably saw the opening of the school as the most important event since the *armistice*, as their village is located in *la France profonde* (rural/deep France), neither on the cultural nor the tourist map. Yet perhaps due to the isolation and remote location, a few villagers considered the sudden diversity spike to be too abrupt a change. In her thesis, Nadia Kergoat, a white French woman working as the receptionist, recalls how "the villagers are cold, often hostile, and most certainly unprepared." She admits that "For the *villageois*, the women are blacks, and sometimes *négresses*." She even remembers that "Once, an elementary school teacher told a pupil: if you don't work you'll end up being a *bonîche* [maid-of-all-work] with the negresses."³⁷ Aside from a white male security guard, all of the school's administrators and teachers were white French women. The rules were strict: students were forbidden to leave the premises during the week, and visits to friends and family were only permitted on weekends.

The workload was also very challenging. Emphasizing discipline, the academic program at Crouy-sur-Ourcq sought to create the perfect domestics; students were encouraged to abide by the school's slogan: *maintenir de l'ordre sur soi et autour de soi* (maintain order on yourself and around you).³⁸ While the students enjoyed a break around mid-afternoon, the school day was relatively long, beginning at 8:30 AM and finishing at 7:00 PM.³⁹ The women attended cooking and cleaning classes, as well as classes on *l'entretiens du linge* (wardrobe management). They learned bed-making techniques and different ways to wash, iron, and sew clothes. They also learned the *service de table*, consisting of arranging tableware for each of the four-course meals served daily, and they memorized an extensive list of wines, cheeses, and desserts, which confirms that the school catered to middle- and upper-class French families that performed these rituals religiously.⁴⁰

Catering almost exclusively to Caribbean women (although there were also a few *Réunionnaises*), the school is an anomaly in the French republican design, which rejects special treatment based on differences of race and gender, because the republic supposedly provides the necessary ingredients to achieve equality for everyone. While this anomaly received very little attention from the mainstream French press, the Caribbean students' press, which has been politically engaged since the interwar period, considered the subject worthy of discussion. *Le Patriote Guadeloupéen*, a Guadeloupean student newspaper, investigated the school and published an article focusing on its pedagogy. It suggested that in theory, the curriculum emphasized three types of specializations: domestic worker, *fille de salle* (nurse's aide), and administrative officer. In practice, however, the school trained women to become maids.[41]

Each of the offered specializations corresponded to the growing need for unskilled and semi-skilled labor in Paris. The *fille de salle* training aimed to channel Caribbean women into the Parisian public health sector, which suffered from a shortage of unskilled workers because judicial barriers prevented the hiring of illegal immigrants, who typically performed these tasks.[42] The emphasis on administration corresponded to the increasing number of administrative opportunities for women. Ideally, the training in office work would allow Caribbean women to compete with other working-class French women for the modest clerical positions readily available in the growing public and private sectors. However, after interviewing the students and the school officials, the Guadeloupean university students concluded that making the women administrators was not part of the agenda, for the administration vigorously promoted the domestic-training track:

> There is a huge propaganda to influence the students. The director and the other administrators argue that it is easier for the students to find employment as domestics and that it drastically reduces the cost of living. The propaganda for *fille de salle* is as intense. However, they discourage administrative training because they claim it leads to longer job searches and unemployment. Thus, even if some students had previously worked in an administrative setting, the school officials direct them into the domestic track.[43]

In many ways, the school at Crouy-sur-Ourcq expanded its mission beyond training Caribbean women. It followed BUMIDOM's mandate, which sought to educate and inculcate the young jezebels with proper moral behavior. Indeed, in what appeared to be a civilizing enterprise, in its newsletters BUMIDOM promoted enrolling Caribbean women in centers that offered professional training and advice about living in France.[44] Thus, uniting French educators and the migrants under the same roof in a faraway village, the school provided a forum for intervening in the private lives of Caribbean women. In other words, as inferred by the proponents of the migration, the French educators were also expected to improve the lives of their "colonial sisters," who supposedly lacked savoir-faire and proper moral behavior. Exemplifying the continuing colonial hierarchies that separated the *métropolitaines* (French women) from Caribbean women, in a report outlining her professional experiences at the school, a twenty-two-year-old French administrator reveals that her colleagues interacted with the students as if they were still children. She claims that she "felt uncomfortable relating to these older women like a mother since many of them are mothers themselves with a lifetime of rich experiences ... [and she] tried to understand their compliance and longing for affection, as well as [her] colleagues' overprotective behavior."[45] For the administrator, the unequal relationship between the migrants and the school officials was embedded in the national structure and related to the process of migrating from the global undeveloped South to the industrialized developed North. Indeed, she affirms that

> [When] they arrive they immediately realize that they don't know much about life in France, and consequently, they surrender their lives to the monitors, who offer the knowledge that allows them to work. From the start, the relation between the monitors and the students is "they know everything and I don't," which is amplified by the fact that they receive free room and board. They receive everything without giving anything. In fact, we only ask them to be on time and participate in the housework. They have to eat, they may not skip meals, and must obey the rules.[46]

Although Caribbean women were treated as *grands enfants* (big children), a stereotype that clearly limited their professional potential, they attempted—with some success—to obtain employment that yielded more prestige and personal freedom than being a maid. A year and a half after its opening in 1965, the school at Crouy-sur-Ourcq had admitted over a thousand women who overwhelmingly desired to become administrative workers. That this dream came true for only twenty-five women does not mean that the others failed to achieve their goals. Indeed, unable to attain their first objective, many women gravitated towards becoming *filles de salle*, their second wish. By 1967 more than one-third of the students graduated as *filles de salle*, thereby securing a position offering more job security and personal freedom than a typical household placement.[47]

Nevertheless, during the postwar period there was a very thin line between being a *fille de salle* and being a household worker, as the former were also responsible for preparing meals; serving, feeding, carrying, and bathing the patients; making the beds; folding the linen; cleaning the floors; washing the dishes; and performing various other menial tasks.[48] One Caribbean woman claims that cleaning constituted an important part of her daily tasks: "In those days it was difficult. We did not know anyone and we had to work very hard. We cleaned a lot. . . . They would give us bars of soap rather than liquid soap, and we often had to scrub the floor on our bare knees."[49]

Despite the hard work, Caribbean women who became *filles de salle* felt enthusiastic about the possibility of climbing up the social ladder. BUMIDOM had outlined a *cycle de promotion sociale* (plan for social promotion) for the women who chose a career in the medical field, and Caribbean women often viewed being a *fille de salle* as a steppingstone toward becoming a nurse. But in actuality, this *cycle de promotion sociale* was almost impossible to accomplish. The women had to work long hours; they remained under probation for more than a year, during which they were evaluated and screened. They subsequently became nurse's aides and often worked nights. As the details of the program suggest, the *cycle de promotion sociale* promoted stress, social stagnation, and exploitation:

> In the first phase the candidate works in a hospital and is responsible for the general maintenance and cleaning the patients' rooms. Eventually, she will also be responsible for cleaning the patients. This first phase, which is generally extremely demanding, is designed to test the candidate's resistance to hard work. The women who successfully pass the 15 months probationary period take an exam to determine if they qualify to enroll in nurse's aide classes. The candidates who passed the exam may enroll in either nurse's aide or *assistante hospitalière* classes, which last one year. The following year the nurse's aide or *assistante hospitalière* prepares for the entrance exam to the nursing school. The student must prepare for the exam after work. Additionally, while preparing for the exam the student must work numerous night shifts. After this preparatory year, the student can finally take the exam. If she passes, she will continue taking nursing classes while receiving the equivalent salary of an *aide hospitalier*.[50]

As the Crouy-sur-Ourcq experiment indicates, the experiences of Caribbean women are unique, different from those of white French women and Caribbean men. The latter migrated to diverse geographic areas, where they served in the military or worked in factories, the construction industry, and hospitals, or as low-ranked skilled civil servants. In its first year of operation (1962) BUMIDOM placed 58 percent of the women in the Parisian region, but only 11 percent of the men.[51] Nora Absalon claims that, as a result of being concentrated in this region, Caribbean women played a special role in developing the community in Paris. By providing housing and information to friends and family, they facilitated the insertion of other Caribbean people into the city, which subsequently attracted more Caribbean migrants.[52]

While these women played a crucial role in cementing the Caribbean community of Paris, as pioneers they faced unprecedented challenges in the housing and labor markets. Women without the privilege of having a host house for an extended period were often forced to settle for undesirable employment. For instance, a Martinican woman remembers that her adventure to Paris was successful only because she first lived with her older sister in a very small apartment, which allowed her to conduct a nine-month-long search and obtain a job as the first black clerk in a mutual fund company.[53] However, another woman from Guadeloupe who worked in a factory claims that her working conditions were intolerable: she received low wages and was routinely harassed by her supervisor, a severe and cold Frenchman who only reluctantly gave her a bathroom break. When asked why she initially took the job and stayed for five years, she replied, "It was that or the street."[54] Having a friend or family member in the city was thus crucial to the women's professional success and quality of life, especially in cases in which the women had migrated on their own, without any assistance from BUMIDOM. Yet for many women, dependence on kin and social networks for housing was a precarious matter, for if the family member or the friend married, or if conflicts and quarrels occurred, they could suddenly become homeless.

Indeed, the new and often hostile environment that women confronted, the burgeoning but fragile Caribbean network in the Parisian region, low wages, and the fact that many Parisian social institutions failed to acknowledge the importance of additional public assistance for working-class Caribbean women migrants (e.g., housing subsidies, financial compensation) led many women to the street, and for many Caribbean women, the street was a metaphor for prostitution. As early as 1966, *Alizé*, a religious magazine published by Caribbean students based in Paris, reported that Caribbean women were disproportionately represented in Le Nids (the nest), a Catholic institution founded in 1946 that provided shelter to prostitutes while trying to reform their lives through religious teaching.[55] Although *Alizé* did not depict migration as a phenomenon leading to the systematic sexual exploitation of women, it feared that prostitution was nonetheless becoming a mode of social insertion that could continue to affect a small percentage of women, especially single women and single working mothers. The question is why did *Alizé* highlight that unfortunate mode of social insertion while the pundits, INSEE and BUMIDOM officials, seemed unaware of it? Were they really oblivious, or did they remain silent because they believed that Caribbean women were simply prone to such behavior? However, one group that was certainly conscious of Caribbean prostitution in Paris, and was determined to condemn and change this phenomenon via radical politics, was the Caribbean nationalists.

Chapter Five

NATIONALISM AND THE VICTIMIZATION OF WOMEN

Until 1946, "assimilationism," or the quest for full French citizenship, was the dominant political ideology of Guadeloupe, Martinique, and French Guiana. As the 1935 festivities commemorating three hundred years of attachment with France suggest, the interwar period witnessed intense manifestations of admiration and devotion to the *métropole*, only to be surpassed by those during the Vichy period, when young Caribbean patriots risked their lives on *yoles* (small fishing boats) to escape the islands' Vichy representatives and reach neighboring Dominica, where they could enlist with the British forces to fight against "Misié Itlè" (Hitler).[56] Nationalism was simply not on the agenda of French Caribbean people.

As an ideology influencing the political landscape, nationalism surged after departmentalization in 1946, when Caribbean associations and political parties created in the fifties, sixties, and seventies began to advocate for independence or more political autonomy from France.[57] French Caribbean nationalism was the product of unfulfilled expectations and stagnant economic growth. Few changes had occurred after ten years of departmentalization. Poverty remained rampant, unemployment high; the agricultural sector offered the only available jobs—namely, picking bananas and cutting sugarcane. But the youth of the rural communes, who had been educated in the schools of the republic, refused to pick up the machete to cut the *béké*'s sugarcane, which their great-grandparents, the emancipated slaves, had cut under the blazing sun.[58] Moreover, the number of high-ranking French administrators in the islands was also increasing, sparking anger and resentment among many French Caribbean people, who felt cheated because thousands of locals were formally and properly educated to fill these positions, and the rate of children attending school in the islands surpassed France's.[59] These factors led many French Caribbean individuals to believe that the French presence was suppressing their ability to manage their own local affairs and robbing them of available opportunities. By the mid-fifties, fueled by young intellectuals and students who abandoned reading Baudelaire for Fanon and Césaire, popular disenchantment became widespread, and a number of nationalist movements began to emerge.

The nationalists wanted to invent a new political, social, and cultural identity for Guadeloupe and Martinique. They believed that colonial hierarchies continued to structure Franco-Caribbean relations in the administrative, educational, and cultural sphere, and that departmentalization could not solve the high unemployment problem. They desired faster economic growth and control over their own destiny.[60] In 1963, capturing the general mood of the thousands of nationalists in Guadeloupe, Martinique, and French Guiana, the Organisation de la Jeunesse Anticolonialiste de la

Martinique (OJAM), Martinique's largest nationalist organization, comprising at least ten thousand people, declared:

> Beneath the hypocritical mask of departmentalization, Martinique is the Algeria of the past. France economically, socially, politically, and culturally dominates it.... We proclaim that the status of Overseas Department clashes with Antillean interests and makes sustainable economic growth impossible. We want the right to industrialize and exploit the island's resources ... we want the right to redistribute the land and to restructure the sugar and rum factories into cooperative enterprises.[61]

Thus in Guadeloupe and Martinique during the late 1950s and the 1960s, nationalism was a potent ideology and, as people migrated to France, an increasingly important aspect of diasporic politics. Like their counterparts in Martinique and Guadeloupe, the nationalist organizations of Paris wanted moderate political changes, or in some cases, advocated for taking revolutionary steps towards obtaining independence. Founded in 1963 by (mostly male) Guadeloupean students, the Groupe d'Organisation Nationale des Guadeloupéens (GONG) seemed to have been the most revolutionary; one flyer it regularly circulated asserts, "Our organization refuses all compromise and negotiation with France, vows to organize the masses, will use violence when necessary, and will neutralize the opportunists and traitors."[62] But the Front Antillo-Guyanais, founded in 1961 by Marcel Manville, Paul Niger, Marie-Joseph Cosnay, and Edouard Glissant, was by far the largest organization. The Front Antillo-Guyanais advocated for political autonomy on the basis of French cultural hegemony and economic exploitation. The organization attracted Caribbean people from various social classes; however, it was short-lived, as a presidential order dissolved it a few months after its creation.[63] These organizations had three common factors: first, they wanted to reconfigure the islands' and French Guiana's political status; second, the leadership was entirely male; and third, they all agreed that the organized migration to France was highly detrimental to French Caribbean people. In fact, they equated France to exile, viewing the Hexagon as a series of gulags, where exploited colonial workers labored their lives away. According to the nationalists' rhetoric, the migration most victimized women, because in France they became the colonizers' "comfort women."[64]

For the nationalists, the prostitution of Caribbean women in the diaspora symbolized the continuation of colonialism, albeit with the colonial subjects now living in the metropole. Unlike Fanon's depiction of colonial societies as spaces outside France in which "the foreigner comes from another country [and] imposes his rules by means of guns and machines ... [and where] the governing race is first and foremost those who come from elsewhere, those who are unlike the original inhabitants, 'the others,'"[65]

Caribbean nationalists strongly believed that colonial relations also occurred in the metropole, where people from the former colonies, the "wretched of the earth," were marginalized for being unlike the "original" inhabitants.[66] Evidently, the nationalists exaggerated. Although no one spread rose petals on the migrants' path, France was not the gulag of Caribbean people, and prostitution was not as widespread as they contended.

Yet, as a controversial and sensational topic, the prostitution of Caribbean women in Paris became an avenue for discussing and promoting the idea of political sovereignty. Feminist scholars have shed light on the politics of gender and nationalism, especially as it occurred in the Caribbean diaspora of Paris. They suggest that the nationalists' defense of exploited women was a process entangled with the emasculating effect of colonization. According to Cynthia Enloe, male activists, intellectuals, and nationalists from colonized and subjugated spaces highlight the plight of colonized women and present themselves as their "savior knights" not only to antagonize the colonizer but also to reclaim their masculinity, which is obliterated by colonization.[67] Male political resistance through the woman's body thus constitutes a self-reflective process and the expression of hypermasculinity; it is an attitude not necessarily linked to the woman's condition.

Published in 1975, *Confessions d'une prostituée antillaise à Paris*, a novel by the Martinican Roland Larouchez, exemplifies how Caribbean male nationalists reinvented and appropriated the struggle of Caribbean women sex workers in Paris to advance their own political agenda. Larouchez's self-proclaimed *roman vérité* (factual novel) tells the story of a young Martinican woman who is lured into going to France, where BUMIDOM finds her a receptionist position in a doctor's office. After a series of unfortunate events, the protagonist meets Monique, a twenty-six-year-old French woman from the Alsace region with whom she develops a romantic relationship. She then quits her job and moves in with Monique, who offers her a luxurious lifestyle. However, Monique deceives the protagonist and draws her into an underworld of violence and forced prostitution. Despite the danger, the protagonist refuses to return to Martinique, as she has become dependent on the superficiality of material wealth.[68]

In spite of its emphasis on Caribbean sex workers in Paris, Larouchez's *roman vérité* reflects his concern about French political hegemony. His voice (the narrator's) dominates, and throughout the novel the characters often question if departmentalization works for the French Caribbean. For instance, describing a man of Corsican origin soliciting a Caribbean prostitute, he writes:

> For about a couple of years, he observed that Caribbean prostitutes were slowly taking over his neighborhood. At first, they annoyed him. But then he talked to them, asked

them questions, and began to understand them. Perhaps being from the island of Corsica helped him comprehend these women. He knew that any effort to dismantle this modern slave trade would be in vain. He was convinced that the solution to this problem was in the Caribbean, not in France. These women should have the means to earn a living in their islands, or at least they should receive professional training in Paris. All these things troubled his mind as he solicited the services of a young prostitute.[69]

Generally, solicitors of sexual services tend to have something else in mind other than politics, but for Larouchez, the novel's message is not the prostitute's confession, but the structural inequalities between France and the French Caribbean, which he uncovers and analyzes through the protagonist's body and experiences.

The Martinican woman migrant, the disillusioned protagonist, embodies the nationalists' perception of the Franco-Caribbean relation. Her story is a metaphor for what is happening to the author's beloved *Iles aux fleurs* (Martinique), the victim, which is repeatedly raped by France, the "pimp" and colonizer whose subjects, blinded by material desires, become subversive accomplices. Yet, by interweaving his political ideology and the experiences of women, the author perpetuates the notion that the prostitution of Caribbean women in Paris was widespread. He produces a myth that brutalizes the history of the women's migration, for according to Caribbean students monitoring the development of their community, the few prostitutes were young single mothers who already had a job but struggled to make ends meet.[70] They were women readjusting their lives to a foreign environment, and in many cases, resembled their working-class counterparts of the French Caribbean: women raising their children without help from the fathers. Additionally, many Caribbean prostitutes in Paris migrated without BUMIDOM's *encadrement* (help) and thus lacked access to the services it offered. As a former activist and nationalist confesses, "Despite our deep resentment of BUMIDOM, it did provide a cushion for the displaced."[71]

While the nationalists invented a narrative of female migration that suited their own reality, painting Caribbean women as victims of the state, they failed to acknowledge how gender relations within the Caribbean community victimized women. Domestic violence found a niche in post-emancipation Caribbean society, giving men carte blanche to abuse their partners.[72] Moreover, many Caribbean scholars demonstrate that the matrifocal dimension of the French Caribbean family has historically placed a greater strain on women, who, along with their extended relations (mothers, sisters, cousins), become responsible for supporting the family.[73] But whereas the women of Guadeloupe and Martinique utilized the kinship structure to support and raise their children, in the diaspora, where fathers remained orbiting figures and kin were scarce, these women looked to other alternatives for survival. Thus, while racism and colonial relations influenced how the French state inserted Caribbean women into the labor market, gender relations within the Caribbean community also erected barriers, burdening women with more responsibilities, forcing them to live with limited resources, and sometimes channeling single and young mothers into the sexual economy.

In many ways, the discourse of French Caribbean men nationalists was full of paradoxes. While they highlighted France's abusive relationship with Caribbean women, they came from a highly patriarchal society that marginalized women; as men, they often participated in this widespread social phenomenon. The private life of Frantz Fanon, the most influential French Caribbean nationalist, illustrates this fact. Indeed, during my fieldwork in Paris, I discovered that Fanon's private life, especially his relationship with his partner, was punctuated with violence. When I interviewed Paulin Joachim, the writer and journalist from Benin who attended the First International Congress of Black Writers and Artists in 1956 and knew Fanon very well, he admitted witnessing a disturbing event during a social gathering at a café. Mr. Joachim, who had gone out with Fanon and his partner, saw the couple arguing. Eventually the argument escalated into a violent outburst. According to Mr. Joachim, Fanon lost his temper and slapped the woman in the face.

Apparently, this was not an isolated incident. Mr. Joachim asserts, "He used to hit his white wife in the bedroom; he once did it in front me, Ibrahim Seïd, and Ado Maurice. He did it to humiliate her, and he would say, "I avenge myself." He was violent. He was a very violent man."[74] Professor Maryse Condé, who I later interviewed, also mentioned hearing similar stories from the mouths of his family members. Fanon's behavior, however, did not surprise her. She claimed, "I am not surprised because we've learned to disassociate men's private relationships with their partner(s) from their intellectual accomplishments. Sometimes we expect these things."[75]

LA FEMME MATADOR: A DIFFERENT CITIZEN

While the nationalists depicted Caribbean women as virtuous and exploited subjects, the government officials viewed them as jezebels responsible for the islands' uncontrolled demographic growth. These perceptions corresponded to two competing ideologies, namely, the French government's politics of development in the Overseas French Caribbean Departments and the nationalists' quest for independence. However, they both framed the identity of working-class Caribbean women narrowly, failing to acknowledge how patriarchy, colonialism, and racism intersect and influence women's lives (the nationalists emphasized only colonialism and racism). They also dismissed the role of women as *chef de famille*.

By focusing on preconceived and imagined notions, French officials and Caribbean nationalists dismissed an important aspect of Caribbean women's experience at home and in the diaspora. They failed to view the *Antillaise* as *une femme matador*,[76] a French Caribbean term referring to a fighting woman who, evolving within a patriarchal society, courageously resists life's trials and assumes the role of *poto mitan* (pivot of the family) despite the obstacles.[77] From the onset of plantation slavery to the times of *la grande migration*, Caribbean women have based their lives on this paradigm.

Historically, women have had the dual responsibility of managing and providing for the household while contributing to the formal labor market. In fact, in the French Caribbean plantation society, more women than men performed harsh agricultural labor such as cutting sugarcane and carrying the bundles to be processed at the rum distilleries or sugar factories.[78] In addition to working hard, these women, often slaves, served as the family's main protector. Indeed, whereas the French nuclear-family model encouraged men to protect and provide, the matrifocal dimension of the Caribbean family imparted to women this primordial responsibility.[79] Simultaneously, as Bernard Moitt illustrates, they struggled against patriarchy and abuse within their own community, for the institution of slavery provided men, both white and black, carte blanche to terrorize them.[80]

Similar to white French women, Caribbean women evolved (and continue to do so) within a patriarchal society. They were and are considered less intellectual than their male counterparts; they only obtained the right to vote after World War II. They manage the domestic sphere, and until the cultural revolution of the late sixties, they routinely met with stiff resistance when they expressed their sexuality and political opinions. Like white French women of the postwar period, Caribbean women in Paris sought to reconfigure their position within the French patriarchal system by seeking jobs that better matched their professional aspirations.[81] Despite these challenges, Caribbean women have participated in a number of political activities to obtain freedom for themselves and for their children.[82]

The intersection of race, gender, patriarchy, and citizenship has inscribed Caribbean women into French history in a manner that differs from Caribbean men and white French women. When examining French women's history through the lenses of their "darker" sisters from the Overseas Departments, historians need to expand their conceptual framework to include the experiences of, in Pap N'Diaye's words, *une minorité française*. In other words, for French women in particular, the fifties are not only a period during which nationalism fueled pronatalist movements and conservative ideologies about women, and the sixties are not only a period of generational conflict and of increased liberty for women. For the women and French citizens of Martinique and Guadeloupe, nationalism emerged from a Caribbean context and generated other ideas of womanhood. As the experiences of Caribbean women in Paris during the postwar period indicate, the history of French women should also reflect these women's struggle to adapt to a new society, transcend racism and the invisible ceiling of the labor market, and provide for their family despite having access to limited resources.

In the fifties, French officials believed Caribbean women were jezebels, or at best, women suited for domestic work; they viewed the women as black colonial subjects. By the mid-seventies, however, they acquired a more informed perspective. As the female labor migrants proved to be professionally ambitious and demonstrated a strong work ethic, they single-handedly altered French colonial notions of Caribbean women. French officials realized that the women would not be maids in Paris; they realized the women were French citizens entitled to the same opportunities as other French citizens. By the mid-seventies, Caribbean nationalists also changed the gender dimension of their political discourse; they abandoned using the trope of the victimized black woman as a rallying cause, because after all, the vast majority of women were now employed in the public sector and health-care industry. Thus, accusing France of sexual trafficking was no longer an effective political slogan. In the final analysis, the migration of working-class Caribbean women to the Parisian region shows that, despite France's pledge to universal equality, racial and gender differences clearly constrained French citizens. That being said, the migrants were not deterred by racial and gendered barriers. Ambitious and determined Caribbean women found ways to circumvent these obstacles and slowly move up the social ladder.

Chapter 6

Henri Salvador's Music and Working-Class Caribbean Males in Paris of the Sixties

From Athens to Dunkirk all of Europe agrees that Henri Salvador of Guadeloupe is one of the greatest entertainers to hit Europe in the last ten years—but they cannot agree which of his "split personality" talents brings him most acclaim. To millions of record buyers, he is a syrup-voiced crooner, whose tones seductively stroke the attentive ears of listening maidens. To thousands who have seen him in night clubs and music halls, he is hardly a singer at all, but one of the world's greatest living mimics. To top it off, Salvador is presently building up a name for himself as a composer.

—*Ebony* magazine describes how Henri Salvador captured Europe's soul, November 1, 1952

Until the 1950s, Josephine Baker, the American-born entertainer who became a French citizen in 1937, was France's most famous black star. Her rare beauty, talent, and American accent seduced the French nation, already fascinated by African American cultural production. In the words of Phyllis Rose, she embodied the quintessential "Jazz Cleopatra."[1] Josephine Baker and the African American jazz artists of the interwar period broke the color line of the French music industry, paving the way for French Caribbean artists who until then performed at the Bal Nègre, a Parisian dancehall catering to French patrons thirsty for exotic encounters.[2] Henri Salvador, a *flâneur*[3] and the first "made in

France" famous black popular artist, owed much of his success to Baker and her jazz contemporaries in France.[4]

The son of a Spanish man and a Guadeloupean woman of mixed Native American and African ancestry, Henri Salvador (1917-2008) was born in Cayenne (French Guiana) and migrated to Paris with his parents when he was just seven years old. He began his career in the thirties, playing guitar in small cabarets. By the fifties, not only had he recorded several songs (including the first French rock-and-roll in 1956), but he also branched out into comedy and acting.[5] In the following decade, frequently appearing in popular television shows, he had clearly become one of France's most accomplished singers and comedians. But after the tragic passing of his wife in 1976, his popularity faded away. Still a determined artist, he returned to his jazz roots in the eighties, performing at various national and international concerts. Coincidentally, in the late nineties the success of elder Cuban artists (the Buena Vista Social Club) suddenly turned a number of older and forgotten musicians into hot commodities, allowing Salvador to make an outstanding comeback in 2001. As an octogenarian, Salvador matched the success of his youth, selling two million copies of *Chambre avec vue* (A Room with a View) and winning the "Best Male Artist and Album of the Year" at the Victoires de la Musique awards ceremony, a milestone accomplished by very few French artists.[6]

While Salvador loved France and was loved by France, he shared a different relationship with the Caribbean community. In the fifties and sixties, though many French Caribbean individuals liked him, most students and intellectuals did not care much for the man. According to Maryse Condé, many students had discovered the poetry of the negritude writers, and artists like Salvador—artists who projected a complicated image of blackness—did not appeal to their senses.[7] Nonetheless, his national success overshadowed his complex relationship with Caribbean intellectuals and students, as he deeply influenced French society during the postwar period. Indeed, not only did he invite the French to reflect on their conception of modernity, but he also left an indelible mark on race relations in France. Salvador had an impact on French perception of Caribbean migrants; not only did the French see him as a Caribbean man, but his music frequently portrayed Caribbean people and culture. However, contradictions surfaced in his work and, therefore, in the French imagination. His depiction of work, home, citizenship, and love often perpetuated French stereotypes of Caribbean people. There was an obvious *décalage* between the experiences of Caribbean male migrants and Salvador's music. Nevertheless, in their own ways, Salvador and Caribbean male migrants both contributed to decolonizing French notions of Caribbean identities.

Henri l'Exotique

Henri Salvador came from a well-to-do family. In his autobiography Salvador writes, "My origins are Spanish, Incas, and since a few *négrillons* [little Negroes] found their ways into my ancestors' quarters, Black. In any case, my roots are not in one place; on the contrary, they are spread throughout the four corners of the planet."[8] Salvador was truly a humanist; he enjoyed life to its fullest and promoted social equality through his music. For example, when he lived in Brazil, a local white millionaire invited him to an "Indian" hunting party, during which a few indigenous Brazilians were set free to be tracked by the millionaire and his crew. Disturbed by this barbaric practice, and hoping to embarrass the man, Salvador revealed his Native American connection to the Brazilian man, who, with a stoic face, reassured him that these "Indians" were not from his mother's ethnic background. Seeing parallels between the man's thinking process and Nazi Germany, Salvador composed a song glorifying his Native American roots. In his autobiography, he asserts feeling a sense of responsibility to "retaliate," claiming, "After meeting this imbecile I had to write a song portraying my ancestors living freely in their immense forest."[9]

Clearly, affirming his global and multicultural identity, Salvador did not endorse notions of racial and cultural purity. Yet, when he arrived in Paris during the midtwenties he was immediately "blackened." Paris's racialized landscape differed sharply from Cayenne's multilayered society where race, class, color, and ethnicity determined one's social position. In the City of Light, the racial ideology divided people into distinct racial groups, each ranked accordingly on the colonial hierarchy. Aside from the white Creoles, anyone from the French colonies in the Americas was considered black, even if, like Salvador, they had fair skin.

Thus, when Henri Salvador arrived in the port of Le Havre in 1924, like thousands of Caribbean people migrating to Europe and the United States, he began learning how to navigate within a society that considered him a racial other. Recalling his first moments as a black person in France (and perhaps in his life), he writes:

> Each time a Black person showed up in the street, around a corner, it was a spectacle. I immediately realized I would generate curiosity; I was an attraction, an exception, something rare. I heard, look a little Negro! And my mother, with her Indian philosophy and its ancestral fatalism replied, you'll get used to it my son. She was right, with great difficulty, I got used to it.... French racism was not violent, but it was steeped in the idea that Blacks were children. They often greeted us with a "salut Negro! Ça va,

Blanchette?" You can imagine how someone who is just over four feet tall and barely weighs 70 lbs feels about these salutations. Some of these encounters are forever engraved in my memory.[10]

Amazingly, this constraining social climate did not thwart the young and ambitious Henri Salvador. As a child, he had been hypnotized by his uncle's jazz collection, and against his father's wish that he would become a doctor or a lawyer, he decided to pursue a career in music, which truly testified to his strong character because in the Caribbean imaginary, professional musicians embodied the quintessential "bums."

Salvador's debut was punctuated by funny stories. For example, he did not know how to play the drums, yet he somehow landed a gig as a drummer. When he was finally hired as a guitarist, he played in a club whose nightly audience usually included one client, a rich Hungarian man who, drunk on himself, kept tipping and asking for a song that required only a solo violinist.[11] In 1935, Salvador met the famous guitarist Django Reinhardt, who, seduced by his talents, hired him to be his accompanist. As Reinhardt's accompanist, he finally received the exposure that he had wished for. However, the German invasion halted his career, and in 1941 he left Paris for the South of France, where Ray Ventura, a famous Jewish French jazzman fleeing the Nazis for Brazil, offered him a job in his band. Only after the war did Salvador come back to France.[12] He returned to Paris full of ambition and thirsty for fame. Yet, he was still a Caribbean man in a society that still believed in colonial hierarchies, a factor complicating his plans.

Since Caribbean people still figured as colonial subjects, their chances for fame in French society were very slim. Moreover, as French colonial music suggests, the French imaginary was particularly cruel to Caribbean men, depicting them as brutes; lazy, grotesque clowns attracted to white women; or sometimes as children lacking decorum and unable to speak French properly. "A la Martinique" (In Martinique), a song popularized in 1912, embodies this musical tradition:

Y avait un négro	There was a negro
Tout jeune et déjà costaud	Young but already strong
Qui venait de la Martinique	He was from Martinique
Entra comme sa sœur	Just like his sister
Chez une marchande de fleurs	He went inside a woman's flower shop
qu'avait une jolie boutique	She had a beautiful boutique
Il eut comme vêt'ment,	He had a nice costume
un costume tout éclatant	Very fashionable and bright
Elle lui dit, c'est épatant, ça t'rend	She told him, what a nice costume

plus joli que l'costume de ton pays	It flatters you more than the Martinican ones
Le p'tit négro répondit	The lil' negro replied
Yaf yaf yaf à la Martinique,	Yaf yaf yaf in Martinique (laughing loudly)
Martinique, Martinique,	Martinique, Martinique
Icizagici, icizagici, Icizagici	Icizagici, icizagici, Icizagici (here)
Pas de veston pas de pantalon	No shirt, no pants
simplement un petit caleçon	Just little boxer shorts
Y en a du plaisir, du plaisir	There's lot of fun
Jamais malade, yoh!	Never sick, yoh!
jamais mourir, yoh!	Never die, yoh!
On ôte le caleçon pour dîner l'soir	We take off our boxer shorts for supper
Et tout le monde est en noir	And everyone wears black
Yaha Yaha Yaha!	Yaha Yaha Yaha! (laughing loudly)
Au bout de quelques jours	After a few days
Il avait le cœur plein d'amour	He fell in love
Pour sa patronne Mam'selle Blanche	With his boss, Ms. White
Mais n'ayant pas d'espoir	He felt hopeless
Il avait des idées noires	He had dark thoughts
Qui lui causaient des nuits blanches	Sleeplessly he longed for her
Et tout en se moquant, elle lui dit	Mocking him, Ms. replied
Mets des gants blancs,	Put on some white gloves
D'mande la main à mes parents	Ask my parents to marry me
Et puis à la mairie,	And at the City Hall
Tu deviendras mon mari	You'll become my husband
Il lui dit	He replied
Yaf yaf yaf à la Martinique	Yaf yaf yaf in Martinique (laughing loudly)
Icizagici, icizagici, Icizagici	Icizagici, icizagici, Icizagici (here)
Pas d'gants blancs, ni mairie,	No white gloves or City Hall
Ni de parents	No parents
Si t'es décidé, t'y passes dix francs	If you want it, it's ten francs
Y en a du plaisir, du plaisir	There's a lot of pleasure

Chapter Six

Jamais malade, yoh!	Never sick, yoh!
Jamais mourir, yoh!	Never die, yoh!
L'soir on s'embr sse sous les palmiers	At night we kiss under the palm trees
Ça y est on est mariés	And that's it, we're married
Yaha! Yaha! Yaha!	Yaha! Yaha! Yaha![13]

Although French society had changed after World War II, Caribbean males still symbolized the colonial other, which gave them limited opportunities in French society. Consequently, Salvador had to find a way to transcend this complicated legacy, which seemed particularly vivid in the film and music industry. Much to his delight, the globalization of rock-and-roll music facilitated this process. The French youth fell in love with this new musical genre emerging from the United States, and creative and entrepreneurial, Salvador understood how to capitalize on these young bodies ready to twist and shout. He teamed up with songwriter Boris Vian, and in 1956 they gave France its first rock-and-roll song.[14] By then, he had officially become a national star.

Nonetheless, despite gaining national recognition, a sort of Du Boisian double consciousness affected the young entertainer. In other words, his songs and performances often mirrored the French perception of Caribbean culture—namely, happy, clownish, nonthreatening *nègres* accompanied by beautiful, exotic young black women.[15] Interestingly, while the French press, the intellectuals, and certain government officials criticized race relations in the United States, the social climate in France of the fifties and sixties seemed to encourage the black artist to present himself in a very similar fashion to his African American counterparts, who in previous decades played silly, loud-laughing, grimacing characters depicting blacks as buffoons and ignorant individuals.[16] Stepin Fetchit, Willie Best, and Mantan Moreland, three famous African American male actors of the interwar period playing these kinds of roles, actually received much criticism from African American intellectuals like James Baldwin, who asserted angrily, "All of these [actors], rightly or wrongly, I loathed. It seemed to me that they lied about the world I knew, and debased it, and certainly I did not know anybody like them."[17]

Amazingly, the resemblance between characters played by Mantan Moreland and Henri Salvador is striking. Both artists were known for their gestures, grimaces, and especially, for widening their eyes beyond limits.[18] Not only did they entertain audiences with their jokes, but they also presented their black body and Caribbean/African American identity as the joke.

However, unlike Mantan, as a product of the French Caribbean, Salvador was also considered an exotic subject, and for this reason many of his early compositions reflect the public's demand for exoticism. "Dans mon île" (On my island), one of his first hits,

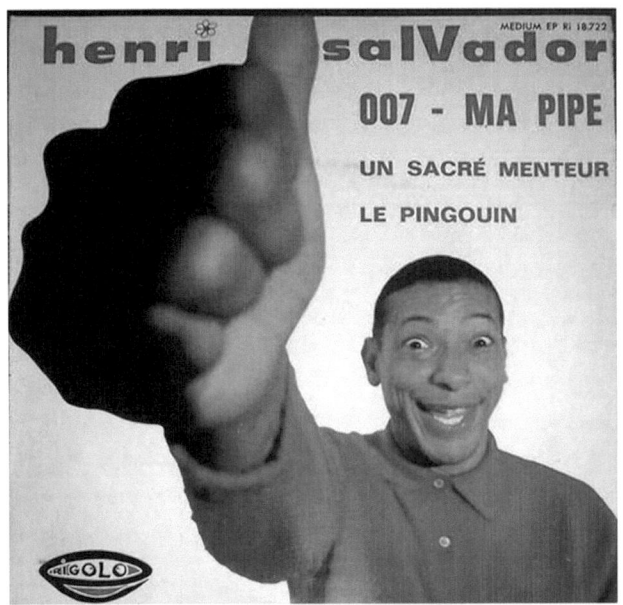

Henri Salvador's album featuring three songs, "Ma pipe," "Un sacré menteur," and "Le pingouin." (Rigolo, 1964.)

Mantan Moreland and mouse, from The Trap, *1946.*

illustrates this point. Accompanied by "tropical rhythms," the song offers his French audience a chance to escape to a beautiful Caribbean island, where one can live freely without the constraints and stress typical of urban France. It appeals to Frenchmen in a subtle manner, generously offering them the exotic island and its sensuous fruits, the sweet, docile, and fragile *doudou* (sweetie), the French Caribbean Woman:

Dans mon île, ah comme on est bien	In my island, ah it's so nice
Dans mon île, on n'fait jamais rien	In my island, no one ever does anything
On se dore au soleil qui nous caresse	We sleep under the sun stroking our skin
Et l'on paresse sans songer à demain	We procrastinate endlessly
Dans mon île, ah comme il fait doux	In my island the weather is so great
Bien tranquille près de ma doudou	Comfortably next to my sweetheart
Sous les grands cocotiers qui se balancent	Under the swinging coconut trees
En silence nous rêvons de nous	In silence we dream of each other
Dans mon île un parfum d'amour se faufileDès la fin du jour	My island smells like love And at dusk
Elle accourt me tendant ses bras dociles	She runs towards me innocently
Douce et fragile dans ses plus beaux atours	Soft and fragile
Ses yeux brillent et ses cheveux bruns	Her eyes shine
S'éparpillent sur le sable fin	Her brown hair rests on the white sand
Et nous jouons au jeu d'Adam et Eve	And we play Adam and Eve
Jeu facile qu'ils nous ont appris	An easy game they taught us
Car mon île c'est le Paradis[19]	Because my island is paradise

While Salvador catered to the French gaze, provoking the desire to travel to the Caribbean and perhaps meet a *doudou aux cheveux bruns*, his song also reveals a desire to explore his origins, a phenomenon commonly found among diasporic communities. In many ways, "Dans mon île" symbolizes Salvador's attempt to deal with being uprooted from the Caribbean; to him, the paradise islands are not merely distant and exotic places, they also represent a distant home. In fact, in his autobiography he genuinely displays regret for not traveling to the French Caribbean and exploring his roots when he lived in Brazil:

In the mid-forties, when I was living in Brazil I cared less that Guadeloupe and Martinique were a boat ride away.... How with my common sense didn't I feel that as long as I am unfamiliar with these islands, I will not know a part of me? I was looking in vain for paradise, but it was over there, in Martinique and Guadeloupe![20]

But despite his longing to connect with his origins, Salvador's music was essentially tainted by exoticism. Not only did his songs portray the French Caribbean as islands full of pristine beaches, beautiful women, and happy people, they also reinforced stereotypes of black people as always happy, docile, and lazy. For instance, when he sang "Le travail c'est la santé / Rien faire c'est la conserver / . . . / Dire qu'il y a des gens en pagaille / qui cour'nt sans cesse après le travail / moi le travail me court après / il n'est pas près de m'rattraper" (working is healthy, but doing nothing is healthier . . . some people run tirelessly after work, but work runs after me and is not about to catch me), he reinforced the French colonial notion of Caribbean identity as lazy.[21] Still, one should keep in mind that Salvador did not create these stereotypes; he was merely a subversive accomplice. As his answers to an interviewer from the *International Herald Tribune* illustrates, he understood the relationship between race and social inequalities in France:

> Here racism is refined. In America it's "Get out, nègre." Here there's a très gentil bonjour, and then they kick you out. There is tacit polite segregation. It may not be violent like in America, they won't burn any crosses, but they mock you. They treat you like a cute little monkey who looks and acts almost like a human being.[22]

Aware of race relations, Salvador promoted social change with art, albeit in a seemingly nonradical and nonthreatening manner. For Salvador, such endeavors often translated into being an excessively charming and funny crooner; sheer physical beauty and humor served as antidotes to the modern plague of anti-black racism and social inequality. Using this unusual combination, he also satirized what he considered to be the nativist and insular ways of French society. Nowhere is this behavior more evident than in the song "Faut rigoler," for which he even shot a video clip, which actually satirizes both French and French Caribbean societies:

Faut rigoler, faut rigoler	You've got to laugh, you've got to laugh
Avant qu' le ciel nous tombe sur la tête	Before the sky falls on our heads
Faut rigoler, faut rigoler	You've got to laugh, you've got to laugh
Pour empêcher le ciel de tomber	To stop the sky from falling on our heads
Nos ancêtres les Gaulois	Our ancestors the Gauls

Cheveux blonds et têtes de bois	They had blond hair and wooden heads
Longues moustaches et gros dadas	Long mustaches and big butts
Ne connaissaient que ce refrain-là	And they only knew this refrain
Nos ancêtres les Gaulois	Our ancestors the Gauls
Inventèrent le tabac	Invented tobacco
Et c'est grâce à ce truc-là	And because of that thing
Qu'ils s' fendaient la pipe à tour de bras	they were always fighting
Nos ancêtres les Gaulois	Our ancestors the Gauls
Eurent tort d'être grand-papas	Were wrong to become grandfathers
Et c'est pour ça qu'on est là	Because here we are
Et qu'on a fait le cha-cha gaulois![23]	Doing the cha-cha gaulois!

The song and video clip is multidimensional. On one hand, paying tribute to the silly ways of the Gauls—the Celtic people who migrated to what is now France, Belgium, Switzerland, and Northern Italy around 1500 BC, and supposedly believed that the sky could fall on their heads—it is a true manifestation of French folklore. On the other, by using an all-Caribbean cast and singing with a heavy French Caribbean accent, Salvador satirizes French Caribbean people seeking to "whiten" their culture. Through music, he encouraged French Caribbean people to reflect on the effect of French colonial policies on the construction of their identity.[24] For example, when Salvador wrote this song, most Afro-French Caribbean schoolchildren recited "Nos ancêtres les Gaulois" (Our ancestors the Gauls), a French version of the U.S. Pledge of Allegiance that emphasizes the citizens' connections with land, culture, and history. But unlike the Pledge of Allegiance, which transcends race, "Nos ancêtres les Gaulois" implicitly praises whiteness. Consequently, as Salvador sings "Nos ancêtres les Gaulois" surrounded by a French Caribbean cast, he alludes to the continuing presence of French cultural hegemony in the Overseas French Departments. Simultaneously, by impersonating the Gauls with black characters, Salvador challenges notions of French citizenship and identity. For him, French citizenship is not only synonymous with whiteness; it must be inclusive and capable of claiming ethnic and racial minorities as children of the nation. In the final analysis, Salvador seems to call for a reorganization of social relations and new modes of identity construction in the French Atlantic so that both the French and their former colonial subjects can transcend the colonial legacy and achieve social harmony. For Salvador, "il faut rigoler," because laughing about the absurdity of colonial logic promotes social progress.

In addition to addressing issues of cultural hegemony, citizenship, and identity, the French Guianese performer also denounced the rapid modernization of France. Like many French intellectuals of the era, he suggested that modernization had a sociocultural cost, especially in the Parisian region, where traditional French homes stood in the shadow of HLMs (*habitations à loyer modéré*), the notorious public housing accommodating thousands of working-class French people, as well as European, African, and Caribbean migrants. Speaking to the changing physical landscape, "Personnalisé," one of his few overtly socially conscious songs, outlines the "depersonalization" of an older, more traditional, and clearly "nobler" France:[25]

Je me promène dans une cité banalisée	As I walk in this mundane project
J'y vois des cubes d'un goût trivial	I see tasteless cubes
Des boutiques personnalisées	Custom-built boutiques
Et un jardin peu végétal	And barren gardens
Je cherche en vain dans les allées	In the alleys I search hopelessly
L'attrait de ce plan quinquennal	For the charm of this five-year-old quarter
Pour m'y dépersonnaliser	I want to remain neutral
Sans retomber, dans les social . . .	Who wants to regress into politics . . .
Façades aussi blêmes que la peau	Pale like skin, the walls are
Graphisme et slogans d'élection	Colored by political advertisements
Balcons fleuris, nul oripeau	The drying clothes garnishing balconies
Témoignent d'une civilization	Symbolize civilization
J'étais venu quérir un toit	I came to look for a roof
Dans une cité qui n'en a pas	In a project that has none
Et le bâtiment F au fond tout droit	But building F in the back
Ne guidera jamais mes pas	Will never attract me
Je pense à la maison de grand-mère en hiver	I think of grandma's house during the winter
Abritée sous un toit de chaume	Of being under a thatched roof
A ses vieux murs rongés de lierre	Of the old walls colonized by plants
Et à l'âtre chaud dans le home	Of the stone-lined fireplace
Je pense à la brume en hiver	I think of the winter mist
A l'odeur de la cheminée	Of the chimney's smell
Aux croix imprimées sur les pierres	Of crosses imprinted on the rocks
Du four où je venais rêver	Of the marvelous oven

Façades de béton sans une âme	Concrete walls without soul
Aux fenêtres glacées d'effroi	With dreadful windows
Vous, les vedettes du grand programme	The residents are the stars of big planning
De la cité des rues sans joie	Of projects full of sad streets
Non je ne pourrai pas m'habituer	No, I could never get used to this
A tous vos cubes banalisés	To your boring cubes
Non je ne pourrai pas m'habituer Au manque d'originalité	I cannot get used to the lack of originality
D'une vie personnaliséea	of a depersonalized life

While Salvador criticized the attributes of French modernity—in other words, rapid urbanization, bureaucracy, and materialism—he also played an important role in changing social behavior, notably in regard to the French attitudes towards interracial relationships. Although France was allegedly more progressive on the issue than other European countries and the United States, the French nation was still close-minded about love across the color line. As Tyler Stovall and Elisa Camiscioli point out, during World War I and the interwar period, white males commonly chastised "men of color" who were romantically involved with white women.[26] Illustrating the tension resulting from interracial relationships in the early postwar period, Salvador asserts, "Les noirs devaient se contenter de vivre et de baiser entre eux" (Blacks could only live and copulate with each other).[27]

To be sure, this racialized characteristic of gender relations has roots in plantation society, when for economic and sociocultural reasons, French males prevented black males from having sexual intercourse with French women.[28] In a study focusing on the legacy of plantation society, Roger Little confirms, "Sociologically, in the French colonies, close transracial relations were forcefully discouraged at the time, as indeed they were until the end of colonization. A clear distinction was made, however, between connivance at the droit de seigneur being transferred to a master's sexual enjoyment of the female slave and horror at the prospect of a negro, traditionally viewed as an animal endowed with unbridled sexual passions and powers."[29] Building upon this analysis, Brett Berliner also makes an important contribution to understanding interracial relationships in the French Atlantic, as well as the French perception of black masculinity. He observes that in contrast to their treatment of Caribbean males, Frenchmen emasculated West African men, a process that occurred when African colonial soldiers remained in France after the First World War. Admittedly, the proximity of "hypermasculine" black colonial subjects to white women generated anxieties, encouraging French males to reinvent their masculinity and sexuality. Thus, prior to World War I, these men were considered "sexual beasts," but after the war they became *grand enfants* (big children), in other words, asexual individuals.[30] In the process, the chocolate powder industry appropriated the image of the African soldier to advertise their products, depicting them as docile and smiling *Tirailleurs*, the good friend of French children. For this reason, black men were certainly not appealing to French women, at least not in popular culture.

However, when Henri Salvador became one of the "hottest" French stars, he single-handedly fashioned another image of black masculinity that did not incorporate the stereotype of the big child or the oversexualized brute. Salvador was a crooner. As Allison McCracken notes, in the United States crooners were "largely non-ethnically marked White men, [who] sang intensely emotional music softly using the microphone to create a sense of intimacy with their audience. Unlike previous male singers, they presented themselves directly to women as objects of desire, and wooed them openly to the bandstands."[31] Thus, like his American counterparts, Salvador sang love songs and promoted his music with his body, refined voice, and smooth personality. However, unlike his non-ethnically marked Euro-American counterparts, he was black. This was truly a unique phenomenon in the West, for blackness was surely not associated with beauty.

With this in mind, one must acknowledge that Salvador's light complexion helped him become a notorious seducer. His fair skin made him more socially acceptable than black men with darker skin tone and gave him an exotic flavor, which he exploited to develop romantic relations with white women. This unique combination—being light-skinned, funny, attractive, and a musician—allowed him to market black masculinity in a way that had never been done in France. Without causing much stir, he packaged and sold black masculinity and invited white women to explore love across the color line, posing on the cover of his albums as a Don Juan seducing them.

These album covers portraying Salvador singing to white women dressed for soirées or wild parties testify to his contribution in helping legitimize interracial relationships and black beauty in France. Thanks to the Guianese artist, black men can be charming or *tombeur*, a term that literally means making women fall into their bed. Ultimately, through his art and demeanor—even though he often reinforced black stereotypes—Salvador challenged conventional notions of black identity, asserting that race, charm, and sex appeal are not mutually exclusive. As he redefined black male identity, in a very subtle manner, he was affirming what had been inconceivable in France, that is to say, "black men are beautiful" and should, like any other males, be entitled to seduce and love women from different racial backgrounds. At the end of his long career, during a tour in Canada, a reporter from a well-established magazine asked him if he really sang for women; he replied, confirming his right to seduce any woman, "Bien sûr que je chante les femmes, je suis un homme après tout" (Of course I sing for and about women, I am a man after all).[32]

Salvador became an important entertainer when conservative social values were resurging in France. Yet through his music and his trademark—the romantic black man—he challenged these values, particularly the notion that race is a barrier to love and sex appeal. But perhaps France accepted Salvador's romantic ways with white women because he was a Caribbean man and consequently figured higher on the colonial hierarchy than sub-Saharan Africans, and especially North Africans, who were highly vilified during the Algerian War of Independence (1956–1962). Nonetheless, as a Caribbean singer and comedian, Salvador had a strong impact on the French imagination of black masculinity and the history of race relations in France. A complex character, he challenged and reinforced black stereotypes while constructively criticizing French society. Ultimately, in ways that one cannot measure, as a Caribbean man and the most famous black artist of the postwar period, Salvador influenced the French perception of working-class Caribbean male migrants by representing them as happy, romantic, and attractive men. He served as a social lubricant, allowing French Caribbean labor migrants to claim a place in French society without much reprisal.

Beyond "Tombeur": French Caribbean Male Labor Migrants' Experiences in Postwar France

Although Henri Salvador's music and performances were an effective social lubricant, he did not depict Caribbean males in ways that mirrored their identity, professional aspirations, and lifestyle. Most of these men had no interest in hypnotizing French women into their beds. Above all, they had migrated to reinvent themselves as middle-class and morally upstanding French citizens. In contrast to Salvador, who seemed grateful for what France gave him—success, fame, and money—many Caribbean males shared bitter social experiences, particularly in the labor market, where they often swelled the ranks of disgruntled workers. This was particularly true for the young men who were skilled in fishing, farming and cabinetmaking—in other words, skills incompatible with the Parisian labor market. These men sought help from BUMIDOM. But BUMIDOM officials often oriented them towards *manœuvre* (menial) and bricklayer

Table 4. Bumidom employment distribution for male migrants in 1962

EMPLOYMENT	# OF MIGRANTS	EMPLOYMENT	# OF MIGRANTS
Hospital attendants	2	Carpenters	12
Mechanical assistants	24	Painters/window cleaners	31
Laborers	2	Plumbers	72
Automobile factory workers	2	Mechanics for agricultural machines	7
Hairdressers	1	Flooring specialists	23
Metal workers	57	Locksmiths	21
Foremen	1	Welders	36
Industrial designers	2	Boilermakers	27
Fishing industry	10	Unknown*	16
Educators	1	Under training†	122
Electricians	36	Diverse trades	26
Domestics	3		

Source: Bureau pour le Développement des Migrations Intéressant les Départements d'Outre-Mer, "Migrations intéressant les Départements insulaires d'Outre-Mer, 1962–1963."
*These individuals received an unknown position with the Association Nationale pour la Formation Professionelle des Adultes.
†These individuals are under training with the Association Nationale pour la Formation Professionelle des Adultes.

jobs, which, as French citizens, they found unattractive and more appropriate for low-skilled migrants from Africa and Europe.

Noting that French Caribbean males looked at these positions apprehensively, in the early sixties BUMIDOM officials channeled Caribbean men into a variety of trade schools for adults (Association pour la Formation Professionelle des Adultes—AFPA), hoping to broaden their professional options. In an excellent study, Stephanie Condon and Philip Ogden note, "From 1962 to 1981, 8763 Caribbean men were sent directly to AFPA courses, of whom thirty-two percent arrived between 1962 and 1965. In addition, 5361 conscripts demobilized in France were sent to AFPA."[33] In theory, channeling the men to trade schools offered more professional opportunities, but in practice, it never occurred; from the early 1960s to the late 1970s, most men enrolling in AFPA programs became bricklayers.[34] As table 4 confirms, this was particularly true for the first wave of Caribbean male labor migrants who arrived in France via BUMIDOM.

By the late sixties, BUMIDOM and the Ministry of the Interior sought to offer Caribbean male migrants more professional options and created a trade school catering exclusively to them. The school opened in February 1968 at Simandres, a city located ten miles from Lyon. It offered specializations in metalwork, carpentry, and electricity. As in the school for Caribbean women at Crouy-sur-Ourcq, its instructors also took the opportunity to teach the students appropriate French social behaviors. In contrast, however, Simandres's internal rules were much looser and the instructors less paternalistic. Even if certain French instructors dared to ask the young Caribbean men if they ironed their clothes or bathed before attending class, they could easily mingle with the students at the school's ping-pong table, weight room, or bar.[35] It seems as if the disparities between the two schools reflected both the gendered division of labor and society's perception of gender roles. Moreover, when colonial relations are factored into this equation, it is clear that the school for Caribbean women intended to manufacture replacements for French mothers and to teach the students proper moral behavior, particularly regarding their sexual lives; in comparison, the school at Simandres upheld the privileges of masculinity, imparting to Caribbean men the necessary skills to become *chefs de famille* (heads of household), even though these skills did not open a path to becoming white-collar workers.

Ultimately, since the military also provided a professional outlet for Caribbean men, the school at Simandres never became as popular as the one for women in Crouy-sur-Ourcq. Only about three to four hundred students registered yearly, and not all of them always attended.[36] Still, the experience of Caribbean males at Simandres generates important questions about the migration. For example, did the collegial and paternal relations that the men encountered at Simandres mirror the experiences of most Caribbean male workers? Did the Caribbean work ethic, which Salvador described as antithetical to the Protestant work ethic, conform to French conceptions of Caribbean identity? How did French Caribbean people negotiate being French citizens of color living at home but technically away from home? How did Caribbean males negotiate anti-black racism? Finally, did they, like the Crooner, believe that laughing was a remedy for their problems?

The following testimonies of Mr. Frank, Mr. Pierre, Mr. Joseph, and Mr. Jean—two soldiers and two health-care workers from Guadeloupe and Martinique—open a window to the experiences and work ethic of Caribbean men in Paris.[37] Interestingly, although they share a similar work ethic, their opinions regarding migrating to France differ; certain Caribbean men are ambivalent about their journey to the metropole, while others relish the opportunity. This distinction is intricately related to their relationship with the French republican ideology of universal equality. Indeed, as descendants of slaves and former colonial subjects, Caribbean people have a complex relationship to the French republican tradition, and without a doubt, the experiences and worldview of the four men below illustrate this phenomenon.

Mr. Frank: From *Agent Hospitalier* to Manager of Ambulatory Ophthalmology Services

In 1963, Mr. Frank proudly passed his *baccalauréat* exam in Guadeloupe. The following year he moved to Paris, hoping to attend medical school. However, coming from a very humble family, Mr. Frank did not have the financial support that other Caribbean individuals applying to university enjoyed, so he decided to look for work. His interest in the medical field led him to apply to the Assistance publique–Hôpitaux de Paris (AP-HP), the agency coordinating Paris's public hospitals. After a few weeks, the AP-HP contacted him to take a placement test, which he successfully passed; the test only consisted of a *dictée* (a basic writing test) and a physical exam, an easy task for someone who possessed the prestigious French *baccalauréat*. Within a couple of months, the AP-HP offered Mr. Frank an *agent hospitalier* position and he happily began his new career in 1964. The position demanded much physical work; it entailed making the beds, cleaning the floors, feeding patients, and changing certain hygiene equipment, notably the *pot de chambre* (chamber pot) used by paraplegic and convalescing patients.[38] Ironically, while the vast majority of French administrators overseeing the Caribbean migration to Paris never received their *baccalauréat*, Mr. Frank obtained a much less lucrative and prestigious position than theirs. During that era, few French people with a *baccalauréat* would have been asked to replace chamber pots.

The following year was a turning point in Mr. Frank's life; he was drafted to fulfill his sixteen-month compulsory *service militaire*. But the military did not destroy his desire or capability to pursue a career in health care. In fact, he took advantage of the educational opportunities offered by this old institution to study nursing, a highly respected profession in France that is not as gender-coded as in the United States. Upon finishing "serving his country," he continued working as *agent hospitalier* for AP-HP, and in 1978, nearly thirteen years after he began the process, Mr. Frank finally became a nurse. A hard worker who always looks for growth opportunities, he transferred to an ophthalmology department, where he became supervisor of the hospital's ambulatory ophthalmology service. By the turn of the twenty-first century, as he approached retirement, he had climbed the social ladder, albeit very slowly. Still, in evaluating his career, Mr. Frank feels successful. He believes anti-black racism did not really affect his chances; for Mr. Frank, one's persistence, capability, and aptitude for work determine one's career path.[39] In other words, he maintains that irrespective of race and ethnicity, the French Republic rewards hard-working citizens.

MR. JOSEPH: AN *AGENT HOSPITALIER*

Like Mr. Frank, Mr. Joseph left the French Caribbean in his early twenties, hoping to start a successful career in the health-care industry. By the late sixties, he became *agent hospitalier* at Saint-Antoine Hospital. In contrast to Mr. Frank, he noted the presence of social tension between French and French Caribbean workers. This tension, he argued, was the product of French paternalism; most French workers at Saint-Antoine Hospital challenged the professional integrity of their Caribbean colleagues, treating them like colonial subjects. As a result, French Caribbean workers retaliated in passive-aggressive ways. For instance, Mr. Joseph observed that many Caribbean workers spoke Kreyol amongst themselves to alienate their French colleagues. In that sense, Kreyol functioned as a defense mechanism. Speaking the language excluded French workers from the conversation and asserted the French Caribbean presence within a white-French-dominated working environment.[40]

Nonetheless, due to the increasing number of Caribbean people at AP-HP and the hospital administration's concerted efforts to improve the dialogue between the two communities, Mr. Joseph notes that tension lessened after a couple of decades.[41] Still, he contends that if Caribbean people did not stand up for their rights by constantly demanding better jobs and to be treated with dignity, they would have continued "holding the devil by the tail," a Kreyol expression signifying that one's life is always characterized by hardship. At the dawn of the twenty-first century, Mr. Joseph was completing the last months of his successful career, yet he was still wondering about the possibility of returning home; in short, after all these years in Paris, he still considers Guadeloupe to be his homeland.

MR. PIERRE: A SOLDIER

Mr. Pierre had been retired for many years when I interviewed him.[42] He was living in a comfortable two-bedroom apartment in Paris's 13th Arrondissement. He had moved into his building prior to gentrification, when the 13th was still populated by Parisians and immigrants from humble social backgrounds. Similar to his old neighbors, Mr. Pierre comes from a humble social background, which is the reason he migrated to France in 1957. But unlike French Caribbean men like Mr. Frank and Mr. Joseph, who journeyed to France without a job, he migrated with the security of a military career.

Originally from Martinique, Mr. Pierre was first dispatched to Poitiers. Initially, he was not sure he had made the right decision. After all, he had left his wife to care for his two children and two stepchildren. He missed his family. He hoped to bring them to France, even if it meant living under Poitiers's cold and wintery gray sky. Still, doubts kept on creeping in. But on his first day, a seemingly unimportant event reassured him; when his superior called out his last name during roll call, a white man emerged from the group, answering with a loud *présent!* Mr. Pierre drew comfort from sharing his name with this man; it gave him a sense of belonging in France.

Mr. Pierre, who is from St. Marie, a small, rural, and picturesque *commune* in northern Martinique, believes staying in his island would have been a professionally unwise decision. He firmly maintains that migrating to France via the military offered him the rare opportunity to see the world (he was stationed overseas for a couple of years) and reinvent himself as a productive French citizen. For him, neither the distance between France and Martinique nor racism seriously affected his life. Moreover, he believes the military, which he truly sees as a family unit, did not encourage judging people based on the color of their skin and origin. Yet despite his successful military career, other factors in Mr. Pierre's life indicate that he actually paid a high price for migrating to France, even just emotionally.

Indeed, when Mr. Pierre traveled to Martinique in the early seventies, he had been separated from his wife for more than ten years. She and her children never made it to France. The distance between the couple had created irreparable wounds, and Mr. Pierre developed another relationship with a Frenchwoman. He literally began a new life. Meanwhile, seeking a better life for her family, his former wife migrated to New York City with the children. Caught in the tentacles of his professional life, deeply in love with his French *amoureuse*, much to his regret, Mr. Pierre ultimately lost contact with his children.[43] In 2003, more than forty years later, this chapter in Mr. Pierre's interesting life story weighs heavily on his conscience, as he feels the burden of unfulfilled paternal responsibilities.

Admittedly, leaving his daughters behind was both morally disturbing and emotionally painful. But for his Martinican wife, the separation came at an emotional, social, physical, psychological, and financial cost. Her life was punctuated with daily battles. She struggled to make ends meet, working full-time as a nurse's aide and part-time as a cook. She actually "held the devil by the tail," raising four girls in New York City on the humble salary of a nurse's aide. In many ways, the story of Mr. Pierre and his family is one of the numerous untold stories of family separation that occurred throughout the fifties and sixties, when young men left women and children behind to look for opportunities in France. It is a sad episode in French Caribbean history, which neither scholars nor government statistics can possibly measure.

Mr. Jean: A Retired Officer

Mr. Jean started his military career in the early fifties. But unlike Mr. Pierre, he recalls that racism often tainted his relationship with other French soldiers, particularly the superior officers. As a soldier, he routinely felt pressured to perform his tasks better than his white counterparts. "Above and beyond," his professional motto was merely a mechanism to deal with the double standard constantly at play. Indeed, he felt as if white soldiers earned more praise for doing the same work as Caribbean soldiers. For that reason, Mr. Jean is certain that if it were not for the color of his skin, he would have retired at a higher rank.

Despite the social exclusion and the racism he encountered in the military, Mr. Jean had a vibrant social life. He never really cut the umbilical cord with Martinique. As a general rule, he gravitated towards a Caribbean circle of friends.[44] On Sundays, or during the major holidays, he always hosted or attended a Caribbean gathering; without these events, he claims his life in France would have been unbearable. Like many other Caribbean migrants, although he lived in France for more than fifty years, Mr. Jean still considers Martinique to be his home. Throughout our conversation, he told me countless stories about his hometown of Rivière-Pilote, as if he had actually never left. To be sure, along with his feelings of exile, romantic notions of the homeland crawled into his stories. When discussing his life, Mr. Jean admits that France offered him a successful military career. Simultaneously, he claims migrating to France stole something from him—perhaps the opportunity to enjoy the multiple fruits of one's homeland.

Messieurs Jean, Pierre, Joseph, and Frank's testimonies speak to the heterogeneous characteristics of the Caribbean male migration. Mr. Pierre's and Mr. Frank's professional and social lives reflect those of many Caribbean people who were initially skeptical about migrating to France, but who built their lives and careers in a France that they now call home. On the other hand, having experienced racism and social alienation at the workplace, Mr. Joseph and Mr. Jean express reservations about migrating to France—a widespread feeling within the French Caribbean diaspora of that generation. Still, although they clearly understood and reacted to racism and other social challenges in France differently, these four men share a common characteristic: they all believe in working hard, and sometimes, harder than the French.

These two different patterns of social insertion are intricately linked to French Caribbean political philosophy. As descendants of slaves and colonial subjects, many French Caribbean individuals developed two related but distinct political philosophies, which speak to their relationship with French republican traditions. Although not all

French Caribbean people conform to the following description, most of them are what I call "pragmatic conformists" or "disillusioned conformists." In general, the pragmatic conformists strongly identify with the French republican tradition, which they believe is inherently anti-racist. This belief flourished during the mid-nineteenth century, when Victor Schœlcher, the famous French abolitionist, spread the idea that liberty and equality should be applicable to any individual pledging allegiance to France. For that reason, Marie-José Jolivet notes that many French Caribbean individuals developed a true cult of Victor Schœlcher in the decades following the abolition of slavery (1848), or what Edouard Glissant calls *le schœlcherisme*.[45] However, beneath this blind love for Schœlcher, the "great emancipator," lay an infatuation with the ideals of the Third Republic (1870-1940), which Afro-French Caribbean people viewed as their Trojan horse to battle the conservative local white Creole elite—the *békés*—who constantly sought to keep them in subservient positions.

The support of a rising class of Afro-Caribbean politicians for the French policy of assimilation during the interwar period further spread pragmatic conformism among French Caribbean people.[46] These politicians viewed French bureaucracy as a way to secure employment for the growing black middle class and an avenue away from the plantation economy, which only offered sugarcane and banana harvesting jobs to the majority of the population. However, in the final analysis, it is Charles de Gaulle's opposition to the Vichy regime that solidified pragmatic conformism as a French Caribbean political philosophy. Indeed, during World War II, avid Vichy supporters ruled Guadeloupe and Martinique with an iron fist. These Vichyites and Nazi sympathizers frequently violated human rights and supported the local white Creole elite all too anxious to reestablish their political hegemony. As a result, de Gaulle's stand against the Nazis and the subsequent creation of the Fourth Republic, which praised universal equality, convinced many Afro-French Caribbean people that French republican ideals truly coincided with their best interests.[47] In sum, the dialectics between the white Creoles' quest for socioeconomic and political hegemony and the possibilities of growth and social equality offered through the auspices of the French Republic have, from the mid-nineteenth century to World War II, encouraged Afro-Caribbean people to become pragmatic conformists—by definition, people embracing the republic who adhere to French codes of social, cultural, and moral conduct, believing this political philosophy and lifestyle translates into climbing up the social ladder.[48] Thus, among the four men discussed in this section, Mr. Frank and Mr. Pierre clearly fit this political profile. They believe racial differences do not interfere with the French meritocratic system. Supposedly, as long as Caribbean individuals work hard, and most importantly, endorse French sociopolitical and cultural values, they will ultimately accomplish their goals.

In contrast to the pragmatic conformists, the disillusioned conformists question the French republican discourse of universal equality. Although they support French republicanism, these French Caribbean people argue that the intersection of race and culture generates different social experiences. Similar to leading postwar black intellectuals and politicians like Aimé Césaire and Léon Damas, the disillusioned conformists often challenge the French Republic, inviting her to put the theory of universal equality into practice. For that reason, the disillusioned Caribbean conformists who live in Paris tend to organize their community to address issues of racism, social inequality, and cultural alienation.[49] In this study, Mr. Joseph and Mr. Jean express the views of disillusioned conformists, as they acknowledge how race and culture affected their professional lives.

Although fundamentally different, these political philosophies encourage French Caribbean people to fit within the French republican mold. The major difference, however, lies in the fact that pragmatic conformists believe respectability and hard work translates into reaping the full benefits of French citizenship, while disillusioned conformists highlight the shortcomings of French citizenship when race and culture are factored into the equation. If one were to speculate about which political philosophy was more prevalent among French Caribbean individuals during the sixties, one would probably suggest pragmatic conformism. However, throughout the past four decades, the French Caribbean sociopolitical consciousness and philosophical outlook has changed. As the social unrest that swept the Parisian suburbs in November 2005 and the protests against the high cost of living that paralyzed Guadeloupe and Martinique in January and February 2009 suggest, disillusioned conformism has slowly crept into the French Caribbean mind, making it the dominant political philosophy.[50]

The Cronner and the Workers' Impact on the French

Henri Salvador spread a new idea of black masculinity that may have facilitated the insertion of Caribbean men into the fabric of French society. Accordingly, the French had no reason to feel anxious about the presence of these black men in Paris, if, as Salvador implied, they were smooth, romantic, funny, and happy. Like the Crooner, these Caribbean men could date across the color line without violent reprisals by disgruntled or socially conservative Frenchmen. This was a major leap forward because a few decades earlier, certain white males did resort to violence at the sight of a white woman in the arms of a black man.[51] Nonetheless, while Salvador presented interracial relationships in a positive light, his music did not emphasize how Caribbean men constantly negotiated colonial relations. He failed to share the story of so many men who flirted with poverty, not necessarily white women. In recalling his first days in France, Mr. Guacide, a retired policeman, illustrates the discrepancy between Salvador's representation of Caribbean males and the men's experience in France:

> I arrived in Paris in 1960. I had no family. I only knew a neighborhood friend. We became very close in France. Every other Sunday, I went to his house. We played dominos and ate a nice Creole meal, even though during that time we hardly found any plantains, yams, or tinin [green bananas]. One Sunday, his wife had invited a beautiful girl from Tivoli [Martinique]; we connected and she eventually became my wife. It was very difficult for us in the beginning. She was working at the hospital, I was in training, and she became pregnant. I tell you, for the first couple of years we hardly had any money. At the end of the month we walked looking down at our feet, hoping to find coins on the ground. That is how we started our lives in France. Today we are retired. We have a home, a nice car, and beautiful grandchildren. But we worked very hard to get there. We still miss our home and want to retire in Martinique, but we can't. You see, if we go home we'll babysit other people's grandchildren.[52]

Interestingly, only grassroots Caribbean musicians sing about the issues that Mr. Guacide, the retired policeman, experienced when he first arrived in Paris. Unlike the Crooner, and for that matter, the historiography of the "Glorious Thirty," these musicians sing about hardship and the sentiments of exile that swept the Caribbean community. For instance, in a song that became highly popular in the Kreyol-speaking Caribbean, Super Combo, a Guadeloupean band from the early seventies, underscores the suffering and disillusionment of many Caribbean people in the City of Light:[53]

Mwen té konprann la vi Pari	I thought the life in Paris
sété Pigal, sété Bawbès	was Barbès and Pigalle
men, lè mwen rivé a Pari	But when I arrived in Paris
Mwen dòmi déwò	I slept outside
Mwen dòmi an dalo	I slept on the floor
Mwen dòmi déwò	I slept outside
Mwen dòmi an tou a metro	I slept in the metro's guts
Wo-y, ka fè fwèt	Gosh, it's so cold
Fwèt kon adan frijidè,	Cold as the freezer
Mwen pa menm tin on vyé pilovè	But I don't even have an old sweater
Mwen vini isi vwè mizè...	I came here to taste misery...

The song suggests that Caribbean migrants had anticipated having a successful professional life in France, but upon arriving in the metropole, they were unable to earn a respectable salary. Migration did not initially translate into climbing the social ladder; on the contrary, it led to deception, poverty, and homelessness, conditions that could only be remedied by hard work, courage, and emotional strength.

In what seems to be a paradoxical situation, the Caribbean migrants who arrived in Paris of the sixties lived in a condition of exile. As French citizens in Paris, they were technically at home, but as French Caribbean individuals, they truly lived away from home. Nonetheless, despite the stress, social alienation, hardship, and limited professional opportunities, most Caribbean migrants of the sixties and early seventies sought to improve their socioeconomic conditions. As reflected in Mr. Frank, Mr. Joseph, Mr. Pierre, and Mr. Jean's testimonies, they continuously worked hard, debunking the stereotypes of Caribbean people as uneducated, lazy, and playful. All things considered, as pragmatic or disillusioned conformists, they participated in the ongoing process of decolonizing France. Whether they clashed with their French colleagues at work or displayed an acute sense of accommodationism, they helped white French citizens unlearn colonial notions of Caribbean identity; however, Caribbean migrants did not only decolonize white-black social relations just by leading respectable lives and having a strong work ethic. There came about a proliferation of community and political organizations within the communities of Caribbean and sub-Saharan African migrants in the Parisian region. These organizations, which sought to improve the living conditions of sub-Saharan African and Caribbean people in France and within their respective countries, played an important role in debunking the colonial continuities that persisted in the postcolonial period.

Chapter 7

French Labor Unions, Black Community and Political Activism, and Decolonization in Postcolonial Paris, 1960–1974

We received your letter regarding your request about our Spanish comrades and the Malian guys living in Barcelona. After all considerations, we realize that we cannot do anything for them. Gérard Esperet, the comrade in charge of finding employment in the Parisian region for these people, is largely unsuccessful. So we contacted other organizations and people helping black Africans. We noticed that many of them are unemployed, sometimes for long periods. Due to these circumstances, we advise you to prevent these Malian comrades from coming to the Parisian region; they would just swell the ranks of the unemployed. Unless you know of employment opportunities in Haute-Normandie, we suggest they return promptly to their country.
—A letter from René Salane, *secrétaire confédéral* of the Confédération Française Démocratique du Travail, France's second largest trade union; dated March 15, 1967

When most black migrants from the lower classes arrived in Paris, they quickly became disenchanted with their quality of life. Many of them only had access to low-wage employment and often lived in insalubrious dwellings. Moreover, continuing colonial relations often characterized their relationship with white French citizens. Angered by these conditions, or simply because they aspired to a better life, a large number of African and Caribbean migrants turned to activism. They joined trade unions and community organizations seeking to improve their living and working conditions. These organizations also helped black migrants deal with nostalgia and sentiments of exile, a common phenomenon within diasporic communities. Similar to the labor migrants, many students and professionals also embraced a life full of activism. However, unlike the workers, their activism was mostly politically oriented. They created vibrant organizations, publishing newsletters, lobbying the French government, and staging a number of demonstrations at strategically selected locations. As a general rule, black students and professionals sought to enhance democratic values in the newly independent African nations and reconfigure the seemingly neocolonial relations between France and her former Caribbean and sub-Saharan African colonies.

The sixties is a unique decade in the history of the African diaspora in France. As in the interwar and early postwar periods (1946-1960), African and Caribbean migrants participated in transnational and transregional politics, addressing issues of decolonization and democracy. But unlike in previous decades, many black migrants began focusing on a number of local issues, usually related to the living and working conditions of the thousands of working-class Caribbean and African individuals flocking to the Parisian region. In many ways, their efforts to curtail these social problems amounted to a new form of black activism in urban France, one suggesting that despite France's tradition of universal equality, ethnic, cultural, and racial differences contributed to the reproduction of social inequalities on French soil.

Like their French counterparts, African and Caribbean migrants viewed the labor union as an ally in the fight for workers' rights. But to their surprise, the unions did not understand their grievances, prompting them to create support systems addressing problems of anti-black racism, poverty, unemployment, and housing quality. Thus, three important African and Caribbean community organizations emerged in Paris, playing an important role in the development of black France. Simultaneously, black political activism continued to flourish, as many African and Caribbean students and workers questioned their leaders' moral integrity and France's relationship to their homeland. The question is to what extent they operated across national, ethnic, or even racial lines. Did Pan-Africanism still influence their goals? What is certain, however, is that community activism promoted the insertion of Caribbean and African migrants into France as equal members of society and black political activism challenged the colonial relations between France and her former colonies that persisted in the postcolonial era.

African Migrants in French Trade Unions

After World War II, French officials clearly stated their unwillingness to recruit workers from sub-Saharan Africa to rebuild France; they preferred European migrants. However, because capitalist systems seek to reduce the cost of labor and production to maximize profit, the private sector often looked beyond racial criteria, effectively recruiting "cheap labor" from various sub-Saharan African colonies. This practice angered French labor-union representatives. They feared that colonial workers from sub-Saharan Africa would deflate wages and undermine the strength of the French working class.[1] Thus, union leaders looked at seasonal colonial workers with contemptuous eyes, arguing that they were useless allies against the government and the increasingly powerful private sector always trying to depress wages.[2] However, by the late forties, French trade unionists changed their perspective, as a distinct community of West African labor migrants emerged in Marseilles.[3] Coming to terms with the fact that these black workers were becoming an integral part of the city's social fabric, they began to view them as potential recruits capable of strengthening the union.

The Confédération Générale du Travail (CGT), the largest French labor union, was the first one to establish contact with the community of African labor migrants. Usually dockworkers who labored alongside Frenchmen and other European migrants, these men played a crucial role in France's thriving import-export economy, as they tirelessly loaded and unloaded cargo boats traveling from Marseilles to the colonies. Because CGT showed interest in the condition of African dockworkers, African activists looking for support began to gravitate towards the union; in fact, it is in this context that the legendary Senegalese novelist and filmmaker Ousmane Sembène, at the time a young dockworker, joined the union.[4]

An autodidact, gifted speaker, and devout anticolonialist, Ousmane Sembène believed CGT could help him organize African workers while pursuing his main political agenda, namely, independence for Senegal and the other sub-Saharan African French colonies. He was following the path of other African activists who utilized the union as a springboard for a political career.[5] As the CGT's steward in Marseilles, and, by default, the leading spokesman of the African community, Ousmane Sembène's activism was both local and transnational; he aimed to end colonialism in Africa, while fighting to improve conditions for African workers in Marseilles, which he noticed were drastically different from those of the educated black middle class of Paris.[6] Indeed, in contrast to the capital, where most African migrants were either professionals or students, the vast majority of Africans in Marseilles—the dockworkers—worked for French employers

Chapter Seven

unwilling to pay fairly. Thus, for Ousmane Sembène, CGT represented an ally truly committed to empowering and protecting African workers from abusive employers.

However, by the end of the fifties, the happy marriage between the union and African workers took a turn for the worse. Due to the Algerian War, the Mediterranean city was flooded with hundreds of thousands of Pieds-Noirs (Jewish and white French settlers), who literally turned the city into a quasi-refugee camp. As a result, feelings of exile, resentment, and anguish conquered Marseilles, a city renowned for its jovial character.[7] But most importantly, this sudden and unforeseen migration had an immediate impact on the labor market. The few jobs that African workers had secured became highly coveted by Pieds-Noirs seeking to provide for their families in distress. For that reason, Marseilles was no longer a "haven" for migrants from sub-Saharan Africa. Instead, Paris, which offered a plethora of low-wage jobs, became the new magnet for young African workers with few professional avenues at home. Ironically, as the number of African labor migrants in Paris increased, their relationship with CGT grew quite cold.

Generally, the union focused on issues affecting the French working class and the larger communities of new migrant workers arriving from Spain, Portugal, and Italy. CGT Paris published pamphlets in Portuguese, Italian, and Spanish to attract European migrants. The union also organized workshops and conferences to figure out how to help new European migrants adapt to their new working environment. For example, during a conference on Spanish steelworkers in Paris, CGT advocated for wage equality, better labor contracts, equal social rights (insurance and financial help for large families), as well as access to professional development for all migrant workers.[8] For CGT, reaching out to European migrants prevented the government and the private sector from using them to stabilize wages. Yet, since the state and the private sector could not use the smaller community of African workers as wage stabilizers, CGT did not cater to them. For that reason, many African workers gravitated towards other French labor unions, notably the Confédération Française Démocratique du Travail (CFDT), the second largest trade union in France, which was created in 1964 when the majority of the members of the Confédération Française des Travailleurs Chrétiens (French Confederation of Christian Workers) decided to become secular.

CFDT took an active interest in the community of African labor migrants. Similar to what CGT had done in Marseilles, CFDT recruited African activists to serve as intermediaries with their community. Drawing from their observations, the union quickly realized that African workers in Paris faced many obstacles. By 1966, when it organized a conference on migrant workers in Paris, it had already sponsored a research group that was supposed to present findings on the conditions of African migrants in Paris. At the conference, Mr. Khlidou, the African delegate, informed CFDT that African workers shared a unique experience. He noted that African labor migrants faced longer periods of unemployment than their European counterparts. For Mr. Khlidou, racism was the barrier preventing Africans from enjoying the fruits of the booming economy. He argued that the problem was structural, claiming, "Even when they routinely attend the unemployment office at the Department of Labor, African migrants still have difficulties finding a job."[9]

By giving a voice to representatives of the African community, CFDT opened a window onto the lives of African workers in Paris. Admittedly, CFDT understood that African migrants faced more difficulties than other migrants, especially European migrants. As committed trade unionists willing to help struggling comrades, CFDT members encouraged Africans to join the union, claiming, "[We] provide a forum to remedy illiteracy, housing, and hygiene problems. When you participate in the union's activities . . . your condition will improve."[10] Convinced that social class and professional training predicated success, CFDT leaders ignored the relationship between racism, colonial continuities, unemployment, and poverty in the African community. Perhaps their shortsighted analysis was related to their own preconceived notions of African identities. Indeed, *Perspective Socialiste*, the union's voice and monthly magazine, had published articles hinting that Africans still lived primitively. The magazine suggested that traditional African values and customs conflicted with the exigencies of the industrial world, ultimately preventing the migrants from working efficiently in France. According to *Perspective Socialiste*, "The factory, the office, or the workshop requires a strong work ethic and demands the ability to work alone, which is unlike the typically free character and communitarian aspect of life in rural Africa."[11] Hence, in the most ironic twist, by framing Africans as unprepared for the demands of the French labor market, the union actually held the same discourse as many French employers who discriminated against them based on imaginary characteristics.

Notwithstanding its reservations about African migrants' capabilities to function in France, CFDT was still soliciting their membership. The union thought all comrades should join the struggle against capitalist exploitation, especially African comrades, the quintessential victims of capitalism. Indeed, for CFDT, recruiting and empowering African labor migrants was a symbolic victory because it reaffirmed their commitment to protecting all workers against the French industrialist community, which had grown in size and strength during the "Glorious Thirty." But in reality, CFDT was not very successful in the community of African workers. Many workers failed to see the advantages of being unionized, since it rarely translated into significant changes in their professional or social lives. For instance, Mr. Gissoko, a retired transnational Malian worker, who now lives in Mali and travels to France for health reasons, recalls that in the early sixties, trade unionists had asked him to represent his community.

After hesitating, he joined because he found the idea of participating in a workers' organization empowering and attractive. However, within a few months he felt as if the union's rhetoric outweighed its actions, and like many other African migrants, he left without remorse.[12]

By the mid-sixties, the French government also implemented a series of rules and regulations deterring Africans from joining trade unions. For instance, it criminalized the participation of immigrants in politically oriented strikes; in the event that the Ministry of the Interior determined that migrants had participated in political manifestations, they were branded as political agitators and could face immediate deportation. In fact, after the May '68 events, the Ministry of the Interior deported seven hundred migrant workers for chanting the same protest songs as their French counterparts.[13] The Union Générale des Travailleurs Sénégalais en France (UGTSF), an African workers' association, actually confirmed that the French police used this strategy to intimidate many of its members. According to the association's representatives, high-ranking police officers frequently summoned Africans and other foreign workers to police precincts, where they threatened to deport them within eight days if they did not stop participating in strikes or any other "political activities."[14]

In addition to threat of deportation, a law stipulated that immigrants could only join or elect a representative to the *comité d'entreprise* (work council) after they had worked in France for at least five years. This law prevented Africans from having a voice at the workplace and the trade unions, since many of them led transnational labor-migrant lives, frequently shuttling between France and Africa. Sally N'Dongo, the UGTSF's leader, argued that the law clearly marginalized African workers throughout Paris's industrial belt. He claimed to know certain factories where Africans constituted close to 80 percent of the personnel, yet could not elect a representative because most of them had been working in France for less than five years.[15] Thus, throughout the sixties, the law, police intimidation, the unions' obvious preferential treatment of European migrants, as well as the union representatives' preconceived notions of African identities deterred African workers from joining either CFDT or CGT.

In contrast to the fifties, when CGT's support for decolonization attracted African workers and activists, during the sixties Africans saw CGT and CFDT as allies fighting their battle half-heartedly. Africans understood how the unions dismissed the effects of racial discrimination and served immigrant communities unevenly. In truth, only after the press covered the infamous *drame d'Aubervilliers* (the Aubervilliers disaster), where five African workers died asphyxiated in an overcrowded basement on January 2, 1970, did CGT and CFDT seem to take a more serious interest in the plight of African workers in the Parisian region.[16] But here again, the line between seizing the moment to inject union politics into the national arena and doing something about the struggle of

Protest following the funeral of African workers who died at Aubervilliers, 1970. (Photo by E. Lamy, Agence de Diffusion nouvelle photographique, used with permission of Archives CFDT [Confédération Française Démocratique du Travail], 6E/1970/8439.)

Africans was blurred. One wonders if, in the heat of the sensationalized Aubervilliers disaster, as CFDT and CGT literally handed the mic to its African members, giving them the space, audience, and attention they needed to voice their community's problems, the unions were not merely capitalizing on this sad episode to portray themselves as the "guardian angels" of all workers in France.[17]

A picture taken in the aftermath of the Aubervilliers disaster captures the relationship between African labor migrants and French labor unions. First, it reveals that few Africans participated in the union-sponsored protest. But most importantly, it allows us to reflect on whether the French participants really understood the challenges Paris offered to transnational African labor migrants. Did these French labor activists protest for the sake of protesting? Were they truly committed to participating in the struggle of African migrants? Did they transcend French stereotypes of Africans? In many ways, the relationship between French labor unions and African workers is full of paradoxes. Throughout the forties and fifties, French labor unions supported nationalist movements in the former sub-Saharan Africa colonies by sheltering and providing a forum for anticolonial activists. However, in Paris of the sixties, they did not nourish close relationships with Africans, because union leaders did not acknowledge how colonial continuities kept most African workers at the bottom of the labor market.

French Caribbean migrants shared a similar relationship with the trade unions. Indeed, CGT had also championed the cause of Caribbean workers during the colonial era. However, when French Guiana, Guadeloupe, and Martinique became Overseas Departments, their relationship with Caribbean workers changed for the worse. This phenomenon was evident when thousands of working-class Caribbean individuals migrated to France at the beginning of the sixties, and in a glaring fashion, the unions failed to service this burgeoning community appropriately. French union representatives treated Caribbean workers like foreigners or white French workers, but in reality, according to Caribbean activists, French Caribbean workers were displaced racial minorities with special needs.

Caribbean Migrants and French Trade Unions

In the mid-1880s, CGT opened its offices in the old colonies. Seeing an ally against the wealthy white Creole planters' class, French Caribbean sugarcane workers flocked to the union. With its support, up until the mid-twentieth century, Guadeloupean and Martinican agricultural workers and dockworkers organized countless strikes, demanding better pay and working conditions.[18] But in the postwar period, as local union activists began to participate in emerging nationalist movements and workers moved away from the agricultural sector, the relationship between the workers and CGT slowly deteriorated. Already fragile, the relationship worsened during the "Great Migration" of the sixties. Many Caribbean workers felt disconnected from French trade unionists, who still saw them through French colonial lenses. For example, in a report entitled *Pour défendre plus efficacement les travailleurs immigrés de la métallurgie de la Seine* (To better defend immigrant steelworkers in the Department of the Seine), CGT unscrupulously lumped French Caribbean people with other immigrants, claiming, "Out of the 80,000 immigrants who arrive yearly, 21,950 settle in the Seine region . . . the majority of these immigrants are Portuguese, Italians, Martinicans, Guadeloupeans, and Spanish."[19]

Many Caribbean migrants, particularly activists, deplored this untimely state of invisibility. They believed Caribbean workers in France constituted a racialized diaspora with "special needs," and therefore, counted on the union to promote and facilitate their socioeconomic insertion into France. However, they felt the union refused to address their needs. According to Mr. George Lassare Michalon, it literally took a decade of meetings for French trade unionists to finally acknowledge the ambiguous, and at times precarious, condition of French Caribbean workers in Paris. Indeed, he asserts:

> We were trying to form a distinct group within the union. It was a tough fight. We wanted CGT to recognize that Caribbean workers had specific needs and deserved a special section inside the CGT apparatus. Only in the 1970s, after the number of Caribbean migrants in Parisian hospitals increased, were we able to form our own group. But in the '60s we faced many obstacles. We had countless meetings and confronted French trade unionists who, for the most part, opposed our demands. We were desperately trying to explain that Afro-Caribbean people shared different experiences, but they did not endorse the heterogeneity of the French working class.[20]

All things considered, when Caribbean and African migrants from the lower classes arrived in Paris during the last half of the "Glorious Thirty," CFDT and CGT had become a force to be reckoned with. However, because many trade unionists failed to understand the racialized dimension of the labor market, neither group benefited from their growing strength. Yet, like all working-class labor migrants, they encountered countless obstacles, especially in trying to secure housing and employment. For that reason, black migrants felt compelled to found their own community organizations to address these challenges and compensate for the lack of support from the unions and the French government.

COMMUNITY ORGANIZING IN BLACK PARIS OF THE SIXTIES

Up until the late fifties, African and Caribbean students founded the most prominent black organizations. But decolonization, departmentalization, and the labor migration from the Caribbean and Africa restructured the black organizational landscape. By the late sixties, African and Caribbean workers' organizations seeking to improve the migrants' living conditions were most commonly found in Paris. Usually, these new organizations only serviced members from their own community; one would not find African migrants in Caribbean organizations, or vice versa. Nonetheless, despite the apparent ethnic and national fragmentation, these postcolonial community organizations played a crucial role in inserting working-class black migrants into the social fabric of the city. Thus, by examining their structure and the scope of their activities, we can better understand the process of African diasporic formation in postcolonial France, and the ways in which new forms of black activism influenced French society.[21]

Most African and Caribbean community organizations often shared similar goals and a similar infrastructure. Only the size of the organization—whether they were small or large—created differences (a small organization would have less than five hundred members). For example, l'Union des Travailleurs Mauritaniens en France (Mauritanian Workers' Alliance in France—UTMF) embodies the quintessential small-scale African organization of the sixties. Born in the mid-sixties, UTMF was mostly comprised of Toukouleurs and Sarakolé migrants from Mauritania, although a couple of members came from neighboring countries (they were usually Toukouleur or Sarakolé people). Overall, UTMF aimed to gather the Mauritanian diaspora under its umbrella to become an important lobbying force and offer Mauritanians a sanctuary where they could reconstruct their community and network with each other. Like most African and Caribbean community organizations, UTMF embraced bureaucratic values and featured a highly hierarchical structure, qualities that it probably inherited from the colonial period. In that respect, it had a president, a vice president, a general secretary, an assistant to the general secretary, a treasurer and his associate, an account secretary and his associate, and a public relations representative.[22]

Although the organization never became a powerful lobbying force, by offering members information about the Parisian housing and labor landscape—for example, what were the best or worst places to work in the city—UTMF was instrumental in helping Mauritanian migrants survive in Paris. However, due to financial hardship, organizations like UTMF often struggled. They obtained funding from a small membership fee, forcing them to establish their headquarters in basements of private households, which often put them at odds with their French landlords. Certain landlords had not anticipated having large groups of black men attending lively or heated meetings. In fact, it was not unusual that these landlords' discomfort with a large group of African migrants escalated into complaints about the "noise and smell," or the "overcrowdedness" of the meetings. The UTMF's landlord, for example, sued them for abusing the capacity of his property. The judicial fight, which turned malicious at times, lasted four years; the landlord even wrote a letter to the Minister of the Interior, reminding him that France is a small country, and that these "fictive" and "unstructured" associations were not following the law.[23]

Small associations such as UTMF struggled to survive. But large ones, specifically, the Comité d'Action Sociale en Faveur des Originaires des Départements d'Outre-Mer en Métropole (CASODOM), l'Amicale des Travailleurs Antillais et Guyanais (AMITAG), and the Union Générale des Travailleurs Sénégalais en France (UGTSF), thrived. Their size, vibrant leadership, and the government subsidies they received—CASODOM and AMITAG obtained some funding from the Ministry of the Interior and, initially, UGTSF received a grant from Senegal—made them quite influential in their respective communities. These organizations played an important role in black France of the sixties; not only did they come into being for very similar reasons, but somehow they imparted to their members certain notions of entitlement. African and Caribbean migrants passing through these organizations slowly came to realize that, like the French, they also deserved decent housing, respectable jobs, and the right to be treated with dignity.

The idea for CASODOM, the oldest of the three organizations, germinated in the mid-fifties, when poor Caribbean migrants started arriving in the Parisian region at a rate of five thousand per year, a number that actually doubled when BUMIDOM began operating in 1962.[24] Since many migrants had difficulty finding employment and respectable housing, Caribbean activists sought help from the Services Sociaux des Nord-Africains (Social Services for North Africans—SSNA) and the Service Social d'Aide aux Emigrants Etrangers (Social Services for Foreigners—SSAEE). To their dismay, their request fell upon deaf ears. Luckily, Mrs. Dancenis, a Martinican woman working at SSAEE, took interest in the men's quest. She knew that many of her compatriots had found themselves homeless and unemployed soon after they arrived in the Parisian region. Determined to help her community, despite having professional responsibilities, she began laying the foundation for an association catering to disadvantaged Caribbean migrants. Mrs. Dancenis sacrificed her weekends and evenings, conducting research on the migrants' conditions to develop an action plan. Ultimately, her commitment and dedication encouraged other Caribbean activists to participate in the process, which lead to the creation of CASODOM in 1956. Still, in the final analysis, it is her work, sacrifice, and perseverance that was vital to creating the organization.[25]

CASODOM had a huge impact on the lives of many migrants. For one, by serving as a liaison with potential employers, the organization drastically reduced unemployment in the community. Moreover, it helped individuals who migrated before World War II to finally purchase a ticket and visit home. Yvette St. Luce, a privileged Martinican woman who arrived in Paris in the late twenties, recalls that some of these people had migrated in their twenties and were approaching retirement age, yet they never had the opportunity to travel home and see their family.[26] Thus, by providing a humble subsidy to allow people to visit their long-lost home, CASODOM played an important role in the community's "emotional economy."

A decade after Madame Dancenis and her colleagues launched the organization, *Alizé*, the Caribbean student newsletter, noted how it provided a safety net to the community, claiming, "Essentially, CASODOM provides all the services migrants may expect from a welfare institution; it serves as a liaison with potential employers; orients them towards specialized services; grants loans and assists with their social security dossier."²⁷ Additionally, and perhaps most importantly, CASODOM helped decrease the number of Caribbean homeless in the beautiful City of Light, usually people who had stowed away on transatlantic ships and, for lack of assistance, found themselves in the streets. This situation was particularly difficult for Caribbean migrants because they perceived homelessness as a deviant behavior, and of course, no one wanted to bear the weight of such stigma. Consequently, by helping migrants in this predicament, the organization provided much-needed financial and housing assistance, and most importantly, psychological support to a fragile community.

In 1960, just four years after CASODOM, Caribbean community activists founded AMITAG, the second largest organization, which short of offering loans provided the same services as CASODOM. Partly funded by BUMIDOM, AMITAG successfully connected potential employers from the private or public sectors with members looking for employment as administrative assistants, electricians, or carpenters—jobs that they considered acceptable—or as gardeners or maids, jobs that they did not necessarily like. AMITAG provided a range of services. It helped homeless migrants, offering them a place to sleep in a *foyer* of four hundred beds; it offered free legal advice; it organized cultural activities to raise money for the needy and the sick; and it generously lent a large hall for wedding ceremonies, which actually proved quite useful to many young migrants without discretionary income.²⁸

Similar to CASODOM and AMITAG, l'Union Générale des Travailleurs Sénégalais en France (UGTSF) was very influential in the African community.²⁹ It drew its success from its inclusive philosophy and the high number of Senegalese migrants in the Parisian region. Unlike other organizations, which usually accepted members based on national, ethnic, and ideological criteria, UGTSF welcomed Senegalese migrants and a few Africans from neighboring countries. But above all, it may have been Sally N'Dongo, the organization's charismatic leader, who made UGTSF so popular. Mr. N'Dongo was a well-connected and gifted speaker from Senegal who gained much experience in community organizing when he worked with the *Ligue Internationale Contre le Racisme et l'Antisémitisme* (LICRA), a French humanitarian organization that had grown popular in the aftermath of World War II and the Jewish Holocaust. Hoping to connect isolated Senegalese migrants and improve the deplorable living and working conditions of many African individuals throughout the Parisian region, N'Dongo elected to put his experience in community organizing at their service.

UGTSF was officially established in 1961. Following N'Dongo's agenda, it aimed to regroup Senegalese workers scattered throughout the city, improve their quality of life, and facilitate their insertion into the housing and labor markets. Although the organization was primarily concerned with housing, employment, and health issues, it also assisted members with their social security dossiers and residential status, offering them much-needed advice on legal and immigration issues. In some rare cases, UGTSF provided financial assistance to its members.[30]

Occasionally, as one might expect from an organization operating with limited funds, quarrels erupted between members. Unlike their Caribbean counterparts, the ethnic background and political affiliation of members often generated clashes in certain African organizations, including in UGTSF. For example, Toukouleur members often felt silenced by the Sarakolés, the organization's largest ethnic group.[31] But ultimately, as UGTSF flirted with Pan-African ideals and aimed to empower all African workers in France, it successfully sidestepped the ideological and ethnic barriers, at least throughout the sixties and early seventies. According to Jean Pierre N'Diaye, a famous Senegalese journalist and author, in these days UGTSF held enthusiastic and inspiring meetings, trying desperately to carve out a space in the French Republic for the growing sub-Saharan African community. Attending these energetic meetings, Mr. N'Diaye describes them as "democratic in form and jazz-like in style."[32]

UGTSF helped many African migrants navigate the treacherous waters of postcolonial Paris, and in the process fomented resistance and opposition to social injustice. For example, it imparted to many migrants the strength and confidence needed to confront unfair employers and French administrators who managed African foyers with a colonial fist.[33] Essentially, as they constantly addressed housing and employment issues, UGTSF and the other smaller African community organizations manufactured a new social and political consciousness within the community of African migrants in postcolonial Paris. Indeed, despite the national rhetoric, which still framed Africans as colonial subjects and foreigners, UGTSF advocated for equal opportunity and social equality with other blue-collar European and French workers. In that sense, UGTSF and its counterparts played a crucial role in helping the migrants transition from a state of colonial subjectivity—one in which they passively accepted the notion that they were "inferior, uninvited guest workers"—to one in which they actively battled the social barriers that not only kept them in a state of colonial subjectivity, but also prevented them from achieving their socioeconomic goals. Thus, by empowering African workers, community organizations like UGTSF were the engine behind the decolonization of Franco-African social relations in "postcolonial" France.

While Caribbean and African community organizations such as CASODOM, UGTSF, and AMITAG grew out of the challenges the migrants encountered in the housing and labor markets, other organizations emerged out of political discontentment. In the Caribbean community, new conversations about the impact of departmentalization on the French Caribbean revived the anticolonial beliefs that many intellectuals espoused during the interwar period. Eventually, these conversations led to the creation of organizations seeking independence or autonomy from France.

Chapter Seven

Similar to French Caribbean migrants, Africans also denounced French neocolonialism. But, unlike their counterparts from the Americas, as citizens of independent countries, they also contested the authoritarian characteristics of the new regimes leading their nations. For these reasons, Caribbean and African professionals and students in Paris created political organizations, once again making the French capital a hub for transnational politics.

The Fight against Neocolonialism: Political Activism among Africans in Paris

Africans in Paris have always used the press as an outlet for political activism. During the interwar period, they created and participated in a number of journals that discussed the implications of French colonialism in her colonies and outlined new concepts of black identity.[34] This tradition continued into the postwar period, as Alioune Diop created *Présence Africaine*, and the Fédération des Etudiants d'Afrique noire en France (FEANF), among other student organizations, published their powerful quarterly journal, *L'Etudiant d'Afrique Noire*. In 1960, independence did not tame activism at the press. As the number of students and workers in Paris increased, African organizations multiplied and political activism at the press continued to blossom. Students' organizations often published quarterly newsletters to voice their opinion on a variety of African sociopolitical issues. They looked at their continent through avant-garde lenses, foreshadowing the political discourses and development strategies outlined by organizations such as UNICEF, Human Rights Watch, and Doctors without Borders. Illustrating this phenomenon, *L'Etudiant du Gabon* (*The Gabonese Student*) dedicated one of its publications to Gabonese women, questioning how social policies, or the lack thereof, affected poor women in rural and urban areas.[35] Criticizing certain "traditional" values and practices such as arranged marriages, which they deemed anachronistic and particularly detrimental to young women, the students proposed several initiatives to increase women's participation in the formal labor market and within the political sphere. But they refrained from painting Gabonese women as men's victims; on the contrary, they emphasized their agency in society by showing how they successfully organized a series of protests against police brutality without any assistance from Gabonese men.

Problems of governance in Africa sparked the most protests by far among African students in France. Thirsty for democracy and transparency, the students published essays criticizing their own governments for serving the interests of the French and the

African elites. By the early sixties, in addition to fighting at the press, the students also organized public demonstrations at African embassies. For them, demonstrating at the embassies symbolized their anger against corrupt African government and France's persistent domination over her former African colonies. These demonstrations ranged from peaceful, nonviolent protests at the embassies' doorsteps, to spirited takeovers, where demonstrators wrecked offices passionately. For instance, on May 24, 1964, hoping to capture the attention of the international community, which seemed to have forgotten the African continent since the independence wave of 1960, dozens of students from the Association of Senegalese Students in France stormed the Senegalese embassy, declaring their government a corrupt puppet of France and denouncing the police brutality against their counterparts in Senegal.[36] In many ways, these protest statements in the press and at the embassies signaled the start of a campaign against neocolonialism, an expression coined by Ghanaian independence leader and statesman Kwame Nkrumah, which essentially suggests that former colonial powers still held the reins of African countries.[37]

The frequency of protests at African embassies increased after May '68, as African students cleverly took advantage of the "anti-statist" social climate in France to advance their own political agenda.[38] Thus in a variety of ways, by the turn of the seventies, African student organizations from Mali, Haute Volta, Senegal, Chad, Mauritania, and Gabon had manifested their dissatisfaction at their respective embassies.[39] Without a doubt, they truly disturbed African despots pretending to be democratically elected presidents. But most importantly, they were bringing a fresh perspective into the discourse of international relations between France and sub-Saharan African countries. Unlike French media, which presented France as a beacon of prosperity for Africa, they highlighted how she still bred violence, poverty, and corruption in her former colonies. The students held a discourse that truly disturbed the power structure and challenged the status quo.

However, because African students did not threaten established Franco-African foreign relations—they were merely flies in the face of Goliath—the French government opted to "impartially" monitor their activities. In contrast, certain African governments reacted swiftly and aggressively against this type of transnational political activism. For instance, after heated protests at their embassy, in August 1971 the Gabonese government nullified all student associations in France, declaring them threatening and illegal. In 1973, in a personal letter addressed to the Ministère d'Etat, Bongo, the Gabonese president, encouraged the French government to suppress the students' political activities and deport those refusing to comply back to Gabon, where they would presumably assume the consequences of their actions. Subsequently, a few Gabonese students created a new association, the Association des Etudiants et

Chapter Seven

Elèves Gabonais (AEEG). Supporting the reactionary political leader, AEEG became the only Gabonese student organization eligible to receive government fellowships.[40] Indeed, in the postcolonial era, not all African students adopted a critical stance toward authoritarian governments. Students from military and government families, many of whom belonged to the upper classes, often supported these questionable governments.

Nevertheless, in the scheme of transnational, oppositional politics, by the early seventies most African students in Paris strongly voiced criticism against authoritarian governments. However, the landscape of African student political activism had changed. Unlike in the fifties, when FEANF was the dominant organization, and ideals of Pan-African unity motivated the students' agenda, by the early seventies FEANF had lost its notoriety. African student organizations were fragmented, caring mostly about national, regional, or even local issues. As in the African workers' associations, members of student associations often belonged to the same nation. Unlike in the fifties, when FEANF united all students in the fight against colonialism, these smaller and newer student organizations battled for a variety of postcolonial issues concerning their respective homelands. Political activism among African students had been balkanized. Moreover, a growing number of young French leftists interested in "Third World" issues began to forge connections with certain African student organizations. For example, l'Association des Etudiants Tchadiens had denounced France's relationship with François Tombalbaye (1918–1975), a former trade unionist, who after becoming Chad's first president, dissolved the opposition and governed autocratically. Their voice of dissent had motivated young French leftists to protest against his administration.

These interracial cooperations disturbed French authorities. The Parisian police, in particular, wanted to prevent immigrants from flocking to *extrême gauche* (far left) organizations and regulate transnational political activities on French soil. Thus, on November 14, 1969, when thirty young Europeans threw Molotov cocktails at the Chadian embassy in the name of a free Chad, the French police intervened and began strategizing to prevent further protests.[41] But the police had limited options to deal with the French insurgents. They could incarcerate them for forty-eight hours, which would not prevent them from protesting again. In other words, the police were unable to regulate interracial political cooperations denouncing France's marriage with the Chadian dictatorship. Nonetheless, only a small number of French leftists got involved in transnational African politics, leading the French police to conclude that interracial alliances between French leftists and African student organizations hardly threatened national security.[42]

But even if the French police and their colleagues from the Ministry of the Interior deemed these alliances nonthreatening, they still worried about the impact of transnational African politics. After all, France's interest often depended on the survival of authoritarian regimes, which African students and intellectuals generally denounced for violating human rights and democratic principles. Thus, under the supervision of the Ministry of the Interior, Paris's Préfecture de Police continued to closely monitor certain African students' and workers' organizations in Paris, routinely sending spies to their meetings and cultural events. As table 5 indicates, the French government was essentially hoping to map their ideological orientation and determine if their activities warranted intervention.[43]

Table 5 also reveals that students' organizations were much more politically oriented than workers' organizations like UGTSF, which essentially provided social assistance to their members. But here again there were exceptions. For example, the Amicale des Guinéens en France (Association of Guineans in France) and the Regroupement des Guinéens à l'Extérieur (Guinean Union in the Diaspora), two seemingly apolitical organizations, vehemently opposed Sékou Touré's administration.[44] In fact, members of these associations used Paris as a laboratory to spread anti-Sékoutouréism, constantly demanding that the international community pressure him to step down.

All in all, during the sixties and early seventies, many African students and professionals participated in some form of political activism. As outlined above, they yearned for social progress, equality, democracy, and political stability in their homelands. But in their quest for efficient and modern African states, many students, activists, and professionals lost sight of the Pan-African ideals that had previously united them. Their political activism reflected the political fragmentation that ensued after independence; only FEANF remained faithful to the concept of African unity. Yet the notorious student organization, which had challenged colonialism throughout the fifties and forced French officials to closely monitor their activities, was losing its influence on the community. As Sékou Traoré notes, by the late sixties, the French secret service agents who still spied on FEANF were actually spying on a dying organization.[45] Political activism survived, but the proliferation and fragmentation of African student organizations along national lines weakened their political clout.

Another story was unfolding within the Caribbean community. Unlike the Continental African diaspora, many Caribbean students, intellectuals, and workers united their efforts to found new political organizations that embraced a common political agenda. Initially, these organizations advocated for national sovereignty, believing that it would translate into faster and more sustainable economic growth for Martinique,

Table 5. French Police officials map African organizations in Paris

ASSOCIATIONS	START	POLITICAL ORIENTATION
Fédération des Etudiants d'Afrique Noir en France	1950	Marxist-Leninist student organization
Association des Etudiants Sénégalais en France	1953	Anti-Senghor—stormed the Senegalese embassy on May 24, 1964
L'Association des Etudiants Tchadiens en France	1954	Anti–Francois Tombalbaye gov't
Union nationale des Etudiants de Côte d'Ivoire	1964	Anti-Ivorian government
Jeunesse du Mouvement Populaire de la Révolution	1967	Supports Mobutu's party
Association des Etudiants et Stagiaires Maliens	1968	Anti-gov't demonstrations in 1969 and 1970, occupying the Malian embassy four times
Mouvement des Etudiants de Côte d'Ivoire	1969	Pro-Ivorian government
Association des Etudiants Voltaique en France	1969	Originally pro-gov't, then switched and aligned with the more radical FEANF
Le Regroupement des Guinéens à l'Extérieur	1970	Anti–Sékou Touré
Association des Stagiaires et Travailleurs Guinéens en France	1973	Work and networking
Association des Travailleurs et Etudiants originaire du Madagascar	No specific dates given	Anti-capitalist, anti-imperial, and critical of the status quo
Comité National Malgache	No specific dates given	Pro-government
Union Générale des Etudiants Mauritaniens	No specific dates given	Opposes Mauritanian gov't
Association Générale des Etudiants Soudanais en France	No specific dates given	Apolitical
Union Générale des Etudiants Elèves et Stagiaires Sénégalais	No specific dates given	Anti-Senghor
Association Sportive des Etudiants et Stagiaires Togolais	No specific dates given	Sports and fun

Source: Archive de la Préfecture de Police, Paris, "Afrique Noire: Déplacement de personnes," box GaA9.

Guadeloupe, and French Guiana. However, by the mid-sixties, the increasing number of Caribbean migrants in the Parisian region also encouraged these newly born Caribbean nationalist organizations to lend a helping hand to struggling members of their community. Still, by criticizing French economic policies and French cultural hegemony in Martinique, Guadeloupe, and French Guiana, they played a crucial role in developing an anticolonial political consciousness within the growing Caribbean diaspora in the Parisian region.

Political Activism in the French Caribbean Diaspora in Paris

Unlike Guadeloupe and Martinique, employment opportunities were more plentiful in French Guiana during the fifties and sixties, leading most Guianese individuals to endorse departmentalization. Only the communists held a nationalist discourse. It took the independence of neighboring British Guiana in 1966 and the global recession of 1973 to lure many French Guianese individuals into nationalist parties.[46] This phenomenon, however, had already occurred among many Guadeloupean and Martinican individuals in France. Indeed, by the mid-fifties, the Association Générale des Etudiants Martiniquais (Martinican Student Association) and the Association Générale des Etudiants Guadeloupéens (Guadeloupean Student Association) had begun to express their disenchantment with departmentalization. Aware of France's rapid industrialization, they felt the French Caribbean should move beyond the agrarian economy, which they inherited from plantation slavery. They claimed departmentalization was a euphemism for colonization, and despised having so many French administrators at home when each island possessed her own intelligentsia. Additionally, they wanted a more efficient educational system. Why, they asked, did Guadeloupean and Martinican students need to travel to France for higher studies? Why was regional history absent from the high school curriculum?[47]

Motivated by these claims, in the late fifties, French Caribbean student associations in Paris began to advocate for independence. Convinced that France did not truly represent Martinique's and Guadeloupe's interests, they sought to obtain a political status giving them more agency in their own affairs. However, while the students' quest for self-rule seemed clear, their plan to implement that goal was a bit murky. Reflecting their youthful spirit, the students elaborated ideas of a government that, at best, seemed simplistic. For example, members of the Martinican Student Association argued that Martinique should have a government comprised of a sovereign local assembly that would be under the authority of an executive body; or, during a conference in 1960, the Guadeloupean Student Association called for establishing a new government comprised of a legislative assembly and an executive body.[48] These demands suggested that French Caribbean students had developed a new political consciousness—they wanted to control their destiny and no longer saw France as the "motherland" and a beacon of prosperity—but as their simplistic notions of government indicated, their quest for a national identity still remained at the rhetorical level.

In 1961, the situation took a new turn. The generation of Caribbean intellectuals and professionals who had arrived in Paris in the late forties and early fifties—people like Edouard Glissant, Paul Niger, Marcel Manville, and Marie-Joseph Cosney—began to play more prominent roles in their community. These individuals had participated in anticolonial demonstrations and Pan-African events like the First Congress of Black Artists and Writers and had grown tired of departmentalization. Thus in 1961, Glissant, Niger, Manville, and Cosney, two writers and lawyers respectively, joined hands to create the Front Antillo-Guyanais, the first Pan-French Caribbean nationalist organization in France.

On April 22 and 23, 1961, they organized a symposium in Paris, where presidents of Caribbean student organizations and notable Caribbean administrators gave speeches in support of independence. In a report summarizing the symposium, the organizing committee noted that 85 percent of the audience was comprised of "enthusiastic" and "boisterous" students; only ten Europeans, mostly members of the Communist Party, attended the event.[49] They also signaled the presence of a few delegates from other Caribbean and African organizations, including l'Union des Etudiants d'Afrique Occidentale, les Etudiants Dahoméens de Dakar, les Etudiants Progressistes Français de Dakar, l'Association Nationale des Prisonniers de Guerre du Sénégal, l'Union Générale des Travailleurs du Sénégal, l'Union des Femmes Sénégalaises, l'Union du Peuple Sénégalais et les Jeunesses U.P.S., le Mouvement de Libération des Etudiants Réunionnais, and le Faisceau Féminin de Haïti. To some extent, the event was a successful display of Pan-Africanism.[50]

The international presence at the symposium was certainly not coincidental. The conference unfolded in an era when many intellectuals and students from the former French colonies still believed in the concept of linked fate among all people of African descent, and particularly among all subjects dominated by European powers, including war-torn Algeria and the Overseas French Departments. For them, the liberation movements that swept sub-Saharan Africa should have been extended to all French colonies.

More than seven hundred people attended the closing remarks.[51] By any measure, it was a successful symposium. Yet, in spite of the "brotherly" atmosphere reigning over the event, it appears that postcolonial geopolitical realities interfered with the symposium's Pan-African appeal. The Front Antillo-Guyanais's organizers faced the same challenge that Diop had encountered during the second Congress of Black Writers and Artists, which took place in Rome in 1959. Like Diop, they had invited important black figures, including many leaders and ambassadors from various African countries. But to their dismay, these political figures shunned the event, sending letters of apology. The new African political elites had privileged diplomacy over Pan-Africanism, reassuring France, their most important trading partner, and ironically, political ally, that they did not support citizens who challenged her authority. For the new African leaders, Pan-Africanism existed in the symbolic realm. This was a major setback for the organizers who had hoped to receive support from the leaders of the former colonies. Only Michel Leiris and Frantz Fanon made a humble appearance, perhaps out of courtesy to the organizers, whom they knew as friends and colleagues.

During the conference, the Front Antillo-Guyanais accused France of keeping the Overseas French Caribbean Departments in a state of colonial subjectivity. This was not an unusual outcry. But the participants may have gone too far when they voiced support for a free Algeria. This bold move encouraged the French government to dissolve the Front Antillo-Guyanais and place Glissant, apparently the one who had played the most prominent role in organizing the symposium, under house arrest. The Front Antillo-Guyanais disappeared as quickly as it had emerged on the political landscape. However, dissolving the Front and restricting Glissant's movements did not thwart the movement. The other founding members refused to give up their quest for sociopolitical change and proceeded to create another organization, the Amicale Générale des Travailleurs Antillais et Guyanais (AGTAG).[52]

Due to increasing government scrutiny, the new organization denied having any affiliation with political parties or labor unions. Threats from the French government, and most importantly, the growing number of Caribbean labor migrants in Paris, had forced the political activists to focus on issues of social insertion. Moreover, Marcel Manville, one of the founding members of the Front Antillo-Guyanais, had become the most visible political activist, and though he still wanted to reconfigure his islands' political status, he steered the organization in a new direction.[53] Charismatic and politically savvy, Manville encouraged AGTAG to become more moderate and pragmatic than the Front Antillo-Guyanais. Thus, unlike its predecessor, the organization refused to advocate for full-fledged independence; instead, it argued for political autonomy, a status granting the Overseas Departments more power at the local level. But most importantly, the organization turned its attention to the Caribbean diaspora in France.

Manville's preference for grassroots social movements and community empowerment appealed to the burgeoning community, which felt that someone was defending their material interests. With the support of hundreds of migrants, the organization began a decade-long quest to obtain certain social benefits for the French Caribbean diaspora. Hoping to make traveling to Martinique, Guadeloupe, and French Guiana easier for the migrants, AGTAG began to advocate for cheaper flights between Paris and the Overseas French Departments. Because certain migrants could not afford housing, the organization lobbied the city of Paris to create a *foyer* for Caribbean people managed by Caribbean people. AGTAG also lobbied the Ministry of the Interior and the Ministry of Labor on behalf of Caribbean workers in the public sector. The organization demanded that every two years, Caribbean workers in Paris be offered the opportunity to visit their families in the Caribbean. It argued that workers needed an extended paid vacation to complete the expensive journey across the Atlantic. Last but not least, AGTAG routinely asked the Ministry of the Interior and the Ministry of Labor to create jobs in Martinique, Guadeloupe, and French Guiana for skilled Caribbean workers "stuck" in France. In other words, the organization also believed that social integration meant empowering Caribbean workers to return home and contribute to developing their homeland.[54]

By 1965, however, organizations that embraced a purely nationalist agenda resurfaced in Paris. Following clashes between the French police and workers in Guadeloupe, in 1963 a few Guadeloupean individuals in Paris created the Groupe d'Organization Nationale pour la Guadeloupe (GONG), an organization seeking complete independence from France. GONG members literally viewed themselves as the wretched of the earth taking their destiny into their own hands. They embraced Fanon's and Malcolm X's teachings. For GONG members, Guadeloupe had remained a French colony, a condition warranting immediate action, including, if necessary, armed resistance. Eventually, by 1965 a number of GONG members also joined AGTAG, which created tension because most Martinicans favored autonomy over complete independence. Certain Martinicans, who endorsed moderate political views and favored working on issues of social insertion in France, left the organization to found the Regroupement de l'Emigration Martiniquaise.[55]

Nonetheless, galvanized by disenchanted Caribbean students, the nationalist movement remained strong until the early seventies. Not only did slow socioeconomic growth in the French Caribbean radicalize the students, but transnational black intellectual currents denouncing Eurocentric education and anti-black racism also influenced them. Like their counterparts in the United States, Caribbean students wanted to transcend the status of second-class citizenship. They wished to reform the educational system and adopt a curriculum that reflected their own regional history and experiences. The calls of the Black Power movement resonated loudly within their community.

The Association Générale des Etudiants Guadeloupéens (AGEG) was particularly attracted to the Black Power movement. Conflating the cultural nationalism of the Black Power movement with the self-defense and proletarian appeal of the Black Panther Party, AGEG believed that Caribbean people should unite with the French proletariat and fight against the French bourgeoisie, which promoted an unequal division of labor based on racial and class attributes. Along the line of Black Power rhetoric, they portrayed French Caribbean people as colonized subjects who shared a special mission. They reaffirmed this belief in their newsletter, stating emphatically:

Members of AGEG raising their clenched fists like their counterparts from the United States, September 1971. Note that they covered their faces in fear of retaliation from the French government.

French Caribbean people must fight against French colonialism. They must fight against exploitation in factories and hospitals, where they tirelessly sweep the floor while being treated like dogs. Our proletariat must fight to end this senseless migration to France. French colonialism is a form of political and cultural oppression. Thus, we must promote our culture and the cultures of peoples who have been colonized. The black proletariat in France must promote the development of national consciousness at home and unite with their counterparts in their respective countries to found new societies.[56]

In many ways, the sixties and early seventies represent the heyday of French Caribbean nationalism. Activists and students created organizations that influenced the Caribbean diaspora and the Overseas French Caribbean Departments. By the mid-seventies, however, the nationalist organizations lost their steam. There was just too much infighting; a vociferous minority of Caribbean students and activists wanted to sever all political ties with France. But they could not form solid bonds with Caribbean migrants advocating for more political autonomy under the auspices of the French Republic. As a result, leaders quarreled and left to create their own organizations, a phenomenon that led to the balkanization and the eventual demise of the nationalist movement in France.[57]

Conclusion

Many students, activists, and professionals from the African and Caribbean communities were determined to uplift their nations and empower the lower classes. Africans believed better governance would lead to sustainable development. Caribbean migrants advocated for reconfiguring the departmental status, arguing they would do a better job than the French, who allegedly treated Caribbean people like colonial subjects. But not all Africans and Caribbean migrants were consumed with national politics. Most black migrants worried about surviving in their host society. They worried about finding housing and making a respectable living, the main reason that had brought them to France. Neglected by French trade unions and welfare institutions, under the stewardship of dedicated community activists, black workers joined new associations catering to their social and material needs. In the process, African and Caribbean workers developed a sense of confidence and "entitlement" in a country that usually ignored their challenges or deplored their presence in the capital. Through these organizations, African and Caribbean migrants also challenged French perceptions of black people as big children or "happy" islanders incapable of developing their own institutions.

To be sure, the African fight for better governance in Africa and against inequality in the housing and labor market in Paris, as well as the Caribbean fight for political autonomy, independence, and better social services in Paris, encouraged French labor-union activists, members of the Ministries of Labor and the Interior, law enforcement officials, and other French individuals who interacted with the migrants, to reflect on their colonial notions of blackness. Yet, in addition to the impact of Caribbean and African sociopolitical activism, another event played an important role in shaping Franco-African and Franco–French Caribbean relations. Caribbean and African experiences during the events of May 1968, one of the most memorable years in modern French history, also changed the political consciousness of many African and Caribbean workers in Paris.

Chapter 8

May '68 in Black

The future of the French Caribbean is decided in France. Let's not forget, we are dealing with the same reactionary government and the same police. We also feel the plight of French workers and students, but we feel it more intensely. In fact, we are the product of exploitation. This is a reality that Caribbean students and workers must understand; after all, Caribbean students and workers are two different sides of the same coin. Caribbean workers must participate in the protest. They must join the labor unions in the factories, hospitals, and public transportation. They share the same interest as French workers. However, they must always be aware that French labor unions only see them as workers, not as [displaced] Caribbean people.

—A quote from *Alizé*, a Caribbean student newsletter, May–June, 1968

In May and June 1968, France underwent two months of unprecedented social unrest, during which millions of people, especially students and workers, claimed the streets and university halls to protest for labor and educational reforms. Never seen since the French Revolution, this massive movement for change has generated a vibrant scholarship exploring the causes and implications of the events. For instance, economic historians argue that the events occurred because modernization outpaced social relations, and sociologists suggest that the students' middle-class background and the outpouring of leftist ideologies, as well as students' discontentment with the outmoded university system, spurred the protests.¹ Alain Touraine, the preeminent sociologist of the time, suggested that the student protests and the workers' strikes were new forms of social conflict stemming from the rejection of technocratic values promoted by the state and multinational corporations.² Recently, scholars embracing an interdisciplinary approach have expanded this analysis, highlighting that Third-Worldism (awareness of the plight of the Third World) and a desire for progressive cultural changes spurred the events.³ Shedding light on the symbolic meaning of May '68, they reject the conclusion of notable French historians and sociologists who describe the events as a movement about everything and nothing, one that was invented by the media.⁴ In fact, they contend that May '68 was a watershed in French history and culture, for it allegedly changed labor practices, student culture, and gender relations.⁵

Although this scholarship on May '68 is invaluable, in a glaring fashion it fails to acknowledge the presence and meaning of the events for racialized minorities in France, particularly Caribbean and sub-Saharan African migrants. One must raise certain questions to bring their history out of the realm of invisibility. Indeed, did African and Caribbean migrants protest for the same reasons as their French counterparts? Did they experience the events in the same way? Did black women participate? Were the events a cultural watershed in the history of the African diaspora in modern France, or were they merely a series of protests about everything and nothing? Digging through the archives and gathering ethnographic evidence to answer these questions, I discovered a close connection between the May '68 events and the development of a new black consciousness in the French Republic.

MEMORIALIZING THE BLACK MAY '68

In late summer 2003, en route from Berkeley to Paris, I stopped in New York City to visit family. I knew that Edouard Glissant (1928–2011), the late Martinican philosopher and writer who founded the Front Antillo-Guyanais, was teaching at CUNY's graduate center, so without an appointment I ventured to visit him during his office hours. I was convinced that my research interests and our common origin, Martinique, were a passport to at least a short conversation. As I arrived and settled down in the French department, waiting for my turn, I began to wonder if I had made a mistake. The students and the staff revered the man; he was, after all, of "French academic nobility," so why would he waste his time with a young "serf" like me, a graduate student? After I waited a short fifteen minutes, he agreed to see me. Of course, I nervously walked into his office and, as graduate students do best, I began talking about my research, which at the time focused on issues of citizenship, migration, and racism in the African diaspora in Paris of the sixties. To my joy, Professor Glissant quickly took the reins of the conversation. He recalled his days of political activism, mentioning that he cofounded the Front Antillo-Guyanais in 1961, which was dissolved by government decree six months after its establishment. He confessed that these were very tense years for him because he was put under house arrest and forbidden to travel to the French Caribbean until 1965.[6]

During our meeting, I asked Professor Glissant to share his perspective on the evolution of African-Caribbean relations from the fifties to the sixties. Precisely, I wished to know if during the sixties African and Caribbean scholars and activists still worked on common projects, or if the independence of African countries had created an "interest gap" between the two groups. Without giving me precise examples of collaboration, Professor Glissant stated in a convincing tone, "Of course, we [I assume he meant Caribbean intellectuals] had many African friends!"[7] As I noticed that the subject did not elicit much conversation, I asked Professor Glissant if he could talk about the spirit of the Caribbean diaspora in Paris of the sixties. Did he think the community had integrated well into the fabric of Parisian society? Were there other types of Caribbean protests besides the activities organized by nationalist groups? Interestingly, his answer was brief, but as expected, fascinating.

Glissant painted a picture of the Caribbean diaspora that corresponds with Professor Maryse Condé's description of a community highly fragmented by class differences. According to Glissant, Caribbean intellectuals and students were highly contentious. They disliked that French bureaucrats managed their islands, and they wanted complete control of their political destiny. "We were convinced of our capability to lead when we realized that our credentials overshadowed that of many French public officials in the Antilles," claimed Glissant.[8] However, reflecting his perception of the French Caribbean diaspora as a group of hard-working and exploited people from the lower classes, Professor Glissant argued that the Caribbean sixties of Paris was merely a decade of "bal boudin." For him, Caribbean migrants worked hard throughout the week and looked forward to the weekend, when they organized house or public-hall parties to dance the night away, drinking rum and eating *boudin*, a spicy blood sausage/pudding served religiously during these occasions.[9]

Then, Professor Glissant paused, his body language indicating that our meeting was over. Politely, I thanked him for his time. As I exited his office, he extended a kind and common Kreyol farewell: "Tchimbé red pa Moli," which literally means be tough and don't soften up, to which I conventionally replied, "Sé moli a ki red" (It's softening up that's tough). Although my first interview did not go as planned—I thought it would have offered more information and research leads—I actually left more excited and curious about my research topic than prior to our conversation. Maybe because I know history is always full of contradictions, I thought working-class Caribbean migrants in Paris of the sixties did much more than working hard and going to *bal boudin* soirées. In retrospect, after interviewing Maryse Condé towards the end of my research, I developed a more critical view of the African diaspora in France of the sixties than what Professor Glissant had presented. Indeed, Professor Condé had genuinely confessed that "living in the ghetto of intellectuals and privileged people" did not allow her to fully grasp the challenges of the black working classes.[10] Consequently, I wondered if Professor Glissant was facing the same predicament. Was it possible that Glissant, a participant in the First International Congress of Black Writers and Artists who arrived in Paris in 1946 and orbited around black intellectual circles, had a perspective of working-class black Paris that was informed by his own social class and lifestyle?

In hindsight, after my conversation with Professor Edouard Glissant, I realized that class differences and memory affect writing the history/histories of marginalized and racialized subjects. Indeed, if, from the vantage point of statesmen, community leaders, and intellectuals who created political organizations, one asks, "Which part of history matters most? Or, who makes history?," then much of the history of the African diaspora during the postwar period would be invisible.[11] In many ways, as the participation of black individuals during the May '68 events illustrates, the black sixties were much more than *bal bouding soirées*. The events raised the black migrants' consciousness as exploited people who must stand up for their rights to improve their socioeconomic conditions. Truly a fascinating chapter in the history of the African diaspora in France, the May '68 events helped black migrants demystify colonial notions of French identity and encouraged certain French officials, particularly those who interacted with Caribbean migrants, to reconceptualize their notions of blackness.

May '68 and Sub-Saharan African Workers in Paris

Writing about black experiences in Paris of the sixties without acknowledging how May '68 affected black labor migrants and students would, I believed, raise questions about the study's integrity. Hence, as part of my ethnographic research, I asked certain migrants if they participated in the events. To my surprise, when I invited African migrants to reflect on May '68, they usually asserted that the events did not influence their community. In fact, none of the interviewees recalled participating in the events.

Perhaps I would have obtained different answers if I had asked migrants who worked at the Renault automobile factory about their participation in the events. Renault employed many sub-Saharan African workers. According to Laure Pitti's research on North African workers at the factory, sub-Saharan African workers may have participated in the protests with their French counterparts.[12] That being said, the trail of evidence pointing to the sub-Saharan African presence is quasi-invisible. However, the paucity of evidence does not suggest that African labor migrants did not care about the protests; nor does it suggest that May '68 did not influence them.

As a general rule, my informants mentioned feeling a sense of solidarity with French workers. They believed workers ought to stand up for their rights, and after all, May '68 was first and foremost a massive strike. However, they insinuated that May '68 was a French affair, not an African one. Apparently, in the late sixties, many African workers believed the issues at stake mostly concerned salaried French workers, not transnational labor migrants who did not hold stable jobs. This is a surprising phenomenon because issues such as higher wages, better working conditions, and access to social benefits, which had brought French workers into the streets, also concerned African migrants. In fact, one would argue that they mostly concerned African migrants since they typically worked longer hours in unpleasant conditions and received lower pay. Why, then, weren't African workers lured into the streets swarming with disillusioned French workers?

There are three possible reasons explaining why most Africans stayed home during the demonstrations. First, many African workers were not formal members of French labor unions. They usually orbited around CFDT and CGT for a short period and left. They left because their professional lives had remained stagnant. That being said, the invisibility of African labor migrants in the union affected their participation rate in the protests. Indeed, the unions had played a key role in organizing the protests. Not only did they impress upon French workers the urgency to protest, but they also provided institutional support, a much needed element for successful and long-lasting protest. However, since Africans remained on the periphery of union life, they were not pulled into the fray.

Second, citizenship stood in the way. African labor migrants who participated in the heated strikes and protests risked deportation. This outcome would have had severe ramifications for African workers and their families, which often depended on remittances for survival. Third, from a financial standpoint, joining the masses of discontented French workers seemed irrelevant. After all, African workers usually worked as manual laborers or "non-specialized workers." They were literally the "mules" of large factories and small businesses, earning a fraction of their French counterparts' salaries. Consequently, they knew that marching in protest, blocking the streets, and refusing to work would not significantly alter their working conditions, especially if they worked for a small company, or worse, toiled as day laborers at cold construction sites. For these workers, "job flight" was still the most effective strategy for increasing their income and improving their working conditions. Thus, throughout the events most African workers remained in the foyers. They sympathized with French workers and felt the wind of change, but for logical and practical reasons they stayed away from the marching mob.

However, as most African workers elected to stay clear of the protestors' path, a very interesting phenomenon occurred. In a temporary reversal of fortune, the very people who had been subjected to the French gaze were now observing the French coping with adversity. African labor migrants who had satisfied the curiosity of filmmakers and been scrutinized by journalists, city officials, public health workers, and social scientists, were now observing the French, and to their surprise, realized that many French individuals could not cope with the impact of the general strike on their personal lives. For instance, Mr. N'Diaye, one of my informants, was shocked to see how Parisians were affected by having limited access to transportation and the other amenities of a modern city.[13] He was shocked because he and many African workers often lived with the bare minimum. They constantly experienced the hardship Parisians discovered during that one month, yet they endured their suffering—including not having enough money to pay the metro fare, or sometimes, eat—with dignity and pride. Thus, witnessing the French struggle with the reality of their daily lives was in many ways a demystifying moment for African migrants. Used to leading a harsh life in Paris, they began to see their former colonizers through different lenses, and ostensibly felt a sense of "superiority" over French citizens in disarray. To put it bluntly, Africans had always perceived the French as "winners," people who by virtue of bearing the fruits of modernity were invincible; however, during May '68 they also viewed them as "whiners."

Although most sub-Saharan African workers did not participate in the May '68 events, the spectacle of class struggle and protest for higher wages and university reforms raised their consciousness about workers' and human rights in France. *Le Monde*, the leading French newspaper, noted a correlation between unrest in the foyers and the events, arguing that the African threshold of tolerance for abuse and exploitation had decreased. It also added that African workers had grown more oppositional at the workplace. Supposedly, after '68 they were more likely to voice their anger against abusive employers. In fact, according to the newspaper, incidents of physical resistance against French employers also increased after May '68. To support this argument, *Le Monde* pointed to the case of Mr. Boubacar Bathily, a resident at an ASSOTRAF (Association pour l'Aide Sociale aux Travailleurs Africains) foyer in St. Denis, who had threatened to kill the French manager. Apparently, Mr. Alix, the manager, was notorious for disrespecting African residents.[14]

Thus, for African workers, May '68 engendered new ideas of French identity that did not correspond to what they had previously imagined. Ironically, if '68 had subversive intentions—French workers and students sought to change labor relations and the educational system—it actually engendered a less reverential perception of French identity within the Continental African diaspora. Moreover, even if African workers did not take over the streets, the protests had a direct impact on the African community. African students began protesting more frequently against corruption and neocolonialism after May '68. Additionally, as expressed by *Le Monde*, there seems to be a direct correlation between the events and increasing social unrest in African foyers. Indeed, the tension between African residents and French administrators became more palpable, and ultimately evolved into a full-fledged social movement for better housing. The Caribbean diaspora, however, shared a different experience of May '68. In many ways, not only did Caribbean workers, students, and activists participate in the events, but they also gave them a different meaning.

THE FRENCH CARIBBEAN MAY '68

May '68 had a transformative effect on the Caribbean community. Unlike their African counterparts, French citizenship shielded Caribbean migrants from threats of deportation. Many Caribbean workers were card-carrying union members, even if they felt that CGT and CFDT failed to appropriately represent their interests. Thus, they actively participated in the protests. Only a marginal group of French Caribbean migrants—usually the devout de Gaulle supporters—were not swept up in the national wave of protest for educational and labor reforms. Faithful to de Gaulle, the one who liberated Guadeloupe and Martinique from oppressive Nazi supporters, certain Caribbean migrants chose to stay in the comfort of their homes. For these Caribbean individuals—pragmatic conformists to the bone—de Gaulle's regime was irreproachable, and staying home was merely the expression of their political philosophy.

Nonetheless, the Caribbean migrants who chose to stay home and support de Gaulle's administration did not share the feelings of anger and dissatisfaction permeating the Caribbean community. According to *Alizé*, annoyed by the administration, the private sector, and the educational system, most Caribbean migrants had opted to passionately voice their anger against the system. They protested against capitalism, the government's domestic and international policies, Parisian institutions catering to migrants, and the educational system, which they felt ignored Caribbean experiences.¹⁵ Moreover, Caribbean nationalists, people who truly saw France as a colonizer, were seduced by the Third-Worldist sensitivity of the young French participants. The chants emanating from university halls, which denounced France's neocolonial relations with its former colonies, the Vietnam War, and Western capitalist exploitation, appealed to their senses.

The social conditions in France and the French Caribbean had galvanized radical individuals (the nationalists) and transformed many pragmatic conformists—people who believe French republican ideals promote social equality irrespective of gender, cultural, and racial differences—into disillusioned conformists ready and willing to challenge the French Republic to keep its promise of universal equality and opportunity. Similar to the French, as disillusioned conformists or nationalists, Caribbean workers and students took over the streets of Paris, chanting slogans of solidarity like "Le patron a besoin de toi, tu n'as pas besoin de lui" (your boss needs you, you don't need him). They made up a small, distinct group of people among the hundreds of thousands of discontented French citizens conquering the city. Disappearing in a sea of French people, they formed their own contentious island.

Caribbean students felt particularly enthusiastic about joining their French counterparts, who had been protesting against the allegedly conservative and archaic university system at Nanterre University since March 1968. They also joined their comrades at the Sorbonne, the old and prestigious French university where the student outcry against the system has been immortalized on the walls. Even the Fédération Antillo-Guyanaise des Etudiants Catholiques (Federation of Catholic Caribbean Students), a politically neutral Christian organization, openly voiced their support for the millions of French workers and students seeking change.¹⁶ They truly felt united by a sense of common struggle against a conservative university system that did not reflect their values and aspirations.

Yet despite the overwhelming show of solidarity with the cause of French students, there were structural distinctions between the ways in which French Caribbean students and French students participated in the events. For one, unlike French workers and students, who remained distant from each other throughout the events, Caribbean students and workers constantly rubbed shoulders. It seems as if two opposite social phenomena occurred simultaneously. As Kristin Ross suggests, hoping to contain the protests into a manageable affair, the French government had successfully drawn space between French workers and students. She observes that at the beginning of the protests, French students erected barricades to protect themselves against the French police; however, by the end of the protests, the French police used the same barricades to prevent the students from joining the workers.¹⁷ But the situation was

A group of Caribbean workers demonstrating with their French counterparts, May 13, 1968. (Photo by André Bugat, used with permission of Archives CFDT [Confédération Française Démocratique du Travail], 6E/1968/1974.)

entirely different for Caribbean students and workers. For one, unlike French students, who generally came from the middle and upper classes, many Caribbean students who arrived in the sixties originated from humble social backgrounds and saw their fate as intricately linked to Caribbean workers. They interacted with workers during weekend *bal boudin* parties, and most importantly, they realized that a university degree did not preclude them from facing the same challenges as the labor migrants, namely, finding jobs at home. Both groups had been displaced and longed to return home, a condition that united them in a common fight.

Unlike their French counterparts, Caribbean students and workers protested for the same reason; they expressed dissatisfaction with departmentalization and the labor migration organized by BUMIDOM. Many students, workers, and activists felt that BUMIDOM and departmentalization engendered poverty in France and conditions of economic dependency in Guadeloupe, Martinique, and French Guiana. GONG and AGTAG, the independentist and autonomist organizations respectively, crystallized this quest for a new political status. Moreover, even if Caribbean students and workers did not belong to either GONG or AGTAG, as people originating from the Caribbean basin, they had been influenced by the Cuban Revolution, and admittedly, wished for a similar political transformation in the Overseas French Departments.

The students' proximity to the workers, as well as their quest for independence and affinity for Marxism, motivated them to found the Comité d'Action des Travailleurs et Etudiants des Territoires sous Domination Coloniale Française (Committee of Workers and Students from the Colonized Territories). Born in the wee hours of the events, the Committee of Workers and Students from the Colonized Territories was affiliated with the Sorbonne Occupation Committee and actively reached out to Caribbean workers.[18] Unlike French students, who from a distant perspective wanted to end the plight of the Third World and abolish the obvious neocolonial relations between France and its former colonies, many Caribbean students advocated for independence in Martinique, Guadeloupe, and French Guiana for personal reasons; for them, the quest for independence, cultural empowerment, and economic development truly hit close to home.

Thus, the Caribbean *soixanthuitards* fought two battles simultaneously (*soixanthuitards* is a term referring to the youth who participated in the events). They joined the general fight against the system in Paris's streets and universities, demanding an improved educational system, higher wages, and social benefits, but they also led their own crusade against the French institutions in charge of managing the Caribbean diaspora. BUMIDOM, in particular, was their sworn enemy. Many students believed that the state-sponsored organization played an active role in keeping Caribbean migrants in a state of colonial subjectivity. Transferring the unemployed Martinican and Guadeloupean youth to France, they argued, was an extremely counterproductive development strategy; instead, they favored imparting competitive skills to the youth and creating jobs in the French Caribbean. Even *Alizé*, the Catholic student newsletter that typically endorsed moderate views, echoed their disenchanted Caribbean counterparts, asserting:

> They are constantly saying the migration improves the Antilles' economy, but they do not mention that it transplants the youth to France. Young individuals are the most capable and productive members of society, yet they leave without contributing and giving back to their own societies. The Antillean youth must stay in the French Antilles to foster its development. By decreasing the number of adults living in Martinique, Guadeloupe, and Guiana, the migration gives the illusion that the French Antilles have a much higher GDP. In reality, it only masks the poverty and prevents making a fair comparison between the Antillean and the French GDP.[19]

For many Caribbean *soixanthuitards*, the fiercest battles occurred at BUMIDOM and AMITAG, the two institutions that played the most important role in bringing and "inserting" Caribbean migrants into French society. BUMIDOM was particularly targeted for its alleged paternal treatment of Caribbean migrants and its role as a placement agency. Indeed, not only did Caribbean students and community activists despise the jobs it offered the migrants, but they had also heard disturbing stories about the ways in which certain staff members related to their clients. Apparently, many BUMIDOM workers who previously worked in the former African colonies had trouble adapting to the realities of the postcolonial period. Colonial notions of Caribbean identity were still flowing throughout the institution's "veins," affecting staff relationships with the clients. During an interview, a former employee confirmed this unpleasant condition. He confessed how his own notion of Caribbean identity had changed since the sixties, when he merely viewed the migrants as uneducated islanders, literally hyperventilating at the sight of the French capital:

> I was one of the people in charge of picking them up at the airport. Come to think of it, I was their first contact with France. I have so many stories to tell, I don't even know where to begin. You see, in those days it was pretty funny. Antilleans arrived in Paris all year long; usually, when they got off the plane they were scared, intimidated, and sometimes, not appropriately dressed. Once, I picked up a young lady at the airport, who was so nervous I did not know what to do; she was hyperventilating, I think she almost fainted. After calming her down, I gathered that she was just an island girl who had never been to the city. Everything impressed her. Trust me; there are stories, which are funnier than this one.[20]

Thus in May and June 1968, hoping to reform the employees' behavior and improve the institution's strategy of social insertion, dozens of Caribbean migrants occupied BUMIDOM, the foe par excellence. AMITAG, the Caribbean organization that collaborated with BUMIDOM, was also stormed, although the occupation barely lasted seventy-two hours. The insurgents came from diverse backgrounds: they were students from the Committee of Workers and Students from the Colonized Territories, disenchanted workers, community activists, and nationalists who believed these institutions supported a deceitful French government. Despite sharing different political outlooks and being at BUMIDOM and AMITAG for different reasons—certain insurgents wanted better service from these institutions while others wanted to close them down—the protests were seemingly well coordinated. Much of this success was due to the connection between the Committee of Workers and Students from the Colonized Territories and the various cultural, community, and nationalist organizations that had recently sprouted throughout the Parisian region. The students, workers, and political activists shared common social networks, which facilitated organizing the community and staging the protest at BUMIDOM. Mr. George Lassare Michalon, a member of the Amicale

Générale des Travailleurs Antillais et Guyanais (AGTAG), the autonomist organization created in 1962 by former members of the Front Antillo-Guyanais, participated in the protest. According to him, gathering Caribbean people at BUMIDOM had occurred fairly smoothly; supposedly, a few comrades simply called each other, and within hours, a crowd of insurgents grew at the organization's doorstep.[21]

Caribbean students, workers, and community and political activists occupied the institution with a rage that had been brewing for years. At BUMIDOM, instead of the tricolor blue, white, and red French flag, they erected a red flag, revealing their affinity for communist and Marxist ideals.[22] Similar to millions of students and activists from various regions of the world, they had grown increasingly tired of capitalism and saw leftist movements as a means to successfully bridge the gap between the social classes. In raising the red banner, they also reaffirmed their rootedness in transnational Caribbean politics, expressing the sentiments that dissatisfied youth in Caribbean countries such as Grenada, Surinam, and Dominica had been feeling. Simultaneously, by choosing BUMIDOM as a site of contestation, the politics of the flag became entangled in the old tradition of lobbying and protesting to change French laws and institutions that allegedly harmed French Caribbean people.[23]

Robin Kelley's study of African American communists during the interwar period, which demonstrates how they utilized communism to achieve a black nationalist agenda, gives yet another perspective as to why French Caribbean insurgents raised the red banner. Kelley claims, for "African-American communists, like American Jewish and Finnish communists, whose cultural and national identities constituted a central element of their radical politics, ethnic nationalism and internationalism were not mutually exclusive."[24] In other words, following Kelley's logic, the French Caribbean protestors apparently raised the red banner to show their allegiance and sympathy for the various leftist movements opposing imperialism and capitalism, but on the battleground, the gesture had very little significance. French Caribbean people did not storm and occupy BUMIDOM to advance a communist agenda; they stormed it because they believed the organization implemented policies that maintained the French Caribbean islands and the Caribbean diaspora in a state of colonial subjection. In the French Caribbean imagination, BUMIDOM symbolized the French government, and to be sure, the occupation was a call for a real commitment to develop Martinique, Guadeloupe, and French Guiana into self-sustaining Overseas Departments or independent nation-states.

French Caribbean insurgents occupied BUMIDOM until the end of June. At the beginning of the occupation they held a few administrators hostage, but since they were targeting the system, not the employees, they quickly released them.[25] During the entire occupation, they prevented French administrators from resuming their work, chanting Kreyol songs and showing their anger by vandalizing the offices. Madame Janine Martin, the former BUDIMOM archivist who began working with the organization in the early seventies and graciously introduced me to a number of documents (some of which had never been previously consulted), underscored that the insurgents destroyed many BUMIDOM publications. When she introduced me to the documents published prior to May '68, I observed that the insurgents' destructive spurts were encoded with symbolic gestures, which reaffirmed their anger against the ways in which the institution related to its clientele and channeled the migrants into the labor market. Indeed, they had ripped up the employment contracts of Caribbean domestic workers, indicating how seriously they opposed giving women this kind of work.

In short, three themes had fueled the protest. First, the insurgents demanded better jobs for Caribbean people who migrated via BUMIDOM. They condemned giving women domestic positions, because after all, this pattern reminded them of plantation slavery. They also desired that women who chose a career in the health-care industry be channeled into different positions. More specifically, they did not want women to only receive *fille de salle* positions—which they thought trapped employees into a profession demanding hard work but offering low wages and no avenue for professional growth. Second, they were expressing their frustration against the continuing colonial relations between France and the Overseas Departments. In fact, not only did many students and political activists consider departmentalization to be a pseudonym for colonization, but they also believed the French had not changed their perception of Caribbean culture and identity. Third, they considered the labor migration to be a form of exile, and thus demanded that government officials also facilitate the migrants' return to their respective homelands.

All things considered, the protest at BUMIDOM helped many Caribbean migrants debunk colonial notions of France and French identity. They realized that France, so to say, was not what it was cracked up to be. Above all, it signaled that many black citizens from Guadeloupe, Martinique, and French Guiana understood the importance of standing up for their rights to force French institutions to practice French republican values promoting equality. In other words, for French Caribbean people, the storming of BUMIDOM is a cornerstone in the fight for equal opportunity. For Mr. George Lassare Michalon, the former Caribbean community activist who participated in the 1968 takeovers, the events clearly had a strong impact on the formation and evolution of the community's identity and political consciousness, as he cleverly notes:

> We had been anti-BUMIDOM for a while and I with a few friends decided to protest at the headquarters. We wanted Aimé Césaire there, but he feared the situation could potentially escalate into a much larger problem and cautioned us not to go. We went

Chapter Eight

anyway, and occupied BUMIDOM like our French counterparts were occupying other buildings. For us, it was a demystifying moment. We felt as if we brought down what the institution symbolized. In short, the occupation signaled a turning point in our community.[26]

Although the BUMIDOM and AMITAG takeovers are important milestones in the history of the African diaspora in France, the event also influenced French officials in charge of supervising the migration. In truth, the occupation brutalized their preconceived notion of French Caribbean people as uneducated and apathetic individuals sharing a blind affection for France.[27] By fiercely protesting against the institution, which supposedly helped the community, not only did the insurgents encourage French officials to reconsider their perception of Caribbean individuals as naive apostles of the French Republic, but they also forced them to better serve the French Caribbean diaspora. At the end of June 1968, when the protests were over, one had a sense that something had changed at BUMIDOM. The organization's leaders, the ones who had been "calling the shots," had made calming and concessionary speeches. According to Mrs. Janine Martin, senior staff members agreed to implement changes in order to prevent future uprisings.[28] In other words, BUMIDOM officials suddenly realized that Caribbean migrants had professional aspirations of their own; they began to view these black migrants as contentious citizens deserving the same opportunities as working-class French people. For this reason, the protest at BUMIDOM was a turning point in the relationship between French officials and French Caribbean people, which to say the least, had been extremely paternalistic.

Thus, the storming of BUMIDOM and AMITAG had a bigger influence than previously imagined. In fact, in a very subtle manner, the events also affected gender relations within the Caribbean diaspora. During my meeting with Mr. Michalon, I asked him if Caribbean women participated in the takeovers. I also invited him to lend his opinion on the extent to which the events affected the lives of Caribbean women in France. Of course, his answer was quite informative and interesting. After reflecting silently for a few seconds, gently scratching his beard and searching for an answer in the ceiling of his home, he replied with a smile: "After '68 we [Caribbean men] could no longer ignore women. We had to listen to them."[29] This was no surprise, since the few women who participated in the storming of BUMIDOM were, according to Mr. Michalon, more vociferous, determined, and radical than their male counterparts.[30]

In contrast to the previous generation of women activists like Mrs. Dancenis, the woman who helped found AMITAG, these women asserted their desire to actively pursue social change as leaders, not mere followers. Thus, in many ways the AMITAG and BUMIDOM takeovers represent a social laboratory wherein women expressed their political views, and in the process, began to reconfigure gender relations in the Caribbean community. Ultimately, Mr. Michalon's comments on the evolution of gender relations in the French Caribbean diaspora in France correspond with what scholars have observed. Indeed, according to Jean Goossen and Stephanie Condon, two experts in French Caribbean migration, women gained leadership positions in the community through a series of initiatives, including servicing their families and the community, as well as participating in social movement and diasporic politics.[31] Yet women's service to the community and the family as well as their participation in the BUMIDOM takeover are not the only factors that influenced gender relations in the Caribbean diaspora. After all, not all women had children, much less participated in the event.

An informed discussion about the evolution of gender relations within the Caribbean diaspora should also note how the wind of change blowing on French women affected French Caribbean women. This wind of change had been blowing particularly hard since the late fifties. Women activists had been protesting, leading France to pass a law allowing women to work without their husbands' permission in 1965, and a law legalizing contraception in 1967. These civil rights landmarks reflected the increased awareness of women's rights, an awareness that became even more pronounced during the tumultuous '68 events.

In retrospect, the intersection of race, gender, and regional origin generated a unique legacy for Caribbean women of the sixties, and particularly for the women who participated in the BUMIDOM takeover. As women, they were riding on the wave of French feminism fighting against gender inequality in French society; as people of African descent and former colonial subjects, they were demystifying France's "hypocritical" tradition of universal equality. As active participants in the construction of a diasporic community, May '68 offered Caribbean women a forum to challenge French Caribbean cultural norms, which usually restricted women's leadership to the domestic sphere; even intellectuals like Fanon, Glissant, and Césaire had failed to acknowledge the deleterious effects of patriarchy. Thus, when Caribbean women participated in the takeover, they became agents of sociopolitical change, leaders in their own right, encouraging their male counterparts to acknowledge their existence.

May '68 left a palpable legacy for Caribbean women. Without a doubt, the protest at BUMIDOM changed the ways in which the organization inserted female migrants into the labor market. Before '68, as the school for Caribbean women in Crouy-sur-Ourcq indicates, BUMIDOM favored giving women domestic jobs. But after '68, due to the anger that this mode of social insertion generated in the community, they no longer considered domestic positions to be the best option. The health-care industry and the public sector—sectors that better corresponded to the migrants' professional expectations—became BUMIDOM's preferred sites of social insertion.

Chapter Eight

Decolonization, the Black May '68, and the Fragmentation of Black France

Unlike their French counterparts seeking to reform labor relations and the educational system, French Caribbean migrants underscored how race, class, gender, and regional origin complicated the attributes of French citizenship. Many protested during May '68 because they aspired to obtain independence for their homelands. They believed France still colonized them, and BUMIDOM, the quintessential "neocolonial agent," had to be closed down. But other Caribbean migrants protested at BUMIDOM to enjoy the fruits of the French Republic; they wished for better employment opportunities in order to finally transcend their condition of second-class citizenship. In the end, the protest resulted in changing BUMIDOM's relationship with Caribbean migrants. French officials understood the message "treat us better or else." Thus, by the early seventies, the institution began channeling Caribbean migrants into positions other than maids in wealthy French households or bricklayers at construction sites. In other words, May '68 had a decolonizing impact on both French officials and Caribbean migrants. Indeed, not only did Caribbean migrants receive better employment, but as Mrs. Janine Martin confirmed, by the early seventies, senior BUMIDOM employees reformed their overtly paternalistic behavior. Moreover, the institution made a conscientious effort to employ new staff members, people like Mrs. Martin, a French woman who related to migrants with the proper dosage of respect.

May '68 also had a transformative effect on the Continental African diaspora. For one, the national protest heightened social unrest in the African foyers. From the late sixties to the mid-seventies, African migrants constantly challenged the administration of the *foyers Africains*, demanding better service, affordable rent, and to be treated with respect. But most importantly, the effects of national unrest on Parisians were actually an eye opener for many African migrants. As the first generation enjoying an independent Africa, Africans in Paris had nonetheless inherited colonial ideas of French identity. Most of them still considered the French to be intellectually superior individuals who controlled their socioeconomic and political destiny. But when these materially deprived African labor migrants observed the French negotiate the chaos of May '68, they slowly demystified their preconceived notions of French identity. In other words, May '68 allowed many Africans to transcend colonial notions of French identity, which tended to paint the French as more modern, resilient, and intellectually superior subjects.

Caribbean and African experiences in France of the postwar period are entirely different. On the one hand, citizenship allowed Caribbean people to migrate to Paris, where they initially received positions that were not necessarily better than their African counterparts'. For this reason, Caribbean nationalists argued that the migrants were deceived into coming to France, where they lived in exile as colonial subjects. Nonetheless—despite these allegations of deceit—through hard work, protest, and community activism, not only did Caribbean labor migrants carve cultural and social spaces into the Parisian region, but they also secured better employment than bricklayers in construction sites or maids for the Parisian bourgeoisie.

Africans, on the other hand, did not have French citizenship. Unlike many Caribbean labor migrants who were recruited by BUMIDOM, their journey to France was much more uncertain; hundreds were deported back to their homelands, and the vast majority of African workers in the Parisian region toiled at construction sites, or worse, for abusive French employers. However, like their Caribbean counterparts, through hard work, protest, and community activism, African labor migrants carved cultural and social spaces into the Parisian region. Their war for better living conditions in the foyers brought many victories, and in many ways, played an important role in legitimizing the African presence in Paris. Thanks to these battles, Africans forced French officials to treat them as migrant workers, not merely colonial laborers unfit to live in France.

Despite these different stories of migration, African and Caribbean migrants share two common experiences. For one, from a sociocultural and political perspective, the French perception of African and Caribbean identity often conflicted with the migrants' conception of their own identity. In France of the sixties, African and Caribbean migrants, people who viewed themselves as members of sovereign nation-states or French citizens respectively, embodied the quintessential colonial subjects. Yet, it is this very condition of colonial subjectivity that motivated African and Caribbean people to fight for change. The labor and housing markets, in particular, became true anticolonial battlefields. Paradoxically, even if they fought common enemies—colonial relations and anti-black racism—Caribbean and African labor migrants never built bridges between their communities. In France of the sixties and early seventies, achieving racial unity for the greater good of the African diaspora was all but a fleeting illusion.

Chapter 9

Music, Le Pen, and "New" Black Activism in Contemporary France, 1974–2005

The changes from Martin Luther King to Barack Obama occurred in forty years because the U.S. implemented public policies that precipitated such progress. In France, we supposedly have universal equality for over 160 years, yet we have hardly progressed; I would even say that we have regressed. Still, I trust France. I trust France because she has always mobilized against discrimination. If we imagine the riots of 2005 and the creation of CRAN as a turning point in history, I believe that within forty years we can elect a black president. Since the events of 2005 the situation in France has gotten better, at least theoretically. On a practical level, however, the situation can only improve with the implementation of public policies against discrimination. This is why I fight for change.... I fight because I have trust in France.

—Patrick Lozès, former president of the Conseil Représentatif
des Associations Noirs (CRAN), January 2010

Throughout the sixties and early seventies, ethnic identity, class, culture, and nationality created rigid barriers within the African diaspora in Paris. The lives of African and Caribbean migrants rarely intersected; they belonged to different political, cultural, and community organizations. But forty years later, the situation seems to be quite different. For one, the number of blacks born in France or who came to France as children has increased exponentially, making blackness an undeniable part of the nation. Most importantly, this new

Chapter Nine

French ethnicity—the black French—is deploying unprecedented forms of social and political activism. Quintessentially Pan-African, contemporary black-French sociopolitical activism aims to generate awareness about France's role in the tragic formation of the black Atlantic and, unlike the sixties and seventies, improve the lives of all blacks in France.

BRIDGING DIFFERENCES THROUGH MUSIC

Scholars discussing the relationship between the old African diaspora of the "New World" and Africans have elaborated different theories.[1] Molefi Asante, an Afrocentrist and leading African American scholar, suggests that African Americans should also nourish a strong relationship with the African continent. He contends that African Americans should recover their long-lost African identity to combat what he views as a global white-supremacist system.[2] On the other hand, Glissant, the late Martinican poet and philosopher, emphasized how rupture and transplantation led to the creation of new identities. For Glissant, Asante's project is inconceivable. It is at odds with the very formation of the "old" African diaspora. Accordingly, blacks from the Americas share hybrid identities.[3] With regard to the French Caribbean, Glissant states:

> Populations transplanted by the slave trade were not capable of maintaining for any length of time the impulse to revert. This impulse will decline, therefore, as the memory of the ancestral country fades. Wherever in the Americas technical know-how is maintained or renewed for a relocated population, whether oppressed or dominant, the impulse to revert will recede little by little with the need to come to terms with the new land. Where that coming to terms is not only difficult but made *inconceivable* (the population having become a people, but a powerless one) the obsession with imitation will appear. This obsession does not generate itself. Without saying that it is not natural (it is a kind of violence), one can establish that it is futile. Not only is imitation itself not workable but real obsession with it is intolerable. The mimetic impulse is a kind of insidious violence. A people that submits to it takes some time to realize its consequences collectively and critically, but is immediately affected by the resulting trauma.[4]

Here Glissant strikes a chord. For most working-class Afro-French Caribbean individuals, especially during the sixties, France and French culture represented the apex of civilization. Even if many people expressed frustration about departmentalization and French cultural hegemony, they were still caught within the web of mimicry, and though "Djinin" or "kongo" (Africa in Kreyol) inspired curiosity, it was still a source of shame and embarrassment. After all, the negritude movement had not trickled down to the masses, which generally did not have the literacy skills or the time to ponder the complex meaning of Césaire's, Damas's, and Senghor's prose. As a result, throughout the postwar period, most French Caribbean individuals commonly believed that Africans were primitive people, good only at casting spells, paradoxically a French Caribbean obsession.

On the other side of the Atlantic, Africans also shared varied, and at times simplistic, notions of Caribbean identity. In *Black Skin, White Masks*, Fanon shows that during the colonial period, several African migrants sought to elevate their social status by passing for Caribbean people because the latter figured higher on the colonial hierarchy.[5] In the postcolonial era, however, animated by a sense of national pride, certain Africans shared less-reverential views of French Caribbean people. When French Caribbean migrants began climbing up the social ladder through the military, the police, the health-care industry, and Paris's municipality, effectively becoming part of the establishment that marginalized and harassed African migrants, they embodied France's "lackeys" in the eyes of many African people. Thus, by the turn of the eighties, aside from the intellectuals who constantly crossed racial and ethnic boundaries, not only did colonial legacies prevent Caribbean and African people from forging links, but the ways in which the migrants had been inserted into the fabric of the city also hindered the development of healthier relationships.

Music helped change this paradigm. In the late sixties, when the Black Power movement gained currency in the United States, artists like James Brown produced a new genre of music—funk—which combined elements of soul music, R&B, and jazz with empowering sociocultural and political messages. Brown and his contemporaries also dressed stylishly, wearing bell-bottom pants and colorful shirts. An energetic performer, Brown quickly contaminated the postcolonial "black world." Reflecting on Brown's impact on West Africa, Manthia Diawarra, the Malian cultural theorist, asserts, "James Brown's music reconnected Bamako's [Mali] youth to pre–Atlantic slavery energy that enabled them to master the language of independence and modernity and to express a return of Africanism to Africa through black aesthetics."[6] Likewise, the funk energy also spread among the French Caribbean youth; Afros, bell-bottom pants, and Afro-centrist songs converged on the flourishing Caribbean nightlife. Interestingly, these musical crossroads led to the creation of zouk music, and arguably revived *mizik tradisionel* (traditional French Caribbean music). Imbued with political messages, the music of Eugène Mona (1943–1991), an important actor in the popularization of *mizik tradisionel*, and Kassav', a Pan-French Caribbean zouk band, helped many French Caribbean individuals fashion more flattering images of Africa and Africans.

Born in Martinique, Eugène Mona was strongly influenced by local intellectuals under the spell of Césaire's negritude. He gained popularity by skillfully weaving the Caribbean oral tradition and folklore with drum-based Afro-Caribbean rhythms. However, this was not an easy task because the various genres of African-derived drummed music such as *bèlè, gwo ka*, quadrille, and *chouval bwa*, which French Caribbean people refer to as traditional music, were considered peasant or low-class music before he climbed onstage in the early seventies. But Mona worked hard to change this situation. According to Dominique Cyrille, he "repeatedly told his accompanying musicians that he viewed the West African contributions as the cement of the Martinican cultural patchwork."[7] Cyrille thinks he was trying to redeem Martinique's African heritage with traditional music. In some ways, he effectively achieved his goal by incorporating jazz and blues—musical genres that the French Caribbean middle class considered to be "high class/art"—into *bèlè* music, the allegedly unsophisticated Afro-French Caribbean musical genre.

But in addition to melding African American musical genres with traditional French Caribbean music, influenced by a number of politically conscious musicians, Mona added a good dose of political and African-centered messages into his lyrics, thereby inviting French Caribbean people to reflect on the construction of their identity. For instance, calling for Martinican and Guadeloupean people to acknowledge and transcend the color and class issues inherited from plantation slavery, he asserts, "If *Neg* [dark-skinned blacks] have been cursed then *Milat* [mulattoes or light-skinned blacks] are probably not blessed."[8] He continuously defied social norms, and at times, proudly referred to Afro-French Caribbean people as *Iche Kongo*, a Kreyol expression signifying Africa's children. During his concerts, he usually performed barefoot to commemorate his ancestors, who toiled in sugarcane fields without shoes. While many French Caribbean people did not fully grasp the African-centered meaning of his music, he nonetheless invited them to reflect on many important subjects, including their racial and cultural identity, the reproduction of social inequalities in the Caribbean, the role of Afro-Caribbean dances and drumming in their society and history, and ultimately their connections with Africa. His music was a steppingstone towards further decolonizing the minds of French Caribbean people, who were taught to minimize their African heritage and look at Africans, people who often look like them, with contemptuous eyes.

As Mona and other local artists began crafting transnational notions of blackness through traditional music, a number of Caribbean musicians in quest of careers moved to Paris. As in the administrative and industrial sectors, opportunities in the

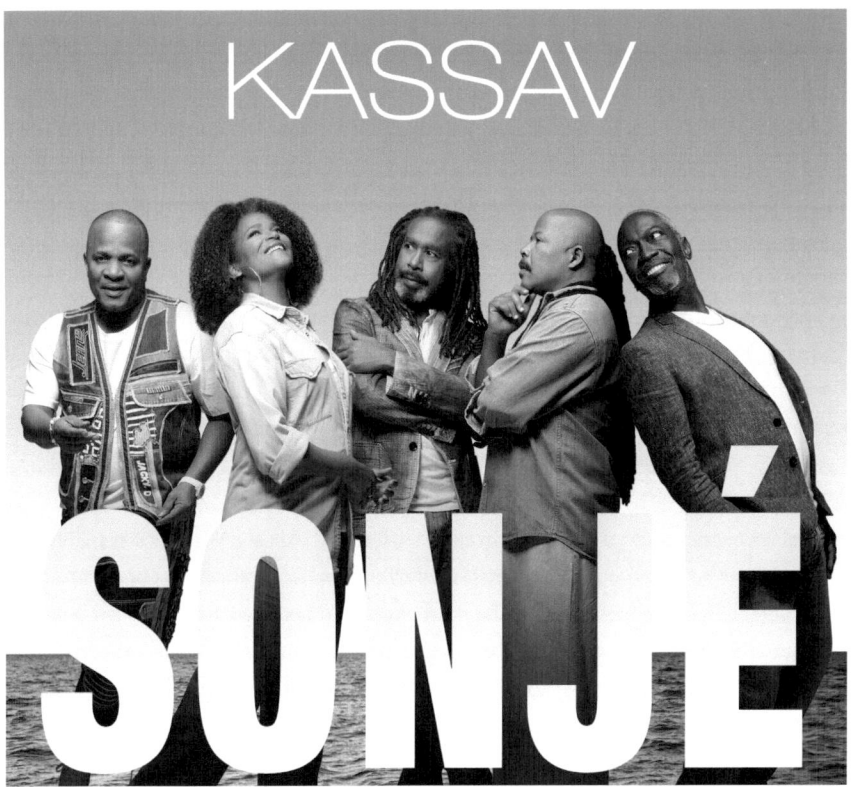

Latest CD by Kassav', Sonjé (Remember), 2013. (Photo by Xavier Dollin, ZOUK 2013, used with permission of Note A Bene.)

music industry were scarce in French Guiana, Guadeloupe, and Martinique, forcing accomplished musicians to live in France, where they were more likely to find work. It is in this context that Kassav', the most popular French Caribbean zouk band, was born.[9] In the mid-eighties Kassav', which combined Haitian *compas direct*, Dominican cadence, and funk with traditional Guadeloupean and Martinican rhythms—the perfect recipe for good zouk—became incredibly popular throughout the Caribbean and Africa, particularly in the Francophone and Lusophone countries. They toured the African Continent, making headlines and filling national stadiums to the joy of audiences consuming zouk, what was then a new, hip, and intoxicating genre of music.

Lamine Sal, a Guinean migrant living in New York City, recalls attending a Kassav' concert in the mid-eighties. Supposedly, everyone in Conakry knew of the event; a combined French presidential and papal visit would not have attracted such a large, enthusiastic audience, he claimed. At the concert, he noted that people were fighting to climb the trees surrounding the stadium just to catch a glimpse of the artists dressed in colorful attire. Jacob Desvarieux, the lead singer with a distinctive, deep voice, was especially popular.[10] For many Guineans, seeing Kassav' was their first encounter with blacks from the "New World." As Mr. Sal suggests, the Kassav' concert invited Guineans to reflect about their descendants across the ocean. During our conversation, he admitted, "We knew that black people lived in the Americas, but we never imagined meeting them. I cannot explain how or why, but seeing the artists play this exiting music elicited emotions and curiosity."[11] Yet, Kassav' not only provided Africans with a window onto diasporic Africa, but it also had a profound effect on French Caribbean people. Although Kassav''s music embraces love themes and promotes partying, a few songs also draw connections with Africa. For example, "An ba chen'n la" (chained) emphasizes the sadness of the Middle Passage and the evolution of African cultures into a distinct Afro-French Caribbean culture.[12] Conversely, "Gorée" seeks to connect Caribbean people to Africa by honoring their ancestors who passed through the dark chambers of the slave castle situated in Gorée, an island just a boat ride away from Dakar, Senegal.[13]

Kassav' also invited African artists to perform on its albums, a practice that opened new avenues of cultural and intellectual exchange between French Caribbean and African people. Thus, by the mid-1990s, the theme of "common roots" was frequently surfacing in different genres of black Francophone music. "Africains et Antillais," a song written by the Martinican artist Ralph Tamar and Idrissa Diop, a famous Senegalese singer, marked this important change.[14] In a smooth bolero rhythm, the song suggests that because the Middle Passage did not erase certain cultural similarities between Caribbean and African people, they should relearn how to appreciate each other. After all, as Diop and Tamar argue, they share family ties:

Idrissa Diop

Antillais et Africains	A long time ago
Ont séparé leurs chemins	Antilleans and Africans
Depuis trop longtemps	Took different paths
Communication coupée	No more communication
Y a plus de tonalité	No more dial tone
Juste un air absent	Just emptiness
Africains et Antillais	Africans and Antilleans
Si proches et si éloignés	So close, yet so distant
C'est une folie	It's insane
D'avoir perdu la mémoire	They have lost their memory
Au point de ne plus savoir	To the extent that they no longer know

Ce qui les unit	What unites them

Ralph Tamar in Kreyol

Wou ki la ka gadé sa	You who are watching me
Ou sav la mwen soti	You know where I come from
Adan fondè mémwa ou	Deep in your memory
Ni rasin' mwen	You can find my roots
Africain et Antillais	Africans and Antilleans
Te pou toujou sa konpwen kote yo soti	Should always know where they come from
Mem lan misik mem koulè, mem soley	It's the same music, same color, same sun
Mem la pli, d'Afrik o zantiy'	Same rain, from Africa to the Antilles

Idrissa Diop

Africains et Antillais	Africans and Antilleans
Café noir, café au lait	Coffee with or without milk
C'est toujours café	is still coffee
100% même origine	100% same origin
Entre cousins et cousines	We are cousins
Pour savoir s'aimer	We should learn to love each other
Antillais et Africains	Antilleans and Africans
Musiciens à quatre mains	Musicians with four hands
D'une chanson d'amour	Playing a song of love
Une mélodie oubliée sur des enfants séparés	A forgotten melody about children separated
Par un long parcours	By a long journey

Ralph Tamar in Kreyol

Mem si mwen pati lot bo dépi bien lontan	Even if I've been on the other side forever
Mwen toujou ni dan tchè mwen	Still, in my heart
Tout rasin' mwen	I have my roots
Antillais et Africains	Africans and Antilleans
ni on rishes ki ta yo	Something so precious belongs to them
Chanté et dansé	Sing and dance to it

Chapter Nine

	Idrissa Diop
Une musique à retrouver	A music to rediscover
Respiration mélanger	A common breath
	Diop and Tamar sing simultaneously
Afrique, Antilles...	Africa and the Caribbean...

As more artists from Africa and the French Caribbean praised black cultures and acknowledged their common roots, rap music, which had emerged from the Bronx, New York, in the late seventies, found an audience among French youth of Caribbean, sub-Saharan, and North African descent. These young individuals strongly identified with African American singers denouncing police brutality, racism, and the reproduction of poverty in the inner cities. Moreover, they loved dancing to the beat of the music. Breakdancing became highly popular in the Parisian suburbs. Initially, in the early eighties, black French and French-Maghrebian (North African) rappers constantly reproduced the beats and lyrics coming from across the Atlantic. However, by the following decade, they had clearly developed their own style and industry. In celebration of cultural diversity and hybridity, which at the time was a highly sensitive topic, black and Maghrebian-French artists often asserted their urban French identity while praising their African or Caribbean parents' culture. Politically defiant, they advocated that racialized minorities should stand together against an oppressive system that deprives people from the *banlieues* (suburbs)[15] from having equal access to resources and employment opportunities.[16] In the process, the black French rappers suggested that cultural, political, and social differences within the growing but struggling African diaspora in France were not as significant as in previous decades. "Banlieusards" (Suburbanites), a song by Kery James, a Guadeloupean-born rapper of Haitian origin who grew up in France, embodies this phenomenon. Truly a response to anti-black and structural racism, "Banlieusards" speaks to the presence of a new collective black consciousness among people of African descent born in France or who grew up in France. In his song, James contends that young, black, and Maghrebian-French people are merely innocent prey who are framed as predators of the nation. Supposedly "leeches" of the state, their road to success is punctuated by hurdles. Still, according to James, it is these very hurdles that trigger strength and pride, as he proudly asserts:

Today, no one denies there are two Frances
I am from the second France
The one of insecurity
Of potential terrorists

Of welfare people
That's what they expect from us
But I've got other projects
Because I'm not a victim
I'm a soldier
Look at me, I'm black and I'm proud.[17]

Although black French people are more likely to welcome the rappers' call for racial unity and dialogue across ethnicity, Caribbean and African migrants are also affected by the catchy lyrics encouraging them to develop a greater sense of solidarity in dealing with social issues like housing, education, and employment opportunities.[18] In other words, even if they rarely interact across culture and community, the concept of linked fate in the face of adversity has fostered some sort of "racial" unity. Somehow, at the turn of the twenty-first century, a black consciousness exists in France without the presence of a homogeneous black community. This black consciousness, which led to a new sociopolitical agenda, was actually heightened by a vigorous far right political movement.

Historically, the far right had been associated with xenophobia and anti-Semitism. In fact, during World War II, the Vichy regime—the far right par excellence—openly embraced anti-Semitism. Vichyites collaborated with Nazi Germany and sent thousands of Jews to horrible death camps.[19] But after the Jewish Holocaust, overt anti-Semitism became unpopular, and xenophobia, at least towards other European migrants, was not as fervent as in the interwar period. Still, many French people had internalized hate. Hate, in a metaphorical sense, became a sleeping monster, which William Schneider argues awoke when migrants from the former colonies settled in France.[20] Ironically, the "monstrosity" of far right political discourse is a key element that helped build bridges between Caribbean and African people.

Unlikely Connection: The Rise of the Far Right and Improvement in African-Caribbean Relations

The contemporary far right political movement owes much to the populist Pierre Poujade (1920–2003), whom leftists facetiously called Poujadolf. Poujade wanted to change French institutions to better serve the interests of small business owners and the *petit Français*, French people from the lower classes. He was also pro–French Algeria, openly anti-Semitic, and a staunch xenophobe. *Poujadisme* peaked in the mid-fifties, drawing more than half a million supporters. However, General de Gaulle, who in a calculating manner returned to power, swept the ultraconservative movement off the national stage. De Gaulle embodied a resilient and victorious France and held a discourse appealing to a nation thirsty for glory and economic growth.[21] He seduced Poujadolf's followers, people desiring a racially homogeneous and powerful French nation. Nonetheless, the damage was done. Poujadolf had carved a space in French politics for pundits arguing that Jews, blacks, and other racialized minorities have no place in France.

In the early seventies, the global recession encouraged France to stop recruiting labor migrants; the government only allowed families to rejoin migrant workers already settled in France.[22] This policy of family reunification brought the wives and children of African workers to Parisian *banlieues*, where the French government had spent millions of francs developing public housing complexes to accommodate the hundreds of thousands of migrants pouring into France.[23] As a result, after the mid-seventies, many Parisian *banlieues* changed from being quasi-religiously and "racially" homogeneous, to heterogeneous spaces comprised of different "races," ethnicities, cultures, and religions. However, the trumpet of xenophobia and anti-Semitism that had been playing its horrific tune during the interwar period, World War II, and the postwar period—the music of Poujadolf—had predisposed many French citizens to feel uncomfortable about this change.

Naturally, the far right, the party of xenophobes, anti-Semites, royalists, ultranationalists, Catholic conservatives, colonialists, and racists, knew exactly how to exploit this malaise. For Jean Marie Le Pen, Poujadolf's apprentice and founder of the ultraconservative Front National political party (1972), the global crisis and immigration issues represented the perfect opportunity to enter politics.[24] Ambitious, he jumped onto the political stage. But to his surprise, the Front National's first years were characterized by failure and unpopularity. Giscard d'Estaing, who in 1974 had been elected on a center-right ticket, drew voters away from the Front National (FN), forcing Le Pen's party to orbit the French political landscape without having much influence on the nation. But Le Pen, charismatic and resilient, refused to let the FN disappear in the pages of French history; in the early eighties he made a surprising comeback. His xenophobic, anti-Semitic, protectionist, and racist political discourse appealed to disgruntled French citizens worrying that immigrants, particularly the most visible ones, took jobs away from them. In other words, the FN became a major political party by popularizing the idea that immigrants from the former colonies and their "extra-large" families represented France's new social problem.

Le Pen's scapegoating politics proved to be quite effective.[25] For white French people clinging to a white and Christian France, migrants from the former colonies and their children—in other words, "people of color"—represented a challenge to their otherwise essentialist conception of the nation. Thus, as people from the former colonies migrated to major French cities like Paris and Marseilles, and the number of "French people of color" increased, the FN's popularity grew exponentially, giving Le Pen carte blanche to voice what many consider anachronistic and hateful thoughts. Indeed, Le Pen had called for the abrogation of the 1972 anti-discrimination law and openly praised the legitimacy of racial and cultural purity. He justified his racist beliefs by suggesting there was nothing racist about "recognizing that there are different races, different ethnic groups, different peoples, who cannot simply be lumped together."[26] These races, he argued, "should preserve their identity as an irreplaceable treasure rather than being merged through indiscriminate interbreeding."[27]

Despite a number of highly racist and anti-Semitic remarks, Le Pen rose in the polls (one can also attribute his success to his racist comments). In the 1988 presidential election, he received a surprising 10 percent of the votes, a number that increased to 15 percent in 1995 and to nearly 18 percent in 2002, or about six million votes. Yet, whether only 18 percent of white French people espoused his views is still very much unclear. *Le Monde* published a poll conducted after the 2002 election suggesting that at least 28 percent of French voters supported the values and ideas of the ultraconservative party.[28] This poll, however, was not consistent with the following presidential election in 2007, when Le Pen finished fourth. Nonetheless, Lilian Thuram, the famous Guadeloupean soccer player and political activist, contends that Le Pen's poor performance does not translate into the declining significance of racism and xenophobia in France. According to Thuram, Le Pen's votes went to President Nicolas Sarkozy, an astute politician who understood that the rhetoric of tougher immigration control and personal responsibility, especially in regard to the social behavior of racial minorities, increased his political capital.[29] Thus, while the FN's leader has not been able to move to the Élysée Palace (the equivalent of the White House), he has successfully advanced his socially conservative agenda, and in the process, contributed to legitimizing misrepresentations of black identities in contemporary France. Even the French media portrays blackness in ways that coincide with FN discourses. For instance, African women (and to some extent Caribbean women) are often stereotyped as leeches of the state; accordingly, in contrast to modern and independent white French women, they depend on their spouses, uphold traditional values, and run away from the conventional labor market. Supposedly, their goal is to bear numerous children and collect "fat" welfare checks. In fact, African mothers embody the quintessential unproductive female migrant who not only depends on the state for survival but also lacks the adequate skills to manage the domestic sphere and raise children appropriately.[30]

The Class (*Entre les Murs*, 2008), the famous film by Laurent Cantet about the black and Arab-French youth in the Parisian school system, which won the Palme d'Or at the prestigious Cannes Film Festival, demonstrates how notions of African mothers as unfit, passive, and barely capable of speaking French have become pervasive in French society. A scene portraying a parent-teacher conference hints that African mothers cannot even parent their children appropriately. The mother embodies traditional Africa, and her son, a rambunctious student, portrays the relationship between young black bodies and the increasing presence of urban pathologies in France. Thus, echoing the far right, the "children of color" figuring in Cantet's film represent a growing liability for France.

Although the film aims to increase awareness about issues of social inequality in France, it does not challenge the far right's political discourse painting these children as a "postcolonial problem." Its themes—namely, the failing school system, the challenges of contemporary teachers, violence and disorder in the classroom, the cultural gap between past and contemporary students—indicate how the far right has normalized the idea that French people of color, even when they are children, represent a burden to society.[31] Yet the rise of the far right and its contaminating rhetoric has not gone unchallenged. "People of color" in France have reacted strongly against the FN. In fact, Le Pen's discourse, which painted black and Maghrebian people in France as illegal immigrants, delinquents, and leeches of the state depleting national resources, has fostered collaboration among these minorities, and sentiments of racial solidarity among black French, French Caribbean, and sub-Saharan African people.

This trend became evident in 1984, when Harlem Désir, a man of Caribbean and French origin, created SOS Racisme, a multiracial organization fighting against racism, xenophobia, anti-Semitism, and for the *sans papiers* (illegal immigrants).[32] Led by its charismatic leader, SOS Racisme organized flamboyant concerts and multiracial rallies during which it called for appreciating a multicultural France. However, by the mid-nineties SOS Racisme's influence faded away. Many people of color in France began to wonder if the organization actually made a difference in their lives. A number of French leftists, people who had been avid supporters of the organization, also started to question the integrity of multiculturalism, suggesting it conflicted with French republican ideals by fostering communitarianism. In their eyes, as Didier Gondola points out, communitarianism reaffirms minority status at the expense of national identification.[33]

Eventually, the far right prevailed, and by the turn of the twenty-first century, many white French citizens still perceived migrants from the former colonies and the new French ethnicities "of color" as a thorn in their nation's side. This explains why many people of Caribbean and African descent living in certain Parisian suburbs—the so-called *zones sensibles* or *zones chaudes* (dangerous or "hot" zones)—feel neglected by state officials who endorse Sarkozy or Le Pen's views. This is particularly true for the black and Maghrebian French youth—people who are imagined to be unproductive members of society; people who are allegedly prone to adopting criminal behavior. In fact, such stereotypical ideas of racial minorities in France may have been responsible for the accidental death of Bouna Traoré, a fifteen-year-old black French teenager, and Zyed Benna, a seventeen-year-old Arab French teenager. On October 27, 2005, the teenagers died by electrocution at a power station in the *banlieue* of Clichy-sous-Bois while running away from the police.[34] Their untimely death triggered protests and riots, which intensified when former President Nicolas Sarkozy, who at the time was Minister of the Interior, insensitively called the black and Maghrebian-French youth of the *banlieues* "la racaille" (scumbags). Yet, it is these types of unpleasant comments from the right that have fueled new forms of Pan-African expression and black activism in urban France. In fact, the Conseil Représentatif des Associations Noirs (CRAN), founded by Patrick Lozès in November 2005 in a climate of despair, anger against the system, racism, and police brutality, embodies this new urban phenomenon.

CRAN AND THE NEW BLACK ACTIVISM IN CONTEMPORARY FRANCE

CRAN, a federation of dozens of Caribbean and African organizations, was founded to promote the socioeconomic and political empowerment of the African diaspora in France. Within a couple of years, the organization gained much visibility in the French media. It also built ties with local politicians and forged transnational connections with other advocacy groups, such as the NAACP in the United States. CRAN drew its immediate success from fighting racial injustice by using the rhetorical weapons of the French Republic. It advocated that liberty, equality, and fraternity should be extended, in theory and practice, to all individuals in France. Pledging allegiance to secularism, CRAN has taken a pragmatic approach that appeals to most individuals across the political spectrum.

CRAN's relationship to secularism is a complicated matter, because, as Joan Wallach Scott observes, praise for secularity can effectively disguise discrimination against "threatening" religious minorities.[35] However, CRAN is not an Islamophobic organization. For the most part, the organization uses social media, government statistics (whenever available), and other social indicators to advocate for black people who routinely confront racial profiling, and housing and employment discrimination. Drafting a law to protect all French citizens against these forms of discrimination figures at the top of its agenda.

Chapter Nine

In January 2010, following an important national debate on the meaning of French identity, I interviewed Mr. Patrick Lozès, at the time the most visible black intellectual and activist in France.[36] In light of the riots that occurred in 2005 and the rising instances of police brutality, as well as the high rate of black poverty in the *banlieues*, I was hoping to better understand CRAN's strategy for curtailing these problems. Additionally, I wished to know if the organization had improved social relations between people from sub-Saharan Africa and the Caribbean. To begin, I asked Mr. Lozès what had compelled him to create CRAN, and much to my surprise, I discovered that his allegiance to French republicanism had played an important role in the process, as he stated:

> At the dawn of the republic France refused to confront racism. Instead of accepting differences, the founding members of the republic ignored them, and by the same token continued ignoring how discrimination affected society. They assumed the ideas of the republic sufficed. Although they are great in theory, in practice they have yet to function. Sadly, many citizens and public intellectuals share a rigid vision of the republic and criticize those who denounce this problem. CRAN was born to provide an institutional space for people who want a better republic. We believe there are other ways of imagining the republic and that it is important to conceive of equality as an objective but not as a given reality. We think that discrimination exists and that society only moves forward by acknowledging and confronting it. In our history, all the groups fighting for equality and the ideals of the republic have initially been repressed. Jews and women exemplify this trend.[37]

In many ways, CRAN calls for reflecting on the gap between idealist discourses of colorblindness and the realities of social stratification based on class, gender, and especially, racial criteria. The organization also believes in participatory activism; it encourages citizens to unite and lobby the government to enact changes at the national level. Accordingly, it advocates implementing affirmative action policies and using statistical data to measure racial, class, and gender diversity in the labor market. Yet this strategy, which displays obvious connections with the United States, has drawn a few skeptical glances. Pundits argue against this strategy, claiming that African Americans and Latinos have remained confined within inner cities, lacking educational and professional opportunities. Aware of this paradox, Mr. Lozès still stood firm on his position, asserting:

> It is true that statistics are merely a diagnosis identifying an existing pathology. But can we treat without diagnosing? I would personally fear a doctor who

prescribes a treatment without consulting the patient. I strongly believe that we must have an idea of what is happening in the labor and housing markets, what we term "statistique de la diversité." For example, when I ask our government officials whether employment or housing discrimination has increased during the last ten years, they are unable to answer me. I contend that statistics improves gauging the efficacy of public policies, particularly in regard to equal employment and housing opportunities. I am currently working with a group of public officials in the parliament to draft a law on "statistique de la diversité." I think that American policies of affirmative action can inspire us; however, we should not try to emulate the U.S. because our society is different. To uplift the majority of underprivileged people in France we must account for regional, class, gender, and racial criteria. This is especially true for urban France, where we have to prevent the impoverishment of people and the formation of ghettos.[38]

Because Mr. Lozès signaled that blacks and other racialized minorities are disproportionally represented in areas of concentrated poverty, I wondered about transatlantic similarities, especially in comparison to the United States. Is the condition of poor blacks in France—particularly their employment situation, educational achievements, and living conditions—affected by racial stereotypes depicting them as criminals and welfare queens?, I asked. In an emphatic yes, Mr. Lozès confirmed that it is precisely these growing similarities that prompted him to create CRAN. In fact, to convince the skeptics, the organization often generates reports on the representation of racial minorities in the media, and uses polling agencies to determine the public's opinion on issues of diversity in France.[39]

Ultimately, Lozès believes that racial stereotyping is a product of fear—the fear of change. According to him, if blacks in France embraced French colonial notions of black identity, they would not figure as unproductive and dangerous individuals.[40] However, by expressing new cultural aesthetics, which departs from "traditional" French culture, they seem to disturb people who endorse rigid notions of the nation. For Lozès, blacks are misrepresented and neglected because they stand up for their rights. He contends, "In demanding equality, our words are often misconstrued and society tends to imagine us differently." As a result, he affirms that CRAN is highly motivated to prove that black people can enrich French society. This goal, he contends, can only be achieved by changing the national consciousness. Once this change occurs, France, he claims, will be a better country.[41]

Interestingly, in reflecting upon CRAN's philosophy, one notes strong connections with the negritude movement. After all, not only were the negritude writers deeply invested in redeeming black cultures—they were pan-African at heart—but they also wrote essays and poems criticizing French universalism. They asserted that French culture should not dominate or eradicate black cultures. According to the writers, cultures should coexist.[42] Thus, in many ways, like the negritude writers, CRAN promotes self-reflection, transformation, and ultimately social harmony. Like the negritude writers, CRAN asks France to question how she (the state apparatus and the nation) relates to people across race, class, gender, and ethnicity. In praising what he calls *la négritude debout* (radical negritude) or the active quest for freedom and equality, Lozès answered my question about the similarities between negritude and CRAN in the following manner:

> Césaire, Senghor, Damas, and even Sartre, shattered conventional notions of black inferiority and paved the way for demanding equality. From that perspective, our work represents a new negritude in France. We are reconnecting with that part of our history, and today, the equality that we are demanding is nothing less than what the elders were demanding—we want black citizens to share the same status as whites—that's all. We are not asking for special treatment. Like Césaire, Damas, and Senghor we are fighting against different types of exclusion affecting blacks in France. We are combating a process of invisibilization (a process of erasing blackness from France), especially in the historical and scientific discourse, in the economy and the labor market, and in the media and in politics. For instance, in the French national assembly only 1 out of 550 deputies from mainland France is black. In the Senate, out of the 330 senators no one is black. Among the representatives of the French government in foreign countries, there are no black ambassadors. There are no black CEOs at the head of large French corporations. Like Césaire, we are saying, *Nous ne sommes pas des citoyens à part entière mais des citoyens entièrement à part* [a French play on words indicating that in reality blacks are second-class citizens]. Similar to the elders, we are highlighting the shortcomings of the republic and pointing to the invisibility of blackness in France. CRAN proposes a new negritude.[43]

Similar to the negritude writers, CRAN adopts a Pan-African outlook and condemns the French Republic for not practicing what it preaches. However, the organization goes further than the writers by proposing a series of initiatives to remedy racial inequalities. According to CRAN, using statistics in the labor market and enacting a law against racial, sexual, and gender discrimination ultimately improves France. Moreover, unlike its predecessors, CRAN capitalizes on the new media (Internet, radio, and television) to effectively change public opinion and advance its agenda in the national political landscape. In sum, CRAN elaborates a new politics of blackness; it advocates for black unity and the integration of the African diaspora into the fabric of the French Republic as equal citizens. In the process, through what one may call black republican activism, CRAN has built bridges between African and Caribbean people.

BLACK ACTIVISM AND *DIVERSITÉ*

Black activism in France has changed tremendously since the sixties. During that period, Caribbean and African students, political activists, and professionals created political organizations to address issues in their respective homelands. In the process, they staged a number of protests at French or African institutions, criticizing authoritarian regimes, neocolonialism, or departmentalization. Most importantly, however, Caribbean and African workers and activists founded many community organizations to facilitate the migrants' insertion into the labor and housing markets. Paradoxically, despite facing common challenges, African and Caribbean migrants did not forge any organization catering to both groups; to be sure, not only did colonial barriers prevent building ties between the communities, but the idea of racial unity seemed trivial to migrants depending on social networks comprised of family members or people from their respective countries, villages, islands, or even foyers.

Three factors changed this situation. First, musical crossroads fostered the development of new black consciousness and cultural exchange across nationality and ethnicity. African American music of the late sixties and early seventies influenced bands like Kassav', which invited Caribbean and African people to reflect on their identity and perception of each other. Additionally, traditional French Caribbean musicians like Eugène Mona also invited Afro-Caribbean people to praise their African heritage, thereby facilitating symbolic encounters between Caribbean and African people. Second, the children and grandchildren of African and Caribbean migrants—the black French—are products of urban France. As a general rule, not only do they embrace the oppositional and Pan-African dimension of rap music, but they are more likely to develop bonds across race and ethnicity. Finally, the far right's attempt to turn Muslims, blacks, and Jews into pariahs of the nation has also encouraged people of African descent to construct political ties. CRAN, for instance, embodies the sort of black political activism that surfaced after the increasing popularity of the far right and the defamatory remarks of moderate right politicians like Sarkozy, who tends to blame the victims without acknowledging the system's role in creating social inequalities.

Distinctively French, this new black political activism draws on French republican values to advocate for equality in the labor, housing, and educational sectors. In the process, following the legacy of negritude intellectuals and influenced by transnational sociopolitical and cultural currents, contemporary black activists such as Patrick Lozès are crafting a new slogan for the French Republic, one that reflects France's cultural, religious, and racial diversity. Indeed, due to France's colonial past, the migration from the former colonies, and the presence of new French ethnicities, these activists suggest that *diversité* should be added to the national slogan praising *liberté*, *egalité*, and *fraternité*; an appreciation for *diversit*é, they argue, would allow France to transcend her colonial legacy and guarantee that all citizens, regardless of their race, gender, religion, sexuality, and class, have, as the Nobel laureate Amartya Sen claims, "the substantive freedoms he or she enjoys to lead the kind of life he or she has reason to value."[44]

Conclusion

In the early eighties, BUMIDOM, the notorious state-sponsored organization that had been dubbed an agent of French colonialism, changed its name to l'Agence Nationale pour l'Insertion et la Promotion des Travailleurs d'Outre-Mer (National Agency for the Insertion and Promotion of Workers from the Overseas Departments). The change was not merely symbolic. The institution had become much more professional. It finally hired Caribbean administrators who connected Caribbean migrants to jobs that better matched their qualifications. To the delight of French Caribbean community activists, the agency also turned to the French Caribbean, hoping to find employment for individuals seeking to return home.

This new pattern of social insertion did not occur without a fight. The Caribbean migrants' work ethic and professional ambition, as well as their protests for better employment, spurred these changes. In many ways, these contentious postcolonial Caribbean migrants owe much to nationalists and community activists who highlighted the contradictions between France's discourse of universal equality and the dire socioeconomic conditions in the Overseas French Caribbean Departments and throughout the Caribbean diaspora of the Parisian region. Indeed, community activists like Mr. Georges Lassare Michalon, Mrs. Dancenis, and Mr. Marcel Manville played an important role in fostering the development of a new sociopolitical consciousness among the migrants. Committed to servicing their community, they recruited disgruntled Caribbean workers into their organizations, encouraging them to stand up for their rights. The activists also lobbied the Ministry of the Interior, forcing French officials to understand that Caribbean migrants were living at home but in exile from home. They argued for lowering the cost of airfare to the French Caribbean and giving the workers extra vacation time to visit family. In combination with the migrants' work ethic and protests for better employment, community activism in the Caribbean diaspora encouraged many French individuals to shed their colonial notions of black identity.

A similar story unfolded in the community of African labor migrants. Although they did not benefit from the shield of French citizenship, through a combination of hard work and protest, African labor migrants also changed French perceptions of African identity. Organizations like l'Union Générale des Travailleurs Sénégalais en France (UGTSF) impressed upon many migrants the need to fight for their rights as blue-collar workers and residents of hostels for migrant workers. The anti-statist and anticapitalist social climate in France of the late sixties also motivated Africans in their quest for better living conditions in the French Republic. That said, after this important black social movement, Africans no longer embodied the subservient colonial subjects—the French viewed them as labor migrants from the former colonies.

However, the evolution of French consciousness does not preclude displays of anti-black racism. If, in the fifties and sixties, many French individuals endorsed colonial notions of African identity—they actually believed France had the moral responsibility to uplift inherently "inferior" African subjects—after the seventies, French people who still emphasized the colonial attributes of African or Caribbean identity were/are merely attempting to minimize and marginalize them. The act is a modern display of anti-black racism. Indeed, much has changed since the postwar era. According to Maryse Condé, when she was living in France during the fifties, most French people were extremely paternalistic towards African and Caribbean migrants; the colonial gaze, she suggests, transcended the boundaries of the colonies to reign freely in France.

For Condé, the fifties connotes a decade of discomfort for black people in the French Republic. She remembers feeling constantly minimized, like she did not belong in France. But today, in 2010, she claims that Frenchness and blackness are no longer mutually exclusive categories. She asserts:

> In the fifties when young children accompanied us, we feared that people would scare them. We were scared that people would exclaim, "Look, a little negress!" It happened all the time, just like Fanon describes. Today, in spite of everything, blacks have a space in France. French people may not like that, but no one will candidly insult you because you're black. They may criticize you, in fact, they will surely criticize black people, but it is done politely. My daughter, who has a two-year-old girl, went to a resort in the

South of France. She told me that people were extremely warm to the child. But forty or fifty years ago it would have been a totally different story. People would be intrigued and surprised—they would probably touch the child, trying to see if they could rub off her skin color. Racism has changed; French people hide their sentiments, the fact that they don't like you. But you see, I live in a ghetto of intellectuals and I am shielded from the racism of the *banlieues*. I can't tell you much about the particularities of this anti-black racism.[1]

Condé's observation truly encapsulates the evolution of white-black relations in France from the postwar period to the turn of the twenty-first century. French people may hide their sentiments and are no longer passing their hands through the hair of black children, but as she suggests, the intersection of race and class still determines one's quality of life in the French Republic. Racism and social inequality, she hints, are more palpable in the "blazing hot" *banlieues*, where dreams of prosperity still elude hundreds of thousands of people of African descent. In the final analysis, however, she admits living in the "ghetto of intellectuals," a place offering a myopic view of the black struggle to transcend antiquated colonial notions of blackness. Thus, she abstained from commenting on the experiences of black labor migrants of the postwar period.

This book offers this missing layer of analysis. It demonstrates that throughout the postwar period, African and Caribbean people from the lower classes have been contentious social agents advocating for their rights; it suggests that black migrants developed a protest tradition that still thrives in France of the twenty-first century. Indeed, if in the sixties, young black workers participated in strikes at foyers for migrant workers or at the BUMIDOM takeover, in the early twenty-first century, when the seeds of oppression flourish to punish innocent people like Bouna Traoré and Zyed Benna, they swarm the streets to protest for justice. Many black community organizations still act as refuges for hundreds of Caribbean and African workers, and as they did during the sixties, they continue to lead a crusade for a better quality of (black) life in France. But unlike the sixties, when class and nationality fragmented the African diaspora, the twenty-first century has witnessed a surge in Pan-African activism. CRAN illustrates this phenomenon; the black organization welcomes people of African descent from any nationality, gender, ethnicity, and sexuality; it also embraces French republicanism, and similar to its counterparts of the sixties, it promotes a climate favorable to achieving liberty, equality, and fraternity across racial boundaries.

Still, if it were not for the struggle and protest of African and Caribbean people who migrated to France during the postwar era, black organizations like CRAN, which continuously encourage France to be more inclusive, would not have existed. As this study underscores, it is important to remember that French people changed their perception of black identities because African and Caribbean people demonstrated an excellent work ethic and demanded to be treated with dignity. The connections between the African and Caribbean migrations, colonial relations, protests, and social change in France are evident.

Black migrants from the lower classes, people who supposedly represented a burden to French society, truly enhanced democratic values and promoted social equality in France. In refusing to accept the attributes of colonial identity—being spoken to in *petit nègre*, for example—these African and Caribbean migrants fought against being labeled *indigènes* in the republic. By negotiating "colonial situations," the impact of underprivileged black migrants on the French may surpass the writings of authors like Aimé Césaire and Frantz Fanon, perhaps the most important anticolonial theorists. Equally important, the social movements and protests initiated by these underprivileged black migrants served as a blueprint for the next generation of black people—people born in France or who came to France at a tender age. In other words, by challenging the colonial boundaries that constrained their lives, the black migrants of the postwar period paved the way for the contemporary generation of French "people of color" to develop new political agendas addressing issues of social insertion and cultural diversity. Because Caribbean and African labor migrants from the lower classes struggled to be treated with dignity and to obtain better housing and employment, people of African descent in contemporary France may now feel entitled to the same benefits and opportunities as white French citizens. However, there is still a gap between the professional goals and the achievements of people of African descent in France. France is no black heaven—perhaps purgatory.

Notes

INTRODUCTION

1. See Todd Sheppard, *The Invention of Decolonization: The Algerian War and the Remaking of France* (Ithaca, NY: Cornell University Press, 2006); Kristin Ross, *Fast Cars, Clean Bodies: Decolonization and the Reordering of French Culture* (Cambridge, MA: MIT Press, 1995); Herman Lebovics, *Bringing the Empire Back Home: France in the Global Age* (Durham, NC: Duke University Press, 2004); Dominic Thomas, *Africa and France: Postcolonial Cultures, Migration, and Racism* (Bloomington: University of Indiana Press, 2013); Rémy Bazenguissa-Ganga and Janet MacGaffey, *Congo-Paris: Transnational Traders on the Margins of the Law* (Bloomington: Indiana University Press, 2000); Pap' N'Diaye, *La condition noire: Essai sur une minorité française* (Paris: Calmann-Lévy, 2008); Vincent Geisser, "Republican Integration: Reflections on a Postcolonial Issue, 1961–2006," in *Colonial Culture in France since the Revolution*, ed. Pascal Blanchard, Sandrine Lemaire, Nicolas Bancel, and Dominic Thomas (Bloomington: Indiana University Press, 2014); Daniel Sherman, *French Primitivism and the Ends of Empire, 1945–1975* (Chicago: University of Chicago Press, 2011); and Gregory Mann, "Immigrants and Arguments in France and West Africa," *Comparative Studies in Society and History* 45, no. 2 (2003): 362–85. Adlai Murdoch's comparative study of Caribbean migrants in England and France also makes an important contribution to understanding how migrants from the former colonies and their descendants are generating new questions about the meaning of national identity and culture in contemporary Europe. His diasporic methodological framework reverberates throughout my work. See Adlai Murdoch, *Creolizing the Metropole: Migrant Caribbean Identities in Literature and Film* (Bloomington: University of Indiana Press, 2012).

2. Jean Fourastié, the scholar who coined the term, frames the *Trente Glorieuses* as a period embodying France's transition from an industrial society to a full-fledged consumer society

Notes

whereby the vast majority of French citizens began to enjoy disposable income allowing them to purchase necessary or unnecessary items. See Jean Fourastié, *Les Trente Glorieuses* (Paris: Fayard, 1979). Readers seeking to have a general knowledge of French history may consult Gordon Wright, *France in Modern Times* (Palo Alto, CA: Stanford University Press, 1995).

3. This study does not focus on Maghrebians, people of North African descent. The study focuses on subjects who throughout centuries of interaction with France have been racialized as black. Additionally, the Algerian War generated a unique social condition for Maghrebians in postwar France that must be examined on its own terms.

4. The last chapter, which aims to demonstrate how changes occur over time, is the only exception. For recent collaborative studies on black France, see Trica Keaton, T. Denean Sharpley-Whiting, and Tyler Stovall, eds., *Black France/France Noire: The History and Politics of Blackness* (Durham, NC: Duke University Press, 2012); Charles Tshimanga, Didier Gondola, and Peter Bloom, eds., *Frenchness and the African Diaspora: Identity and Uprising in Contemporary France* (Bloomington: Indiana University Press, 2009); Pascal Blanchard, Sandrine Lemaire, Nicolas Bancel, and Dominic Thomas, eds., *Colonial Culture in France since the Revolution* (Bloomington: Indiana University Press, 2014).

5. See Ramon Grosfoguel, "Decolonizing Post-Colonial Studies and Paradigms of Political Economy: Transmodernity, Decolonial Thinking, and Global Coloniality," TRANSMODERNITY: *Journal of Peripheral Cultural Production of the Luso-Hispanic World* 1, no. 1 (2011): 14. Grosfoguel's scholarship is in conversation with a number of scholars who examine the legacy of European colonialism in relation to social stratification at the global level. Anibal Quijano and Walter Mignolo figure prominently in his work. For examples, see Anibal Quijano and Michel Ennis, "Coloniality of Power, Eurocentrism, and Latin America," *Nepantla: Views from South* 1, no. 3 (2000): 533–80; and Walter Mignolo, *Local Histories/Global Designs: Coloniality, Subaltern Knowledges, and Border Thinking* (Princeton, NJ: Princeton University Press, 2000).

6. French historian René Colin-Noguès and Oumar Dia attempted to shed light on the sub-Saharan African migration by writing an autobiographical narrative focusing on Mr. Dia's experience from Africa to Paris. Oumar Dia and Renée Colin-Noguès, *Yakaré: L'autobiographie d'Oumar* (Paris: Maspéro, 1982).

7. Interview with Oumar Dia, Paris, June 2004.

8. Ibid.

9. Oumar Dia and Renée Colin-Noguès, *Yakaré: L'autobiographie d'Oumar*, 142.

10. Ibid.

11. Interview with Mrs. Ansel, Paris, March 2004.

12. The MRAP was created in 1949 to prevent France from being recontaminated by Nazism.

13. Interview with Georges Lassare Michalon, Paris, May 2004. One should note that Erik Bleich briefly mentions the existence of such problems in the French capital; see Erik Bleich, *Race Politics in Britain and France: Ideas and Policymaking since the 1960s* (Cambridge: Cambridge University Press, 2003).

14. Archives de la Préfecture de Police, Paris, Box Gabr 47, "Les manifestations actuelles du racisme dans la région parisienne," July 1967, 36.

15. Jennifer Boittin, *Colonial Metropolis: The Urban Grounds of Anti-Imperialism and Feminism in Interwar Paris* (Lincoln: University of Nebraska Press, 2010).

16. One should note the difference between Caribbean and African people from the "lower

classes." During the sixties, the vast majority of Caribbean people migrating to France were mostly young, uneducated labor migrants, people who in their own countries belonged to the lower classes. By contrast, although the French and the African bourgeoisie considered African labor migrants to be from the lower classes, anthropologists and historians paint a more nuanced picture of class and caste in West African societies. Many African labor migrants enjoyed a higher social status in their own communities, one that, unfortunately, was not recognized in France. Chapter 2 discusses this phenomenon in greater detail.

17. Michel Foucault, "The Subject and Power," *Critical Inquiry* 8, no. 4 (1982): 788.
18. Fanon discusses colonial relations quite extensively in *The Wretched of the Earth* (1961) and *Black Skin, White Masks* (1952).
19. The negritude movement flourished in the late twenties when students from the French Caribbean and sub-Saharan Africa discovered the writers of the Harlem Renaissance and began praising their black identities while denouncing the very premise of the French civilizing mission, which sought to change African and Caribbean people into French people. Important figures of the negritude era include Jeanne and Paulette Nardal, Léopold Senghor, Aimé Césaire, and Léon Damas. There are dozens of texts examining negritude, but one of the dominant negritude experts remains Abiola Irele; see Abiola Irele, *The Negritude Moment: Explorations in Francophone African and Caribbean Literature and Thought* (Trenton, NJ: Africa World Press, 2011).
20. Sartre, a French intellectual invested in improving the condition of the "black world," was widely read. However, most people read his most important works, specifically *L'existentialisme est un humanisme* (1946) and *Critique de la raison dialectique* (1955).
21. In the late eighties, Pierre André Taguieff played an important role in creating an intellectual climate for having discussions about anti-black racism in French society. See Pierre André Taguieff, *La force du préjugé: Essai sur le racisme et ses doubles* (Paris: La Découverte, 1988).
22. For examples, see Brent Hayes Edwards, *The Practice of Diaspora: Literature, Translation, and the Rise of Black Internationalism* (Cambridge, MA: Harvard University Press, 2003); T. Denean Sharpley-Whiting, *Negritude Women* (Minneapolis: University of Minnesota Press, 2002); and Tyler Stovall, *Paris Noir: African Americans in the City of Light* (Boston: Houghton Mifflin, 1996).
23. See Jennifer Boittin, *Colonial Metropolis: The Urban Grounds of Anti-Imperialism and Feminism in Interwar Paris* (Lincoln: University of Nebraska Press, 2010); and Philippe Dewitte, *Les mouvements nègres en France, 1919–1939* (Paris: L'Harmattan, 1985).
24. For examples, see Jemima Pierre, *The Predicament of Blackness: Postcolonial Ghana and the Politics of Race* (Chicago: University of Chicago Press, 2013); Paul Gilroy, The Black Atlantic: Modernity and Double Consciousness (New York: Verso, 1993); and the following edited volume, which offers analysis of identity construction and diasporic connection from both a contemporary and historical perspective: Jean Muteba Rahier, Percy C. Hintzen, and Felipe Smith, eds., *Global Circuits of Blackness: Interrogating the African Diaspora* (Urbana: University of Illinois Press, 2010).
25. Many scholars of African diaspora studies, Africana studies, Africology, or Pan-African studies often explore and emphasize the common struggles of people of African descent. This study of Caribbean and African people in postwar France, however, offers a more nuanced narrative. It demonstrates that racial unity does not always motivate the various political and social struggles of people of African descent. In many ways, the study highlights the unique characteristics of black France.

26. See Hayes Edwards, *The Practice of Diaspora*; Sharpley-Whiting, *Negritude Women*; Stovall, *Paris Noir*; Boittin, *Colonial Metropolis*; and Dewitte, *Les mouvements nègres en France, 1919-1939*.

27. For a few examples, see Michel Giraud, "The Antillese in France: Trends and Prospects," *Ethnic and Racial Studies* 27, no. 4 (2004): 622-40; Rahsaan Maxwell, *Ethnic Minority Migrants in Britain and France: Integration Trade-offs* (New York: Cambridge University Press, 2012); Tshimanga, Gondola, and Bloom, eds., *Frenchness and the African Diaspora*; Blanchard, Lemaire, Bancel, and Thomas, eds., *Colonial Culture in France since the Revolution*.

28. See Kim Butler, "Defining Diaspora, Refining a Discourse," *Diaspora: A Journal of Transnational Studies* 10, no. 2 (2001): 209. For another relevant study, see Tiffany Ruby Patterson and Robin D. G. Kelley, "Unfinished Migrations: Reflections on the African Diaspora and the Making of the Modern World," *African Studies Review* 43, no. 1 (2000): 11-45.

29. For an interesting study of the black migration to England in the postwar period, see Winston James and Clive Harris, eds., *Inside Babylon: The Caribbean Diaspora in Britain* (London: Verso, 1993).

30. According to the Ministry of the Interior, between 1946 and 1962, the number of Africans in Paris fluctuated between 13,000 and 15,000. According to the Institut National de la Statistique et des Etudes Economiques (INSEE), in 1954 there were 37,591 Caribbean migrants in France.

31. The French census (INSEE) notes that in 1975 there were 81,850 African and 121,740 French Caribbean migrants in France. At least 80 percent of the black migrants lived in the Parisian region. Many people estimate that in 2010 there were at least 3 million blacks in France, with the majority of them living in the Parisian region. See John Tagliabue, "French Blacks Skeptical of Race Neutrality," *New York Times*, March 21, 2005. According to INSEE, in January 2009, 2,215,197 people lived in the twenty arrondissements of Paris, and the total population of the Parisian region (the arrondissements and the suburbs) was 11,746,000.

32. See the *New York Times*, June 17, 2008; and Allison Blakely, "The Emergence of Afro-Europe: A Preliminary Sketch," in *Black Europe in the African Diaspora*, ed. Darlene Clark Hine, Trica Danielle Keaton, and Stephen Small (Chicago: University of Illinois Press, 2009).

CHAPTER 1. BLACK INTERNATIONALISM AND STUDENT ACTIVISM IN PARIS OF THE FIFTIES

1. Although her study begins in the fifties, Odile Cazenave discusses this phenomenon. See Odile Cazenave, *Afrique sur Seine: A New Generation of African Writers in Paris* (Lanham, MA: Lexington Books, 2005).

2. Some of these journals include *Les Continents* (1924-1926), *Le Paria* (1926), *Le Libéré* (1923-1925), *La Dépêche Africaine* (1928-1932), *La Revue du Monde Noir* (1931-1932), and *Le Cri des Nègres* (1931-1936), which seems to have circulated longer than its counterparts.

3. René Maran, a black French writer who lived in France during the war, corresponded with Mercer Cook, an African American professor at Howard University. In his letters, Maran wrote extensively about the ways in which the occupation affected black people in Paris. He mentioned that blacks, including African American men, had been interned. See a letter to Mercer Cook dated October 17, 1948, at the Moorland-Spingarn Research Center, Howard

University, in Will Mercer Cook Papers, Series C, Box 157-2, folder 21. For a good text on René Maran, see Fémi Ojo-Adé, René Maran, the Black Frenchman: A Bio-Critical Study (Washington, DC: Three Continents Press, 1984).

4. V. Y. Mudimbe, ed., *The Surreptitious Speech: Présence Africaine and the Politics of Otherness, 1947-1987* (Chicago: University of Chicago Press, 1992).

5. Christopher Miller and Tracy Sharpley-Whiting examine the views expressed in these journals in great detail. Christopher Miller, *Nationalists and Nomads: Essays on Francophone African Literature and Culture* (Chicago: University of Chicago Press, 1998); and Tracy Sharpley-Whiting, *Negritude Women* (Minneapolis: University of Minnesota Press, 2002).

6. *Présence Africaine: Les étudiants noirs parlent* 14 (1953); and David Macey, *Frantz Fanon: A Biography* (New York: Picador, 2000).

7. Bennetta Jules-Rosette, "Conjugating Cultural Realities: Présence Africaine," in *The Surreptitious Speech: Présence Africaine and the Politics of Otherness, 1947-1987*, ed. V. Y. Mudimbe (Chicago: University of Chicago Press, 1992), 11-42.

8. Bernard Mouralis, "Présence Africaine: Geography of an Ideology," in *The Surreptitious Speech: Présence Africaine and the Politics of Otherness, 1947-1987*, ed. V. Y. Mudimbe (Chicago: University of Chicago Press, 1992), 5.

9. Salah Hassan's article offers an amazing intellectual history of the journal from its inception in 1947 to the beginning of the sixties. He argues that initially, seeking legitimization from France's intellectual community, Diop pursued the patronage of notorious French intellectuals such as Jean-Paul Sartre, André Gide, and Albert Camus, who in many ways shared his humanist vision. According to Hassan, the journal became more radical and Pan-African after 1953, when it featured a special issue on black students. In other words, he contends that the students' "obsession with decolonization radicalized *Presence Africaine*." See Salah Hassan, "Inaugural Issues: The Cultural Politics of the Early 'Présence Africaine,' 1947-55," *Research in African Literatures* 30, no. 2 (1999): 194-221.

10. Jacques Howlett, "Présence Africaine, 1947-1958," *Journal of Negro History* 43, no. 2 (1958): 142.

11. Ibid.

12. Howlett, "Présence Africaine, 1947-1958," 147.

13. Léopold Senghor would crystallize this train of thought with his controversial statement "Emotion is negro as reason is Hellenic." See Léopold Senghor, *Liberté, negritude et humanisme* (Paris: Seuil, 1964).

14. Howlett, "Présence Africaine, 1947-1958," 147.

15. Niilo Kaupi, *French Intellectual Nobility: Institutional and Symbolic Transformations in the Post-Sartrian Era* (Albany, NY: SUNY Press, 1996).

16. Interview with Maryse Condé, New York, March 2010.

17. Nicol Davidson, "Alioune Diop and the African Renaissance," *African Affairs* 78, no. 310 (1979): 8.

18. *Le Monde*, September 20, 1956; and *L'Humanité*, September 19, 1956.

19. For an amazing study on Dunham's performances as intellectual history, see Véve Clark and Sara Johnson, *Kaiso! Writings by and about Katherine Dunham* (Madison: University of Wisconsin Press, 2006).

20. Davidson, "Alioune Diop and the African Renaissance," 9.
21. Hassan, "Inaugural Issues," 194-221.
22. *Alizé*, December 1965; and Michel Sot, *Etudiants africains en France, 1951-2001* (Paris: Karthala, 2002). Robert Delerm notes that the number of African students was growing rapidly; by 1962 they numbered 12,000. See Robert Delerm, "Population noire en France," *Population* 3 (July 1964).
23. For example, see Ama Ata Aidoo, *Our Sister Killjoy* (London: Longman, 1977); and Gisèle Pineau, *L'exil selon Julia* (Paris: France Loisirs, 1996).
24. Interview with Maryse Condé, New York, March 2010.
25. Ibid.
26. Ibid.
27. See the AMS quarterly newsletter *Trait d'Union: Bulletin de l'Association des Etudiants de la Martinique*, which from its creation in 1947 to the early fifties covers local Martinican news, and advertises and promotes social activities for Caribbean students in Paris.
28. See Richard D. E. Burton, *La famille coloniale: La Martinique et la mère patrie, 1789-1992* (Paris: L'Harmattan, 1994).
29. Interview with Georges Lassare Michalon, Paris, May 2004.
30. *Trait d'Union: Bulletin de l'Association des Etudiants de la Martinique*, May 1957.
31. See Nicolas Armand, *Histoire de la Martinique*, vol. 1, *Des Arawaks à 1848* (Paris: L'Harmattan, 1996).
32. See Oruno Lara, *De l'oubli à l'histoire: Espace et identité Caraïbes* (Paris: Maisonneuve et Larose, 1998); Laurent Dubois, *A Colony of Citizens: Revolution and Slave Emancipation in the French Caribbean, 1787-1804* (Chapel Hill: University of North Carolina Press, 2004); and Edouard Glissant, *Caribbean Discourse* (Charlottesville: University of Virginia Press, 1989).
33. *Trait d'Union: Bulletin de l'Association des Etudiants de la Martinique*, May 1957.
34. *Alizé*, December 1965.
35. Quoted from Julien Valère Loza, *Les étudiants martiniquais en France: Histoire de leur organisation et de leurs luttes* (Martinique: Editions 2M, 2003), 64.
36. *Présence Africaine: Les étudiants noirs parlent* 14 (1953).
37. Ibid.
38. Many authors have taken on the task of writing about primitivism in France during the twenties and thirties. Essentially, they demonstrate that French artists and novelists reduced African cultures and societies to being "primitive," yet simultaneously the artists hinted that Europe, which had become too advanced and industrialized, could benefit from the "primitive" ways of African people. Africans, so to speak, could help Europeans loosen up. For interesting monographs on the subject, see Carole Sweeney, *From Fetish to Subject: Race, Modernism, and Primitivism, 1919-1935* (New York: Greenwood Publishing, 2004); Petrine Archer-Straw, *Negrophilia: Avant-Garde Paris and Black Culture in the 1920s* (London: Thames and Hudson, 2000); Dana Hale, *Races on Display: French Representations of Colonized Peoples, 1886-1940* (Bloomington: Indiana University Press, 2008). For a more theoretical and general overview, see Tzvetan Todorov, *On Human Diversity: Nationalism, Racism, and Exoticism in French Thought* (Cambridge, MA: Harvard University Press, 1993).
39. *Présence Africaine: Les étudiants noirs parlent* 14 (1953): 18.

40. See "Jeunes Africains à Paris," a show about African students in Paris that aired on national TV on September 12, 1963. The show was an episode of *L'avenir est a vous*, a television series focusing on French youth.
41. Albert Franklin, "Le paternalisme contre l'étudiant africain," in *Présence Africaine: Les étudiants noirs parlent* 14 (1953).
42. Ibid., 75.
43. Amady Aly Dieng, *Les grands combats de la FEANF* (Paris: L'Harmattan, 2009).
44. Political activism in the foyers of students from the colonies also occurred during the twenties. In many ways, the foyers for Indochinese students were the lungs of their anticolonial movement. See Amady Aly Dieng, *Les premiers pas de la Fédération des étudiants d'Afrique noire en France (FEANF), 1950-1955: De l'Union française à Bandoung* (Paris: L'Harmattan, 2003).
45. Hakim Adi and Marika Sherwood, *Pan-African History: Political Figures from Africa and the Diaspora since 1787* (New York: Routledge, 2003).
46. See Elikia M'Bokolo, *Afrique noire: Histoire et civilisations du XIXe siècle à nos jours* (Paris: Hatier, 1992); and Gabriel Lisette, *Le combat du Rassemblement Démocratique Africain* (Paris: Présence Africaine, 1983).
47. Sékou Traoré, *Les intellectuels africains face au marxisme* (Paris: L'Harmattan, 1983).
48. Sékou Traoré, *La Fédération des étudiants d'Afrique noire en France* (Paris: L'Harmattan, 1985).
49. Some of the most important scholars offering an analysis of FEANF's social and political activism include Sékou Traoré, *La Fédération des étudiants d'Afrique noire en France* (Paris: L'Harmattan, 1985); Amady Aly Dieng, *Les premiers pas de la Fédération des étudiants d'Afrique noire en France (FEANF), 1950-1955: De l'Union française à Bandoung* (Paris: L'Harmattan, 2003); Fabienne Guimont, *Les étudiants africains en France, 1950-1965* (Paris: L'Harmattan, 1998); and Charles Diané, *Les grandes heures de la F.E.A.N.F.* (Paris: Editions Chaka, 1990).
50. Dieng, *Les grands combats de la FEANF*.
51. Ibid.
52. Fédération des étudiants d'Afrique noire en France, *Le sang de Badoung* (Paris: Présence Africaine, 1958).
53. Dieng, *Les grands combats de la FEANF*.
54. Schofield Coryell, "Africa in Paris," *Africa Today* 8, no. 9 (1961): 12.
55. The police documented this event. See "Afrique noire déplacement de personnes," Archives de la Préfecture de Paris, Box GaA9.
56. See Jean-Pierre N'Diaye, *Enquête sur les étudiants noirs en France* (Paris: Editions Réalités Africaines, 1962); and Diané, *Les grandes heures de la FEANF*.
57. See Stephen Castle and Mark Miller, *The Age of Migration* (London: Macmillan Press, 1998); Douglas Massey, *Worlds in Motion: Understanding International Migration at the End of the Millennium* (Oxford: Clarendon Press, 1998).

CHAPTER 2. AFRICAN MIGRATION TO PARIS OF THE SIXTIES

1. Jacques Marseille, "Les images de l'Afrique en France (des années 1880 aux années 1930)," *Canadian Journal of African Studies* 22, no. 1 (1988): 121.
2. Ibid.
3. See Teresa Hayter, "French Aid to Africa—Its Scope and Achievements," *International Affairs* 41, no. 2 (1965): 236–51.
4. One should note that African social structures coexisted alongside the French colonial social structure. For a discussion of social hierarchy and migration in West African communities, see François Menchuelle, *Willing Migrants: Soninke Labor Diasporas, 1848-1960* (Athens: Ohio University Press, 1997).
5. Patrick Weil, *La France et ses étrangers: L'aventure d'une politique de l'immigration, 1938-1991* (Paris: Calmann-Lévy, 1991).
6. Ibid.
7. "Main d'œuvre immigrée," Archives de la Confédération Générale du Travail, Box Immigrés Travailleurs en France, n.d., Paris.
8. Avis et Rapports du Conseil Economique et Social, "Problèmes posés par l'immigration des travailleurs Africains en France," *Journal Officiel de la République Française*, July 24, 1964.
9. Ousmane Sembène, *Black Docker*, trans. Ros Schwartz (London: Heinemann Educational Books, 1987), 41–42.
10. Hayter, "French Aid to Africa—Its Scope and Achievements," 236–51; Frederick Cooper, "From Imperial Inclusion to Republican Exclusion? France's Ambiguous Postwar Trajectory," in *Frenchness and the African Diaspora: Identity and Uprising in Contemporary France*, ed. Charles Tshimanga, Didier Gondola, and Peter Bloom (Bloomington: Indiana University Press, 2009).
11. "Main d'œuvre étrangère: Réglementation générale, statistiques," Direction de la Population et des Migrations, Centre des Archives Contemporaines, Fontainebleau, Box 810201, art. 3.
12. Following Alfred Sauvy and Michel Debré's wishes, ONI had set up satellite offices in Spain, Portugal, Italy, and Morocco, but in a glaring fashion, it shunned the former sub-Saharan African colonies, forcing Africans seeking job opportunities in France to migrate, for lack of a better term, "illegally."
13. Jean Fourastié, *Les Trente Glorieuses* (Paris: Fayard, 1979).
14. Although young males constituted the majority of the migrants, many African women also found their way to Paris, albeit under different circumstances. One should also note that many of these migrants were from the Soninke ethnic group. Timera Mahamet completed an important anthropological study on the Soninke migration, focusing on the role of Islam in their community and their professional experiences in France. See Timera Mahamet, *Les Soninké en France: D'une histoire à l'autre* (Paris Katharla, 1996).
15. Ministry of the Interior, Direction de la Population et des Migrations, Centre des Archives Contemporaines, Fontainebleau, Box 19760133, art. 133.
16. For the Portuguese migration, see Maria do Ceu Cunha, *Portugais de France: Essai sur une dynamique de double appartenance* (Paris: L'Harmattan, 1988); and Yvan Gastaut, "Les bidonvilles, lieux d'exclusion et de marginalité en France durant les Trente Glorieuses," *Cahiers de la Méditerranée* 69 (May 2006).

17. Claude Arnaud, Jean Claude Bringuiernon, and Jean-Luc Leridon, *Ouvriers noirs de Paris* (Collection le Monde en 40 Minutes, 1962)
18. "Main d'œuvre étrangère: Réglementation générale, statistiques," Direction de la Population et des Migrations, Centre des Archives Contemporaines, Fontainebleau, Box 810201, art. 3 and 10–12.
19. For France's open-door policy regarding the postwar Portuguese migrants, see Jorge Rodriguez-Ruivo, *Portugais et population d'origine portugaise en France* (Paris: L'Harmattan, 2001).
20. Victor Pereira, "L'Etat portugais et les Portugais en France de 1958 à 1974," *Lusotopie* 2 (2002): 13.
21. Avis et Rapports du Conseil Economique et Social, "Problèmes posés par l'immigration des travailleurs Africains en France," *Journal Officiel de la République Française*, July 24, 1964.
22. Roger-Henri Guerrand, *Hygiène* (Paris: Editions de la Villette, 2001).
23. Fabrice Virgili, *Shorn Women: Gender and Punishment in Liberation France* (New York: Berg Publishers, 2002).
24. See Kristin Ross, "Starting Afresh: Hygiene and Modernization in Postwar France," *October* 67 (Winter 1994): 27.
25. See Maghan Keita, *A Political Economy of Healthcare in Senegal* (Leiden, Netherlands: Brill, 2007); and Rita Headrick, *Colonialism, Health, and Illness in French Equatorial Africa, 1885–1935* (Atlanta: African Studies Association Press, 1994).
26. For example, see "Rapport du Professeur Brocard," *Revue de Tuberculose et de Pneumologie*, October 9, 1962; and the special issue of the journal *Hommes et Migrations*, which republished many articles on the health of Africans in Paris, *Hommes et Migrations: Approche des problèmes de la migration noire en France* (Paris: Esna, 1965).
27. See William Schneider, *Quality and Quantity: The Quest for Biological Regeneration in Twentieth-Century France* (Cambridge: Cambridge University Press, 1990).
28. Lucien Petit, *Les travailleurs noirs dans la région parisienne* (Paris: Préfecture de la Seine, 1964).
29. Ibid., 22.
30. Rita Headrick observes that during the colonial period, the French also viewed African bodies as weaker than French bodies. She claims they believed in improving public health in Africa to increase the population's longevity, yet they reluctantly invested in the public health sector. Simultaneously, in what may have been a paradoxical belief, the French believed the African climate was actually detrimental to their bodies. See Headrick, *Colonialism, Health, and Illness in French Equatorial Africa, 1885–1935*.
31. Petit, *Les travailleurs noirs dans la région parisienne*, 22.
32. Ibid., 23.
33. *Le Monde*, March 28, 1963.
34. Avis et Rapports du Conseil Economique et Social, "Problèmes posés par l'immigration des travailleurs Africains en France," *Journal Officiel de la République Française*, July 24, 1964, 563.
35. M. Jourdan, "Conférence sur l'état sanitaire chez les travailleurs originaires d'Afrique Noire" (Paris: Préfecture de la Seine, 1965), 68.
36. Prefecture de la Seine, "Enquête sur les travailleurs africains," Centre des Archives Contemporaines, Fontainebleau, Box 19780262, art. 11.

37. Direction Générale de la Santé Publique, "Travailleurs Noirs: Carnet de santé," Centre des Archives Contemporaines, Fontainebleau, Box 19780262, art. 11.
38. Jourdan, "Conférence sur l'état sanitaire chez les travailleurs originaires d'Afrique Noire," 69.
39. The idea that certain African ethnic groups had evolved more slowly than others dates from the Enlightenment period, when French philosophers and scientists invented hierarchies of African cultures and peoples. Jacques Carlos, "From Savages and Barbarians to Primitives: Africa, Social Typologies, and History in Eighteenth-Century French Philosophy," *History and Theory* 36, no. 2 (May 1997).
40. Ibid., 69.
41. Amelia Lyons also writes about a civilizing mission at home. She demonstrates that from the late forties to the end of the Algerian War, French officials offered "special" social services to Algerian immigrants to bolster France's image as a leader in human rights and teach Algerians about French principles of liberty and equality. She cleverly argues that French officials sought to "remake" Algerians, hoping that this would facilitate their insertion into the fabric of French society. See Amelia Lyons, *The Civilizing Mission in the Metropole: Algerian Families and the French Welfare State during Decolonization* (Palo Alto, CA: Stanford University Press, 2013).
42. See *La Croix*, December 12, 1962; *La Croix*, December 14, 1962; *Le Monde*, December 31, 1962; *Le Monde*, February 21, 1963; *Le Monde*, March 28, 1963; *Le Figaro*, April 4, 1963; *Echos*, July 24, 1963; *La France Catholique*, August 16, 1963; *Echos*, January 7, 1964; *Liberation*, March 26, 1964; *Le Monde*, June 24, 1964; and *L'Humanité*, July 3, 1964. Here I list only a few articles. However, one should note that dozens of other articles describing the poor condition of African people in Paris were published between 1964 and 1970.
43. The following is a short list of some of the articles about the African migration during the first four years after the independence of sub-Saharan countries: "Africains en métropole," *Le Figaro*, February 22, 1963; "Le professeur Lépine réclame un contrôle sanitaire très stricte des Africains venant travailler en France," *Le Monde*, March 28, 1963; "3,000 travailleurs africains s'entassent dans 65 hôtels de la région parisienne," *Aurore*, April 4, 1963; "40,000 noirs vivent en France, la plupart dans des conditions épouvantables," *Echos*, July 4, 1963; "Les travailleurs noirs en France: Un sous-prolétariat pitoyable et déraciné," *Le Figaro Littéraire*, November 2, 1963; "Les négriers des bidonvilles," *L'Express*, October 26, 1964; and "A Montreuil, Mamadou le Malien a dit: "Ce sont nos frères," *L'Humanité*, November 23, 1964.
44. *Le Monde*, February 21, 1963.
45. *La Croix*, December 14, 1962.
46. *Le Figaro*, December 23, 1963.
47. *Le Figaro*, December 10, 1963.
48. *La Croix*, December 14, 1962.
49. *L'Humanité*, December 4, 1964.
50. *L'Humanité*, November 23, 1964.
51. AFTAM has evolved over time. In the twenty-first century, this organization is much different than when it first saw light. To avoid any confusion, I am reiterating that this manuscript only examines the relationship that AFTAM maintained with African migrants during its first decade of existence.
52. Association pour la Formation Technique de Base des Africains et Malgaches, "Travailleurs Africains en France," Pièce 9433, Bibliothèque de Documentation Internationale

53. In 2010, as a nonagenarian, Hessel published *Indignez-Vous! (Time for Outrage!)*, a pamphlet that sold more than three million copies across the globe. In his pamphlet, Hessel, a man of Jewish ancestry, criticized the power of the rich over the media, the shrinking social safety net, and Israel's treatment of Palestinians. See Bruce Weber, "Stéphane Hessel, Author and Activist, Dies at 95," *New York Times*, February 27, 2013.
54. Association pour la Formation Technique de Base des Africains et Malgaches, "Travailleurs Africains en France," Pièce 9433, Bibliothèque de Documentation Internationale Contemporaine, Nanterre.
55. Ibid.
56. Roland Lovatt, Christine Whitehead, and Claire Levy-Vroelant add that "the term *foyer* is rarely used on its own. Instead it is coupled with a word describing the relevant group to which it caters, such as migrant workers, children in need of protection, ex-offenders, and lone mothers. The designation of the type of *foyer* is determined by the attributes of the group that lives there." See Roland Lovatt, Christine Whitehead, and Claire Levy-Vroelant, "Foyers in the UK and France—Comparisons and Contrasts," *European Journal of Housing Policy* 6, no. 12 (August 2006): 151–66.
57. One should note that many Africans, including l'Union Générale des Travailleurs Sénégalais en France (UGTSF), the largest African organization in Paris, welcomed the new foyers as a protection against predatory French landlords. See Union Générale des Travailleurs Sénégalais en France, *Le livre des travailleurs Africains en France* (Paris: Editions François Maspéro, 1970).
58. Association pour la Formation Technique de Base des Africains et Malgaches, "Travailleurs Africains en France," Pièce 9433, Bibliothèque de Documentation Internationale Contemporaine, Nanterre.
59. See "Ressortissants Africains en France," Centre National des Archives Contemporaines, Fontainebleau, Box 1981020, art. 5.
60. Ibid.
61. See Simone Bière, "Les problèmes de l'étranger malade," Centre National des Archives Contemporaines, Fontainebleau, Box 19810201, art. 4.
62. Ibid.
63. The following scholars admit the oil shock of 1973 precipitated more rigid anti-African immigration policies. See Alec Hargreaves, *Multi-ethnic France: Immigration, Politics, Culture, and Society* (New York: Routledge, 2007); Martin Schain, *The Politics of Migration in France, Britain, and the United States: A Comparative Study* (New York: Palgrave Macmillan, 2008); Jane Freidman and Carrie Tarr, eds., *Women, Immigration, and Identity in France* (New York: Berg, 2000); and Pap N'Diaye, *La condition noire: Essai sur une minorité française* (Paris: Calmann-Lévy, 2008).

CHAPTER 3. FRENCH DOCUMENTARIES AND THE REPRESENTATION OF AFRICAN EXPERIENCES

1. Michel Lagié, "La critique de la télévision dans la presse quotidienne de province," *Cahier d'études de radio-télévision*, December 20, 1958, in *La télévision des Trente Glorieuses: Culture et*

Politique, ed. Evelyne Cohen and Marie-Françoise Lévy (Paris: CNRS Editions, 2007).

2. See Richard Kuisel, *Seducing the French: The Dilemma of Americanization* (Berkeley: University of California Press, 1993).

3. See Jean-Noel Jeanneney and Monique Sauvage, *Télévision, nouvelle mémoire: Les magazines de grands reportages, 1959-1968* (Paris: Editions du Seuil, 1982).

4. Ibid., 51-52.

5. Ibid., 160-61.

6. For the most important documentaries on African migrants in Paris of the sixties, see Jean Schmidt, *L'Afrique des banlieues* (ORTF, 1967), Institut National de l'Audiovisuel, BNF, Paris; Jacques Krier, *Ouvriers noirs de Paris*, série 5 Colonnes à la une (ORTF, 1964), Institut National de l'Audiovisuel, BNF, Paris; Jean-Luc Léridon, *Travailleurs Africains* (ORTF, 1962), Institut National de l'Audiovisuel, BNF, Paris; Jean Schmidt, *Paris des négritudes* (1970), Institut National de l'Audiovisuel, BNF, Paris; Max Zelenka, *Ibrahima* (Les Ecrans Modernes, 1966), Forum des Images, Paris; *Un Malien d'Ivry* (Série Panorama de Jean Mailland, 1970). *Jeunes Africains à Paris*, a show about African students in Paris, also aired on national TV on September 12, 1963. The show was an episode of *L'avenir est a vous*, a television series focusing on French youth. See *Jeunes Africains à Paris* (ORTF, 1963), Institut National de l'Audiovisuel, BNF, Paris.

7. Jacques Krier, *Ouvriers noirs de Paris*, série 5 Colonnes à la une (ORTF, 1964), Institut National de l'Audiovisuel, BNF, Paris.

8. See Brett Berliner, *Ambivalent Desire: The Exotic Black Other in Jazz-Age France* (Amherst: University of Massachusetts Press, 2002); and Elizabeth Ezra, *The Colonial Unconscious: Race and Culture in Interwar France* (Ithaca, NY: Cornell University Press, 1992).

9. Any deviation from that standard was chastised as non-masculine, and sometimes homosexual. See Christopher Forth and Bertrand Taithe, *French Masculinities: Histories, Politics, and Culture* (Hampshire, England: Macmillan, 2007).

10. Interview with Mr. Gissoko, Paris, April 2004.

11. Interview with Mr. Joachim and Mrs. Diop, Paris, April 2004.

12. *Jeunes Africains à Paris* (ORTF, September 12, 1963), Institut National de l'Audiovisuel, BNF, Paris.

13. See Ministère de la Coopération, *Dix réponses sur l'Afrique: Opinions sur la coopération entre l'Afrique et la France* (Paris, 1963).

14. The French had a different reaction towards relationships involving French Caribbean men and white women. One should also note that French law and colonial administrators in Africa strongly discouraged interracial unions during the colonial period. See Owen White, *Children of the French Empire: Miscegenation and Colonial Society in French West Africa, 1895-1960* (New York: Oxford University Press, 1999).

15. Ministère de la Coopération, *Dix réponses sur l'Afrique*.

16. Interview with Mr. Lafon, Paris, April 2004.

17. See Fédération des Etudiants d'Afrique Noire en France, *Bulletin d'Activité*, no. 1 (1968).

18. Interview with Mr. Lafon, Paris, April 2004.

19. Ousmane Sembène, *Black Girl* (Senegal, 1966).

20. See "Mouvement des populations étrangères," Centre National des Archives Contemporaines,

Fontainebleau, Box 19810201.

21. Fieldwork interviews, Paris, April 2004.
22. Her husband, who was setting up a retirement home in Senegal, died tragically on *Le Joola*, the Senegalese ferry that capsized in 2002, claiming hundreds of lives.
23. Interview with Mrs. Dacosta, Paris, March 2004.
24. Ibid.
25. Ibid.
26. Interview with Maryse Condé, New York, March 2010.
27. See Gwendolyn Mickell, *African Feminism: The Politics of Survival in Sub-Saharan Africa* (Philadelphia: University of Pennsylvania Press, 1997).
28. Ibid.
29. For transnational perspectives on this phenomenon, see the following edited volumes: Filomina Steady, *The Black Woman Cross-Culturally* (Cambridge, MA: Schenkman, 1981); Rosalyn Terborg-Penn and Andrea Benton Rushing, eds., *Women in Africa and the African Diaspora: A Reader* (Cambridge, MA: Harvard University Press, 1996); Heidi Mirza, ed., *Black British Feminism: A Reader* (London: Routledge, 1997).
30. Interview with Mrs. Dacosta, Paris, March 2004.
31. James Genova, *Colonial Ambivalence, Cultural Authenticity, and the Limitations of Mimicry in French-Ruled West Africa, 1914–1956* (New York: Peter Lang, 2004), 22.
32. Thus far, scholars have mostly examined the hegemonic role of French in the literary world, as the publishing landscape often dictates that writers from countries whose primary national language is not French craft their novels and short stories in French. See Gabrielle Parker, "'Francophonie' and 'Universalité': Evolution of Two Notions Conjoined," in *Francophone Postcolonial Studies*, ed. Charles Foredeck and David Murphy (London: Arnold, 2003); Dany Bebel-Gisler, *La langue créole, force jugulée: Etude socio-linguistique des rapports de force entre le créole et le français aux Antilles* (Paris: L'Harmattan, 1976); Christopher Miller, *Theories of Africans: Francophone Literature and Anthropology in Africa* (Chicago: University of Chicago Press, 1993); and Shireen Lewis, *Race, Culture, and Identity: Francophone West African and Caribbean Literature and Theory from Négritude to Créolité* (Lanham, MD: Lexington Books, 2006). Exceptionally, Gisèle Pineau touches on the theme of language and alienation in her novel *L'exil selon Julia* (Paris: Livre de Poche, 2000).
33. Fanon notes that certain French people regularly spoke *petit nègre* to Africans and French Caribbean people, even though the latter possessed French citizenship. See Frantz Fanon, *Black Skin, White Masks* (New York: Grove Press, 1967).
34. Fanon gives a brief example of *petit nègre* when he tells an anecdote about a priest who, during a pilgrimage, told the only black student—"you go 'way big Savannah what for and come 'long us?"
35. Fanon, *Black Skin, White Masks*, 32, 34.
36. Ralph Ellison, *The Invisible Man* (New York: Vintage, 1947).
37. Max Zelenka, *Ibrahima* (Les Ecrans Modernes, 1966), Institut National de l'Audiovisuel, BNF, Paris.

CHAPTER 4. WORK, HOUSING, COLONIAL RELATIONS, AND THE FORMATION OF OPPOSITIONAL IDENTITIES AMONG WORKING-CLASS AFRICAN WORKERS

1. Banine, *La France étrangère* (Paris: Editions S.O.S., Desclée de Brouwer, 1968), 131-32. Banine, a conservative French writer of the postwar period, hardly manipulated the French language à la Pierre-Alexis Ponson (1829-1871) and Paul Féval (1816-1877), two famous French writers of the nineteenth century who promoted conservative views of women and suggested the elites should lead society. Yet, in their tradition, she promoted an intellectual climate that fostered elitism, sexism, xenophobia, and racism.
2. For a good discussion of the French labor market during the postwar economic expansion, see Chris Howell, *Regulating Labor: The State and Industrial Relations Reform in Postwar France* (Princeton, NJ: Princeton University Press, 1992). Regarding the relationship between immigration and the labor market, see Odile Merckling, *Immigration et marché du travail: Le développement de la flexibilité en France* (Paris: L'Harmattan, 1998).
3. It is important to note that unlike the French, who often defined their identity in relation to their trade, Africans in France did not craft their identity in relation to their jobs. For a discussion of French workers' identity, see Lenard Berlanstein, ed., *Rethinking Labor History: Essays on Discourse and Class Analysis* (Urbana: University of Illinois Press, 1993).
4. During my fieldwork, African migrants confirmed that few whites sought their friendship. Only union members approached them frequently.
5. Interview with Mr. N'Diaye, Paris, April 2004.
6. The African workers who I interviewed all echoed this sentiment.
7. "Travailleurs Africains en France," Centre des Archives Contemporaines, Fontainebleau, Box 19780262, art. 11.
8. "Africains dans la région parisienne," Centre des Archives Contemporaines de France, Fontainebleau, Box 19810201, art. 6.
9. Ibid.
10. "Enquête sur les travailleurs africains en France," Centre des Archives Contemporaines, Fontainebleau, Box 19780262, art. 11.
11. Interview with Mr. N'Diaye, Paris, April 2004.
12. See William Cohen, *The French Encounter with Africans: White Response to Black, 1530-1880* (Bloomington: University of Indiana Press, 2003); Raoul Girardet, *L'idée coloniale en France de 1871 à 1962* (Paris: Hachette, 2005); and Emily Lynn Osborn, "'Circle of Iron': African Colonial Employees and the Interpretation of Colonial Rule in French West Africa," *Journal of African History* 44, no. 1 (2003): 29-50.
13. "Enquête sur les travailleurs africains en France," Centre des Archives Contemporaines, Fontainebleau, Box 19780262, art. 11.
14. Ibid.
15. Ibid.
16. This finding comes from my fieldwork interviews in Paris during the spring of 2004. See also Jacques Barou, *Travailleurs africains en France: Role des cultures d'origine* (Grenoble: Presses Universitaires de Grenoble, 1977).

17. See Roland Lovatt, Christine Whitehead, and Claire Levy-Vroelant, "Foyers in the UK and France—Comparisons and Contrasts," *European Journal of Housing Policy* 6, no. 12 (2006): 151–66.
18. One should also note that although North Africans had been ghettoized in squatters' camps throughout Paris's *banlieues*, many lived in the city's 18th Arrondissement.
19. "Ressortissants Africains en France," Centre des Archives Contemporaines, Fontainebleau, 1981020, art. 5.
20. Fond d'Action Social pour les Travailleurs Migrants, Rapport d'activité pour l'année 1966, Centre des Archives Contemporaines, Fontainebleau 19780262, art. 11.
21. Ibid.
22. Mireille Galano, "Immigration: Trente ans de combat par le droit," *Plein Droit* (March 2002): 53–54.
23. For information on the Pieds-Noirs, see Todd Sheppard, *The Invention of Decolonization: The Algerian War and the Remaking of France* (Ithaca, NY: Cornell University Press, 2006); and Jean-Jacques Jordi, *De l'exode à l'exil: Rapatriés et pieds-noirs en France, l'exemple marseillais, 1954–1992* (Paris: L'Harmattan, 2000).
24. Ousmane Sembène, *Black Girl*, video (Senegal, 1966).
25. Interview with Mr. Camara, Paris, April 2004. *Le livre des travailleurs Africains en France*, a book published by the largest Senegalese association in France, provides statements corroborating Mr. Camara's comments. See Union Générale des Travailleurs Sénégalais en France, *Le livre des travailleurs Africains en France* (Paris: Editions François Maspéro, 1970).
26. Ibid.
27. *La Vie Catholique*, July 2, 1969.
28. A copy of the letter is included in Union Générale des Travailleurs Sénégalais en France, *Le livre des travailleurs Africains en France*, 44.
29. "Afrique Noire: Déplacement de personnes," Archives de la Préfecture de Police, Paris, Box GaA9.
30. See Jacques Barou, *Travailleurs africains en France: Role des cultures d'origine* (Grenoble: Presses Universitaires de Grenoble, 1977).
31. Interview with Mr. Camara, Paris, April 2004.
32. "Enquête sur les foyers de la région parisienne," December 4, 1968, in "Afrique Noire: Déplacement de personnes," Archives de la Préfecture de Police, Paris, Box GaA9.
33. Ibid.
34. During my research, I found that very few students lived in the foyers during the sixties. Abdoulaye Gueye suggests that the small number of students who lived in the foyers played a role in the protests against the administration. However, he does not provide compelling evidence, offering only one interview. Thus, perhaps by the late seventies, the number of African students in foyers for labor migrants increased. But in the sixties and early seventies, the period under investigation, few students lived in the foyers. When African students lived in the foyers for labor migrants, they actually played a marginal role in the protests. The foyers' protests are largely the sociopolitical expression of disgruntled African workers. Additionally, one can safely assert that age, seniority, ethnicity, and caste affiliation determined leadership positions in the foyers. The few students who resided with the workers were, at best,

participants in the protest movement, but certainly not leaders. See Gueye Abdoulaye, "The Colony Strikes Back: African Protest Movement in Postcolonial France," *Comparative Studies of South Asia, Africa, and the Middle East* 26, no. 2 (2006): 225–42.

35. "Enquête sur les foyers de la région parisienne," December 4, 1968, in "Afrique Noire: Déplacement de personnes," Archives de la Préfecture de Police, Paris, Box GaA9.

36. "Ressortissants Africains en France," Centre des Archives Contemporaines, Fontainebleau, Box 1981020, art. 5.

37. Interview with William N'Diaye, San Francisco, April 2005.

38. Direction Centrale des Renseignements Géneraux, *L'émigration africaine en France*, May 1971, in "Afrique Noire: Déplacement de personnes," Archives de la Préfecture de Police, Paris, Box GaA9.

39. "Ressortissants Africains en France," Centre des Archives Contemporaines, Fontainebleau, Box 1981020, art. 5. One should note that many French officials argued that Algerians, the older colonial migrants who owned property in the Parisian region, exploited West Africans. However, there are no detailed studies on the subject matter, putting into question such a claim.

CHAPTER 5. CARIBBEAN WOMEN IN POSTWAR FRANCE, 1946–1974

Most of this chapter has already been published in *French Historical Studies*. However, you will find new information about Frantz Fanon, which truly illustrates how the discourse of Caribbean nationalists was full of paradoxes.

1. Françoise Ega, *Lettre à une Noire: Récit antillais* (Paris: L'Harmattan, 1978), 17.

2. For the few studies on the West Indian migration to France, see Alain Anselin, *L'émigration Antillaise en France: Du bantoustan au ghetto* (Paris: Karthala, 1979); David Beriss, *Black Skins, French Voices: Caribbean Ethnicity and Activism in Urban France* (Boulder, CO: Westview Press, 2004); Gary Freeman, "Caribbean Migration to Britain and France: From Assimilation to Selection," in *The Caribbean Exodus*, ed. Barry B. Levine (New York: Praeger, 1987); Jean Goossen, "The Migration of French West Indian Women to Metropolitan France," *Anthropological Quarterly* 49 (1976): 45–52; and Stéphanie Condon and Philip Ogden, "Emigration from the French Caribbean: The Origins of an Organized Migration," *International Journal of Urban and Regional Research* 15 (Spring 1991): 505–23. For novels focusing on the experiences of Antillean women in France, see Gisèle Pineau, *L'exil selon Julia* (Paris: Stock, 1996); Françoise Ega, *Lettre à une Noire: Récit antillais*; Jacqueline Manicom, *La graine* (Paris: Presses de la Cité, 1974); and Michèle Lacrosil, *Cajou* (Paris: Gallimard, 1961).

3. In the context of the French Antilles, I refer to nationalism as the various political movements and organizations that sprouted in the fifties and sixties and advocated for independence from France.

4. For a discussion on how officials from the Institut National de la Statistique et des Etudes Economiques (INSEE) viewed Antillean women's fertility rate, see *Le Monde*, September 18, 1971. Additionally, Jill Leonard's dissertation discusses the French stereotype of Antillean women as it relates to their sexuality and fertility rate; see Jill Leonard, "Martinican Women and the French State: Race and Gender in the Construction of the Colonial Relation" (PhD

diss., University of Illinois, 1997).

5. See Jean Pellier, *Nécéssité et possibilité de l'émigration pour les habitants de la Martinique et de la Guadeloupe* (n.p.: INSEE, n.d.), available at l'Agence Nationale pour l'Insertion et la Promotion des Travailleurs d'Outre-Mer, Saint-Denis, Paris. Published in 1966, the following article captures the mood of the period. It analyzes the growth of the Antillean population by using data from INSEE and concludes that overpopulation is related to the high number of young and single women: Yves Péron, "La population des départements français d'outre-mer," *Population* 1 (1966): 99-132.

6. Consult Patrick Weil's fascinating account about postwar French immigration policies; Patrick Weil, *La France et ses étrangers: L'aventure d'une politique de l'immigration, 1938-1991*.

7. See Karen Adler, *Jews and Gender in Liberation France* (Cambridge: Cambridge University Press, 2003); and Weil, *La France et ses étrangers*.

8. For government policies affecting French women, see William Schneider, *Quantity and Quality: The Quest for Biological Regeneration in Twentieth-Century France* (New York, 1990); Anne Carol, *Histoire de l'eugenisme en France: Les médecins et la procreation XIXe-XXe siècles* (Paris: Seuil, 1995); and Adler, *Jews and Gender in Liberation France*.

9. Weil, *La France et ses étrangers*, 54-55. For the image and role of women during the Fourth Republic, see Susan Foley, *Women in France since 1789: The Meaning of Difference* (New York: Palgrave Macmillan, 2004); and Susan Weiner, "Two Modernities: From 'Elle' to 'Mademoiselle': Women's Magazines in Postwar France," *Contemporary European History* 8 (1999): 395-409.

10. See Monique Milia Marie-Luce, "L'émigration des Puertoricains, des Guadeloupéens, des Martiniquais, et Guyanais de l'après guerre aux années 1960" (PhD diss., Ecole des Hautes Etudes en Sciences Sociales, 2002).

11. In her insightful dissertation, Jill Leonard contends that the Martinican birthrate and matrifocal family structure were "of particular concern to French policy makers." She also observes that in the late sixties, family-planning and birth-control clinics were established in Martinique, contributing to a decrease in the birthrate from 5.6 children in 1960-1964, to 3.9 in 1970-1974. See Leonard, "Martinican Women and the French State," 88-89. For documentation related to decreasing the birthrate via migration, see "Rapport d'activité 1962: Perspective programme 1963," available at l'Agence Nationale pour l'Insertion et la Promotion des Travailleurs d'Outre-Mer, Saint-Denis, Paris; Pellier, *Nécéssité et possibilité de l'émigration pour les habitants de la Martinique et de la Guadeloupe*.

12. For a discussion of Antillean women's representation, see Claudie Beauvue-Fougeyrollas, *Les femmes antillaises* (Paris: L'Harmattan, 1985); Brenda Berrian, "Chestnut Women: French Caribbean Women Writers and Singers," *Encuentros* 42 (2001): 25-32; and Clarisse Zimra, "Rethinking the Calabash: Writing and History in the Francophone Narrative," in *Out of the Kumbla: Caribbean Women in Literature*, ed. Carole Boyce Davies and Elaine Fido (Totowa, NJ: Africa World Press, 1990); Bernard Mirabel, *Négripub* (Paris: Société des Amis de la Bibliothèque Forney, 1987); Marie-Alice Jaccoulet, *De solitude à mélodie* (Martinique: Ibis Rouge, 2005); and T. Denean Sharpley-Whiting, *Black Venus: Sexualized Savages, Primal Fears, and Primitive Narratives in French* (Durham, NC: Duke University Press, 1999).

13. Doris Garraway, "Race, Reproduction and Family Romance in Moreau de Saint-Mery's Description ... de la partie francaise de l'isle Saint Domingue," *Eighteenth-Century Studies* 38 (2005): 228.

Notes

14. See Bernard Moitt, *Women and Slavery in the French Antilles, 1635-1848* (Bloomington: University of Indiana Press, 2001).
15. Mirabel, *Négripub*, 10.
16. Throughout the first half of the twentieth century, French composers and musicians were highly inspired by the French colonies. This particular song is from *Toi et moi*, a popular operetta in Paris. The song features a female voice accompanied by a conga beat emulating the French Antillean Biguine music. Simone Simon, "Moi tout faire pour te plaire" (Paris: Columbia DF 1607 [CL 5043-1], October 10, 1934).
17. In the 1950s *puericulture* was considered a "science" that improved child rearing, women's morality, and physical and psychological health.
18. Pellier, *Nécéssité et possibilité de l'émigration pour les habitants de la Martinique et de la Guadeloupe*.
19. Bureau pour le Développement des Migrations Intéressant les Départements d'Outre-Mer, "Migration intéressant les Départements insulaires d'Outre-Mer," at l'Agence Nationale pour l'Insertion et la Promotion des Travailleurs d'Outre-Mer, Saint-Denis, Paris.
20. Ibid.
21. For a complete description of the origins and structure of BUMIDOM, see Milia Marie-Luce, "L'émigration des Puertoricains, des Guadeloupéens, des Martiniquais, et Guyanais de l'après guerre aux années 1960." One should also note that Pap N'Diaye briefly discusses the Antillean migration of the fifties and sixties; see Pap N'Diaye, *La condition noire: Essai sur une minorité française* (Paris: Calmann-Lévy, 2008), esp. 161-66.
22. One should also note that from the mid-fifties to the late seventies, seeking a better life, each year about the same number of Antilleans migrated to Paris without BUMIDOM's supervision. See Claude Marie-Valentin, *Les populations des DOM-TOM, nées et originaires, résidant en France métropolitaine* (Paris: INSEE, 1990).
23. See Alain Anselin, *L'émigration antillaise en France: La troisième île*.
24. Milia Marie-Luce, "L'émigration des Puertoricains, des Guadeloupéens, des Martiniquais, et Guyanais de l'après guerre aux années 1960."
25. "Compte rendu d'activités décembre 1967," available at l'Agence Nationale pour l'Insertion et la Promotion des Travailleurs d'Outre-Mer, Saint-Denis, Paris.
26. Bureau pour le Développement des Migrations Intéressant les Départements d'Outre-Mer, *Bulletin d'Information* (Paris, 1967), l'Agence Nationale pour l'Insertion et la Promotion des Travailleurs d'Outre-Mer, Saint-Denis, Paris.
27. Ibid.
28. Daiva Stasiulis argues that in major Western cities, domestic staffing agencies increase the demand for household workers. See Daiva Stasiulis, *Negotiating Citizenship: Migrant Women in Canada and the Global System* (New York: Palgrave Macmillan, 2003).
29. For the Pieds-Noirs migration to France, see Jean-Jacques Jordi, *De l'exode à l'exil: Rapatriés et Pieds-Noirs en France, l'exemple marseillais, 1954-1992*; and William Cohen, "Legacy of Empire: The Algerian Connection," *Journal of Contemporary History* 15 (1980): 97-123.
30. See Claire Duchen, "Une femme nouvelle pour une France nouvelle?," *Clio* 1 (1995): 1-8.
31. Bridget Anderson, *Doing the Dirty Work? The Global Politics of Domestic Labor* (New York: Zed Books, 2000). Richard Jobs also notes that by 1960, Travailleuse Familiale, a program

encouraging young women to serve temporarily as household domestics, "underwent a broad professionalization as a social service, that would lead, in 1974, to the recognition of *Travailleuses Familiales* as career social workers." Accordingly, this evolution further rationalized the "need" for having Antillean women domestics. See Richard Jobs, *Riding the New Wave: Youth and the Rejuvenation of France after the Second World War* (Stanford, CA: Stanford University Press, 2007).

32. BUMIDOM, "Migration en métropole de travailleurs des Départements d'Outre-Mer et de leurs familles, février 1964," available at l'Agence Nationale pour l'Insertion et la Promotion des Travailleurs d'Outre-Mer, Saint-Denis, Paris.

33. Ibid.

34. Françoise Ega, *Lettre à une Noire: Récit antillais*, 17.

35. One should also note that during the interwar period, Antillean women willingly responded to job ads seeking domestics in Paris. Hundreds of women traveled to become maids in the City of Light. However, after departmentalization, expectations changed, as Antillean women were more educated and sought to receive jobs deemed more modern. For reference on the interwar "domestic" migration, see "France Has New Rage in Dark Maid," *Chicago Defender*, April 7, 1923.

36. Bureau pour le Développement des Migrations Intéressant les Départements d'Outre-Mer, *Bulletin d'Information* (Paris, 1967), available at l'Agence Nationale pour l'Insertion et la Promotion des Travailleurs d'Outre-Mer, Saint-Denis, Paris.

37. Nadia Kergoat, "Une secrétaire d'acceuil," master's thesis for the Institut National du Tertiaire Social et de la Formation Continue, September 1981, 15, available at l'Agence Nationale pour l'Insertion et la Promotion des Travailleurs d'Outre-Mer, Saint-Denis, Paris.

38. Ibid.

39. Document pédagogique du centre Crouy-sur-Ourq, 1973, available at l'Agence Nationale pour l'Insertion et la Promotion des Travailleurs d'Outre-Mer, Saint-Denis, Paris.

40. Ibid.

41. *Le Patriote Guadeloupéen*, at Université de Nanterre, Bibliothèque de Documentation internationale contemporaine, Pièce F 3825.

42. Claude Marie-Valentin, "Les populations des Dom-Tom en France," *Journal de l'Agence Nationale pour l'Insertion et la Promotion des Travailleurs d'Outre-Mer*, no. 7, supplement (Paris, 1982).

43. *Le Patriote Guadeloupéen*, 13.

44. Bureau pour le Développement des Migrations Intéressant les Départements d'Outre-Mer, *Bulletin d'Information* (Paris, 1967).

45. Genevieve Rouquie, "Y sa va ou," Mémoire promotion Infac (BUMIDOM, 1980), 31, at l'Agence Nationale pour l'Insertion et la Promotion des Travailleurs d'Outre-Mer, Saint-Denis, Paris. One should note that the trope of the *grand enfant* has traditionally been used in relation to the *Tirailleurs Sénégalais* (a term encompassing all the sub-Saharan African soldiers who served in the French army during the Great War). According to Brett Berliner, the French painted the African soldiers as children to appease the anxiety that their imagined masculinity generated in the proximity of white French women. See Brett Berliner, *Ambivalent Desire: The Exotic Black Other in Jazz-Age France* (Amherst: University of Massachusetts Press, 2002). However, because of the Antillean women's colonial and humble educational background,

the French officials of BUMIDOM and the Crouy-sur-Ourcq teachers and administrators also related to the women as if they were children. In many ways, the officials imagined their role as "parents," whose duty was to educate and guide the "migrants/children" into adulthood.

46. Rouquie, "Y sa va ou," 32.
47. Bureau pour le Développement des Migrations Intéressant les Départements d'Outre-Mer, *Bulletin d'Information* (Paris, 1967), available at l'Agence Nationale pour l'Insertion et la Promotion des Travailleurs d'Outre-Mer, Saint-Denis, Paris.
48. Ibid.
49. Mrs. Christiane (nurse's aide at Pitié-Salpêtrière), interview by author, Paris, March 15, 2004.
50. Cited in BUMIDOM, "Migration en métropole de travailleurs des départements d'outre-mer et de leurs familles, février 1964," at l'Agence Nationale pour l'Insertion et la Promotion des Travailleurs d'Outre-Mer, Saint-Denis, Paris.
51. Bureau pour le Développement des Migrations Intéressant les Départements d'Outre-Mer, "Rapport d'activité, 1962," at l'Agence Nationale pour l'Insertion et la Promotion des Travailleurs d'Outre-Mer, Saint-Denis, Paris.
52. One should note that from 1962 to about 1975, about five thousand Antilleans migrated to France yearly via BUMIDOM, and that the same number of people migrated without any state assistance. Men and women were equally represented in both the state and the self-sponsored migration. See Nora Absalon, "Le personnel hospitalier originaire des DOM a l'Assistance Publique de Paris, 1967–1987" (mémoire de maîtrise d'histoire contemporaine, Université de Paris I, 2001), 41.
53. Jacqueline Ansel, interview by author, Paris, February 15, 2004.
54. Madame Gabriel, interview by author, Aulnay-sous-Bois, April 7, 2004.
55. *Alizé*, December 1966. Available at Aumônerie Nationale Antilles Guyane, Paris.
56. See Eric Jennings, "Monuments to Frenchness? The Memory of the Great War and the Politics of Guadeloupe's Identity, 1914–1945," *French Historical Studies* 21 (1998): 561–92. For David Massey's discussion on the Antillean resistance movement during World War II, see *Frantz Fanon: A Life* (London: Granta, 2000).
57. There are two dominant nationalist parties in Guadeloupe and Martinique, the UPLG (Union Populaire pour la Libération de la Guadeloupe), founded in 1978, and the MIM (Mouvement Indépendantiste Martiniquais), founded in 1972. See Robert Aldrich and John Connell, *France's Overseas Frontier: Départements et Territoires d'Outre-Mer* (New York, 1992). In 1999 about 21 percent of Guadeloupeans and 14 percent of Martinicans favored autonomy or independence, a number that has been consistent since the early seventies. See *Le Monde Diplomatique*, December 1999.
58. For a discussion of education in the French Antilles after World War II, see Michel Giraud, *L'école aux Antilles* (Paris: Karthala, 1992).
59. For reference on the number of children attending school, see the documentary *Une île au soleil*, Cinq Colones à la une, April 6, 1960.
60. See Gesner Mence, *L'affaire de l'O.J.A.M* (Fort-de-France, Martinique: Editions Désormeaux, 2001).
61. Julien Valère Loza, *Les étudiants martiniquais en France: Histoire de leur organisation et de leurs luttes* (Martinique: Editions 2M, 2003), 184.

62. "La population antillaise en France," Archives de la Préfecture de Police, Paris, Box Gabr47.
63. See Félix Germain, "For the Nation and for Work: Black Activism in Paris of the 1960s," in *Migration and Activism in Europe since 1945*, ed. Wendy Pojmann (New York: Palgrave Macmillan, 2008).
64. See Mence, *L'affaire de l'O.J.A.M*; and Marcel Manville, *Les Antilles sans fard* (Paris: L'Harmattan, 1992).
65. Frantz Fanon, *The Wretched of the Earth*, 40.
66. See Manville, *Les Antilles sans fard*.
67. See Cynthia Enloe, *Bananas, Beaches, and Bases: Making Feminist Sense of International Politics* (Berkeley: University of California Press, 1990); and also Laura Briggs, *Reproducing Empire: Race, Sex, Science, and U.S. Imperialism in Puerto Rico* (Berkeley: University of California Press, 2002).
68. Roland Larouchez, *Confessions d'une prostituée à Paris* (Fort-de-France, Martinique: Imprimerie Désormaux, 1975). One should note that because it was published by Le Naif, a leftist publishing house, the novel mostly circulated within the Martinican nationalist and communist circles.
69. Larouchez, *Confessions d'une prostituée à Paris*, 125.
70. *Alizé*, December 1966 and January 1967.
71. Georges Michalon, interview by author, Paris, May 7, 2004.
72. See Dany Bébel-Gisler, *Léonora: L'histoire enfouie de la Guadeloupe* (Paris: Seghers, 1985).
73. See France Alibar and Pierrette Lembeye-Boy, *Le couteau seul: La condition féminine aux Antilles* (Paris: Katharla, 1981); and Danielle Crusol-Baillard and Louilot Germaine, *Femmes martiniquaises: Mythes et réalités* (Paris, 1987).
74. Fieldwork interview, Paris, April 2004.
75. Interview with Maryse Condé, New York, March 2010.
76. A matador is a bullfighter, but as one observes in the previous paragraphs, it has an entirely different meaning in the French Antilles.
77. See Bonnie Thomas, "Identity at the Crossroads: An Exploration of French Caribbean Gender Identity," *Caribbean Studies* 32 (2004): 45–62.
78. See Bernard Moitt, *Women and Slavery in the French Antilles, 1635-1848*.
79. For a discussion of matrifocality in the Caribbean region, see Christine Barrow, "Caribbean Gender Ideologies: Introduction and Overview," in *Caribbean Portraits: Essays on Gender Ideologies and Identities*, ed. Christine Barrow (Kingston, Jamaica: University of West Indies Press, 1998).
80. For instance, in a study analyzing the role, contribution, and condition of Antillean women in slavery, he observes that the fear of being raped by other slaves and by white men encouraged women to escape in groups; Bernard Moitt, "Slave Women and Resistance in the French Caribbean," in *More Than Chattel: Black Women in Slavery in the Americas*, ed. David Barry Gaspar and Darlene Clark Hine (Bloomington: University of Indiana Press, 1996).
81. For interesting works on women in postwar France, see Anne Cova, *Maternité et droits des femmes en France (XIXe-XXe siècles)* (Paris: Anthropos, 1997); Evelyne Diebolt, *Les femmes dans l'action sanitaire, sociale et culturelle, 1901-2001* (Paris: Femmes et associations, 2001); and Claire Duchen, *Women's Rights and Women's Lives in France, 1944-1968* (New York: Routledge,

1994).

82. See Arlette Gautier, *Le sœurs de solitude: La condition féminine dans l'esclavage aux Antilles du XVIIè au XIXè siècle*; and Gilbert Pago, *Les femmes et la liquidation du système esclavagiste à la Martinique, 1848-1852* (Petit-Bourg, Guadeloupe: Ibis Rouge, 1998).

CHAPTER 6. HENRI SALVADOR'S MUSIC AND WORKING-CLASS CARIBBEAN MALES IN PARIS OF THE SIXTIES

1. Phyllis Rose, *Jazz Cleopatra: Josephine Baker in Her Time* (New York: Doubleday, 1989).
2. See Jeffrey Jackson, *Making Jazz French: Music and Modern Life in Interwar Paris* (Durham, NC: Duke University Press, 2003).
3. Charles Baudelaire (1821-1867) popularized the concept of the *flâneur*. A *flâneur* is one who strolls throughout the city, contemplating the architecture and observing people. Seeking to decipher the meanings of the city, he is both immersed in and detached from the crowd. See Keith Tester, ed., *The Flâneur* (New York: Routledge, 1994); Edmund White, *The Flâneur: A Stroll through the Paradoxes of Paris* (New York: Bloomsbury, 2001); and Richard D. E. Burton, *The Flâneur and His City: Patterns of Life in Paris, 1815-1851* (Durham, England: University of Durham Press, 1994). Inspired by this definition, black *flâneurs* like Salvador are strollers, loners, and people who by day move comfortably throughout the city, and by night, jump from party to party, drinking, joking, and searching for a sexual escapade.
4. Although other black Francophone artists, singers, and actors such as Habib Benglia had achieved national success, by the sixties Henri Salvador was clearly the most popular black celebrity in France.
5. *New York Times*, November 3, 2008.
6. *New York Times*, February 14, 2008.
7. Interview with Maryse Condé, New York, March 2010.
8. Henri Salvador, *Attention ma vie* (Paris: Editions Jean-Claude Lattès, 1994).
9. Ibid., 37-38.
10. Ibid., 50.
11. "Henri Salvador: Inventaire Montparnasse," *L'art et les hommes*, ORTF (January 1, 1963).
12. Salvador, *Attention ma vie*.
13. Charlus, "A la Martinique," EMG, 1912.
14. *New York Times*, November 3, 2008.
15. During that era, Salvador could hardly escape the essentialist ideas of blackness, which influenced many black performers, artists, and writers. This phenomenon even affected the most notable black intellectuals. According to Marcien Towa, Léopold Senghor, one of the founders of negritude, believed that while whites are rational individuals, blacks are essentially emotional individuals. Towa is quoted in Barbara Ischinger, "Negritude: Some Dissident Voices," *Issue: A Journal of Opinion* 4, no. 4 (1974): 24.
16. See Audrey Thomas McCluskey, *Imagining Blackness: Race and Racial Representation in Film Poster Art* (Bloomington: Indiana University Press, 2007); and Ed Guerrero, *Framing Blackness:*

The African American Image in Film (Philadelphia: Temple University Press, 1993).

17. Charlene Regester, "Stepin Fetchit: The Man, the Image, and the African American Press," *Film History* 6, no. 4 (1994): 502.

18. For an interesting discussion of Mantan Moreland, see Donald Bogle, *Toms, Coons, Mulattoes, Mammies, and Bucks: An Interpretive History of Blacks in American Films* (New York: Continuum Press, 2001), 74.

19. Henri Salvador, "Dans mon île" (Disque Barclay, 1957).

20. Salvador, *Attention ma vie*, 251.

21. Henri Salvador, "Le travail c'est la santé" (Sony, 1965).

22. *International Herald Tribune*, January 12, 1992.

23. Henri Salvador, "Faut rigoler" (Barclay, 1960).

24. For an overview of French assimilation policy in the Martinican and Guadeloupean school system, see Michel Giraud, *L'école aux Antilles: Langues et échec scolaire* (Paris: Karthala, 1992).

25. Henri Salvador, "Personnalisé" (Rigolo, 1967).

26. See Tyler Stovall, "The Color Line behind the Lines: Racial Violence in France during the Great War," *American Historical Review* 103, no. 3 (1998); and Elisa Camiscioli, "Reproducing the 'French Race': Immigration and Pronatalism in Early-Twentieth-Century France," in *Bodies in Contact: Rethinking Colonial Encounters in World History*, ed. Tony Ballantyne and Antoinette Burton (Durham, NC: Duke University Press, 2005).

27. Salvador, *Attention ma vie*, 51.

28. During plantation slavery and the colonial period, Frenchmen opposed interracial relationships to avoid *métissage* and maintain the racial division of labor. Ann Stoler observes that Frenchmen policed love between the colonizer and the colonized with greater intensity when the former was a white woman; they desired to preserve the social structure as much as to keep "their" women for themselves. See Ann Stoler, *Carnal Knowledge and Imperial Power: Race and the Intimate in Colonial Rule* (Berkeley: University of California Press, 2002); and Owen White, *Children of the French Empire: Miscegenation and Colonial Society in French West Africa, 1895-1960* (New York: Oxford University Press, 2000).

29. Roger Little, "From Taboo to Totem: Black Man, White Woman, in Caroline Auguste Fischer and Sophie Doin," *Modern Language Review* 93, no. 4 (1998): 948.

30. Brett Berliner, *Ambivalent Desire: The Exotic Black Other in Jazz-Age France* (Amherst: University of Massachusetts Press, 2002).

31. Allison McCracken, "'God's Gift to Us Girls': Crooning, Gender, and the Re-Creation of American Popular Song, 1928-1933," *American Music* 17, no. 4 (1999): 372.

32. *Voir Ça*, November 27, 2003.

33. Stephanie Condon and Philip Ogden, "Afro-Caribbean Migrants in France: Employment, State Policy and the Migration Process," *Transactions of the Institute of British Geographers*, New Series 16, no. 4 (1991): 450.

34. Ibid.

35. Georges Douay, "Animation au foyer de jeunes travailleurs de Simandres." Georges Douay wrote a report on the school for Caribbean men at Simandres to receive a promotion at BUMIDOM. Although no date of publication is given, one may assume that he wrote his report in the late sixties.

Notes

36. See Georges Douay, "Animation au foyer de jeunes travailleurs de Simandres"; and Pierre Bardet, "Monographe," a brief report on the Simandres school that he also wrote to receive a promotion. One may assume that Bardet wrote his report in 1974, as he details the school's progress up until that year. Documents available at l'Agence Nationale pour l'Insertion et la Promotion des Travailleurs d'Outre-Mer, Saint-Denis, Paris.
37. The four testimonies that I selected come from my ethnographic fieldwork and a study on Antillean workers in Paris public hospitals. For the study, see Lucette Labache, *Les originaires de l'Outre-Mer à l'AP-HP* (Paris: Assistance Publique Hôpitaux de Paris, 2003).
38. Labache, *Les originaires de l'Outre-Mer à l'AP-HP*, 35.
39. Ibid.
40. For examples of scholars discussing the role of Kreyol in the French Caribbean, see Frantz Fanon, *Black Skin, White Masks* (New York: Grove Press, 1967); and Dany-Bebel Gisler, *La langue créole, force jugulée: Etude socio-linguistique des rapports de force entre le créole et le français aux Antilles* (Paris: L'Harmattan, 1976).
41. Labache, *Les originaires de l'Outre-Mer à l'AP-HP*, 47.
42. Mr. Pierre is my step-grandfather. I met for the first time in 2003, when I was completing fieldwork for the book.
43. Fieldwork interview, Paris, December 21, 2003.
44. Fieldwork interview, Paris, March 22, 2004. One should also note that a similar pattern existed in the American military. Racism persisted well beyond the disbandment of the last all-black unit in 1954, and like French Caribbean people, African Americans also clustered together because of cultural similarities and anti-black racism. See Gerald Astor, *The Right to Fight: A History of African Americans in the Military* (Cambridge, MA: Da Capo Press, 2001).
45. For *schœlchérisme* in the French Antilles, see Marie-José Jolivet, "La construction d'une mémoire historique à la Martinique: Du schœlchérisme au marronisme," *Cahiers d'études africaines* 37, no. 148 (1997): 813–37.
46. See Georges Mauvois, *Louis des Etages, 1873–1925: Itinéraire d'un homme politique martiniquais* (Paris: Karthala, 1990).
47. For an excellent analysis of *Pétainisme* in the French West Indies, see Eric Jennings, *Vichy in the Tropics: Pétain's National Revolution in Madagascar, Guadeloupe, and Indochina, 1940–1944* (Palo Alto, CA: Stanford University Press, 2001). For a discussion of *Gaullisme*, see Bernard Lachaise, "Contestataires et compagnons: Les formes de l'engagement gaulliste," *Vingtième Siècle: Revue d'histoire* 60 (October–December 1998): 73.
48. For an excellent analysis focusing on the Martinican white minority, see Edith Kovats, *Les blancs créoles de la Martinique: Une minorité dominante* (Paris: L'Harmattan, 2002); and Juliette Smeralda-Amon, *La racisation des relations intergroupes ou la problématique de la couleur: Le cas de la Martinique* (Paris: L'Harmattan, 2002).
49. For important work on French Caribbean identity, activism, and relation to the French state, see David Beriss, *Black Skins, French Voices: Caribbean Ethnicity and Activism in Urban France* (Boulder, CO: Westview Press, 2004).
50. In November 2005, many young people of sub-Saharan African, Caribbean, and North African origin "rioted" in the suburbs of Paris, protesting against police brutality and the government. From February to early April 2009, Guadeloupeans and Martinicans organized a major strike that paralyzed the public sector and the tourist industry. They protested against the high cost

of living, the high price of imported food and gas, and the unemployment rate, hovering near 25 percent. In short, they pointed out that the French Caribbean reality was very different from France, where food and gas is cheaper and the unemployment rate much lower, usually below 10 percent. During the protests, French Caribbean people argued that racial and cultural differences play an important role in the reproduction of social inequalities.

51. For an analysis of interracial relations and racial violence in early twentieth-century France, see Tyler Stovall, "Love, Labor, and Race: Colonial Men and White Women in France during the Great War," in *French Civilization and Its Discontents: Nationalism, Colonialism, and Race*, ed. Tyler Stovall and Georges Van Den Abbeele (Lanham, MD: Lexington Books, 2003); and Stovall, "The Color Line behind the Lines: Racial Violence in France during the Great War."

52. Interview with Mr. Guacide, Paris, April 2004.

53. Super Combo, "Chalè a Paris" (Debbs, 1977).

CHAPTER 7. FRENCH LABOR UNIONS, BLACK COMMUNITY AND POLITICAL ACTIVISM, AND DECOLONIZATION IN POSTCOLONIAL PARIS, 1960–1974

1. See Martin Schain, "Immigration and Trade Unions in France: A Problem and an Opportunity," in *A Century of Organized Labor in France: A Union Movement for the Twenty-First Century?*, ed. Erick Chapman, Mark Kesselman, and Martin Schain (New York: St. Martin's Press, 1998).

2. See Leah Haus, *Unions, Immigration, and Internationalization: New Challenges and Changing Conditions in the United States and France* (New York: Palgrave Macmillan, 2002).

3. In his study Mar Fall also notes that small communities of Africans were present in Le Havre and Bordeaux. Generally, African migrants who lived in these cities worked on the seaport. See Mar Fall, *Les Africain noirs en France: Des Tirailleurs Sénégalais au Blacks* (Paris: L'Harmattan, 1986).

4. Ousmane Sembène, the most popular and influential African filmmaker, also wrote a novel about African dockworkers in the South of France. This novel is now a classic in African literature. See Ousmane Sembène, *Black Docker* (London: Heinemann Educational, 1987). One should also note that Claude McKay touches upon the theme of the exploited black colonial workers in interwar Marseilles; see Claude McKay, *Banjo* (London: X Press, 2000).

5. In the fifties CGT sympathized with anticolonial activists. In many ways, the activists welcomed the support because they realized the union offered them a great opportunity to reach large audiences. See Elizabeth Schmidt, "Top Down or Bottom Up? Nationalist Mobilization Reconsidered, with Special Reference to Guinea (French West Africa)," *American Historical Review* 110, no. 4 (2005).

6. See Samba Gadjigo, Ralph Faulkingham, Thomas Cassirer, and Reinhard Sander, eds., *Ousmane Sembène Dialogues with Critics and Writers* (Amherst: University of Massachusetts Press, 1993).

7. See Jean-Jacques Jordi, *De l'exode à l'exil: Rapatriés et Pieds-Noirs en France, l'exemple marseillais, 1954–1992* (Paris: L'Harmattan, 1993).

8. "Les travailleurs espagnols dans la métallurgie parisienne" (June 1964), Archives de la Confédération Générale du Travail, Box A 22g, Immigrés travailleurs en France.

9. "Conférence nationale sur les travailleurs immigrés," Archives de la Confédération Française

Démocratique du Travail, Box 7 H 28.

10. Ibid.
11. Confédération Française Démocratique du Travail, *Perspective Socialiste* (January 1964).
12. Fieldwork interview, Paris, April 2004.
13. Union Générale des Travailleurs Sénégalais en France, *Le livre des travailleurs Africains en France* (Paris: Editions François Maspéro, 1970).
14. Ibid., 26.
15. Ibid.
16. For the impact of the disaster at Aubervilliers, see Yvan Gastaut, "Les bidonvilles, lieux d'exclusion et de marginalité en France durant les Trente Glorieuses," *Cahiers de la Méditerranée* 69 (May 2006).
17. Yvan Gastaut, "Figures et présence des immigrés dans les medias," *Confluences Méditerranée* 24 (April 2004). Gastaut's bibliography provides an extensive list of the Aubervilliers media coverage. Some of the most important examples include the documentary *Les dossiers de l'écran*, which aired on January 14, 1970; and the article "Propos de Sally N'Dongo, président de l'UGTSF (Union générale des travailleurs sénégalais en France)," *Le Monde*, January 13, 1970.
18. See Jacques Adélaide-Merlande, *Les origines du mouvement ouvrier en Martinique: 1870-1900* (Paris: Editions Karthala, 2000).
19. "Pour défendre plus efficacement les travailleurs immigrés de la métallurgie de la Seine," January 1963, Archives de la Confédération Générale du Travail, Box A 22g, Immigrés travailleurs en France.
20. Fieldwork interview, Paris, May 2004.
21. Here I am referring to the associations/community organizations they created to advance a particular goal, one that is usually connected to their incorporation into the fabric of the nation. Although a few scholars have discussed this phenomenon, they limit their analysis to the contemporary period. For examples, see Rahsaan Maxwell, "Evaluating Migrant Integration: Political Attitudes across Generations in Europe," *International Migration Review* 1 (March 2010); Michel Giraud, "The Antillese in France: Trends and Prospects," *Ethnic and Racial Studies* 27, no. 4 (2004): 622-40; and Rahsaan Maxwell, *Ethnic Minority Migrants in Britain and France: Integration Trade-offs* (New York: Cambridge University Press, 2012).
22. Association Etrangère en France, Archives Contemporaines de France, Fontainebleau, Box 19870799, art. 24.
23. Ibid.
24. See Bureau pour le Développement des Migrations Intéressant les Départements d'Outre-Mer, *Mises au point* (no month, 1972).
25. CASODOM, *1955-2001: 45ème anniversaire du comité d'action sociale en faveur des originaires des départements d'outre-mer en métropole* (Paris, 2001).
26. Interview with Mrs. Yvette St. Luce, Paris, June 2004.
27. "L'émigration des Antillais vers la France," *Alizé: Bulletin de la Fédération Antillo-Guyanaise des Etudiants Catholiques*, December 1966-January 1967, 20.
28. Bureau pour le Développement des Migrations Intéressant les Départements d'Outre-Mer, *Bulletin d'Information* (Paris, 1967).

29. For a discussion of African activism beyond the sixties and seventies, see Jean-Philippe Dedieu, *La parole immigrée: Les migrants africains dans l'espace public en France, 1960-1995* (Paris: Klincksieck, 2012).
30. Union Générale des Travailleurs Sénégalais en France, *Le livre des travailleurs africains en France*.
31. Ibid.
32. Fieldwork interview, Paris, May 2004. One should also note that Jean Pierre N'Diaye authored a text about African students in 1960s Paris. See Jean Pierre N'Diaye, *Enquête sur les étudiants noirs en France* (Paris: Editions Réalités Africaines, 1962).
33. For a discussion of the social unrest in the foyers, see Oumar Dia, *Yakaré: L'autobiographie d'Oumar* (Paris: François Maspéro, 1982); and Michel Samuel, *Le prolétariat africain noir en France* (Paris: François Maspéro, 1978).
34. Some of these journals include *Les Continents* (1924-1926), *Le Paria* (1926), *Le Libéré* (1923-1925), *La Dépêche Africaine* (1928-1932), *La Revue du Monde Noir* (1931-1932), and *Le Cri des Nègres* (1931-1936), which seems to have circulated longer than its counterparts.
35. "Le role de la femme gabonaise dans la libération nationale," *L'Etudiant du Gabon* (September 1974). I chose this student newsletter to demonstrate how African students were already addressing the social issues that Western organizations began to tackle in the 1990s.
36. Information is available at Centre des Archives Contemporaines, Fontainebleau, Box 19870799, art. 24.
37. In 1964, Sartre published a book that also influenced many African students in France. See Jean-Paul Sartre, *Colonialism and Neo-Colonialism* (New York: Routledge, 2001).
38. This was not an entirely new phenomenon. Similar protests also occurred in the early sixties, albeit not as frequently as after 1968.
39. Centre des Archives Contemporaines, Fontainebleau, Box 19870799, art. 24.
40. Ibid.
41. Ibid.
42. Archives de la Préfecture de Police de Paris, Box GaA9, Afrique noire déplacement de personnes.
43. The list and description of the organization is available at the Centre des Archives Contemporaines, Fontainebleau, Box 19870799, art. 24.
44. For a brief analysis of the Sékou Touré dictatorship, see Rajen Harshe, "Guinea under Sékou Touré," *Economic and Political Weekly* 19, no. 15 (1984).
45. Sékou Traoré, *La Fédération des Etudiants d'Afrique Noire en France: (F.E.A.N.F.)* (Paris: L'Harmattan, 1985).
46. See Serge Mam Lam Fouck, *Histoire générale de la Guyane française* (Matoury, Guyane Française: Ibis Rouge, 2010).
47. Interview with Edouard Glissant, New York, September, 2003.
48. Association Générale des Etudiants de la Martinique, "Extrait du rapport politique du cinquième congrès national de l'Association Générale des Etudiants de la Martinique," December 1961, available at Bibliothèque de Documentation Internationale Contemporaine, Université de Paris Ouest Nanterre, Pièce 9899.

49. Compte-Rendu du Congrès des 22 et 23 Avril, Bibliothèque de Documentation Internationale Contemporaine, Université de Paris Ouest Nanterre, Pièce 9899.
50. Ibid.
51. Ibid.
52. A more or less close translation of AGTAG would be Association of Antillean and Guianese Workers.
53. Marcel Manville, *Les Antilles sans fard* (Paris: L'Harmattan, 1992).
54. Amicale Générale des Travailleurs Antillais et Guyanais, *Bulletin d'Information*, 1964.
55. The Regroupement de l'Emigration Martiniquaise published its own newsletter entitled *La Voix de l'Emigration*. In the second issue, it outlined how members left to better address the issues that solely pertained to the Martinican diaspora and Martinican politics. See *La Voix de l'Emigration*, March-April 1966.
56. "Le role des travailleurs émigrés dans la lutte de libération nationale," *Le Patriote Guadeloupéen* (September 1971).
57. Richard Burton also attributes the decline of nationalist organizations and parties to political development in the French Caribbean. He argues that socialist and communist mayors took away the popular support needed to mount an effective nationalist movement. This was especially true in Martinique, where Aimé Césaire's Parti Progressiste Martiniquais catered to the most dispossessed Martinicans. See Richard Burton, *French and West Indian: Martinique, Guadeloupe, and French Guiana Today* (Charlottesville: University of Virginia Press, 1995).

CHAPTER 8. MAY '68 IN BLACK

1. For an explanation of May '68 following an economic history perspective, see Chris Howell, *Regulating Labor: The State and Industrial Relations Reform in Postwar France* (Princeton, NJ: Princeton University Press, 1992); and Odile Merckling, *Immigration et marché du travail: Le développement de la flexibilité en France* (Paris: L'Harmattan, 1998). For the sociologists, see Pierre Bourdieu, *Homo academicus* (Paris: Minuit, 1984); and Roger Gregoire, *Worker-Student Action Committees, France, May 68* (Detroit: Black & Red, 1970).
2. Alain Touraine, *Le mouvement de mai ou le communisme utopique* (Paris: Editions du Seuil, 1968).
3. For instance, see Margaret Atack, *May 68 in French Fiction and Film: Rethinking Society, Rethinking Representation* (Oxford: Oxford University Press, 1999); and Kristin Ross, *May 68 and Its Afterlives* (Chicago: University of Chicago Press, 2002).
4. See Michael Siedman, *The Imaginary Revolution: Parisian Students and Workers in 1968* (Oxford: Berghahn Books, 2004); Edgar Morin, Claude Lefort, and Cornelius Castoriadis, *Mai 68: La brèche* (Paris: Éditions Complexe, 1988); and Alain Touraine, *The May Movement: Revolt and Reform* (New York: Irvington Publishers, 1979).
5. Kristin Ross in particular demonstrates that the students and the workers succeeded in threatening the political regime, which reacted in the most creative manner to secure its survival and maintain the established social order. See Ross, *May 68 and Its Afterlives*.
6. Interview with Edouard Glissant, New York, September 2003.
7. Ibid.

8. Ibid.
9. Ibid.
10. Interview with Maryse Condé, New York, March 2010.
11. These are some of the questions that Geneviève Fabre and Robert O'Malley ask when they examine the role of historical consciousness and imagination in African American culture. See Geneviève Fabre and Robert O'Malley, *History and Memory in African-American Culture* (Oxford: Oxford University Press, 1994).
12. See Laure Pitti, "Ouvriers algériens à Renault-Billancourt de la guerre d'Algérie aux grèves d'OS des années 1970" (PhD diss., Université de Paris VIII, 2002).
13. Interview with Mr. N'Diaye, Paris, April 2004.
14. *Le Monde*, July 24, 1969.
15. *Alizé: Bulletin de la Fédération Antillo-Guyanaise des Etudiants Catholiques* (May–June 1968).
16. Ibid.
17. Ross, *May 68 and Its Afterlives*.
18. Fieldwork interview, Paris, June 2004.
19. *Alizé* (December–January 1966).
20. Interview with Mr. Kayzer, a retired BUMIDOM employee, Paris, May 2004.
21. Interview with Mr. George Lassare Michalon, Paris, May 2004.
22. *Alizé: Bulletin de la Fédération Antillo-Guyanaise des Etudiants Catholiques* (May–June 1968).
23. This tradition predates the French Revolution, as numerous *gens de couleur*, including the Haitian Vincent Ogé, traveled to France to claim more rights for the free people of color in St. Domingue. See John Garrigus, "'Thy Coming Fame, Ogé! Is Sure': New Evidence on Ogé's 1790 Revolt and the Beginnings of the Haitian Revolution," in *Assumed Identities: The Meanings of Race in the Atlantic World*, ed. John Garrigus and Chris Morris (College Station: Texas A&M University Press, 2010).
24. Robin D. G. Kelley, "'Afric's Sons with Banner Red': African-American Communists and the Politics of Culture, 1919-1934," in *Imagining Home: Class, Culture, and Nationalism in the African Diaspora*, ed. Sidney Lemelle and Robin D. G. Kelley (New York: Verso, 1994), 37.
25. Secrétariat Général des Départements d'Outre-Mer, "Mise au point," available at l'Agence Nationale pour l'Insertion et la Promotion des Travailleurs d'Outre-Mer, Saint-Denis, Paris.
26. Interview with George Lassare Michalon, Paris, May 2004.
27. For relevant studies on the relationship between French Caribbean people and France, see Eric Jennings, "La dissidence aux Antilles, 1940-1943," *Vingtième Siècle: Revue d'histoire* 68 (2000): 55-71; and Richard Burton, *La famille coloniale: La Martinique et la mère patrie, 1789-1992* (Paris: L'Harmattan, 1994).
28. Interview with Madame Janine Martin, the former BUMIDOM archivist, Paris, November 2003.
29. Interview with George Lassare Michalon, Paris, May 2004.
30. Ibid.
31. Jean Goossen, "The Migration of French West Indian Women to Metropolitan France," *Anthropological Quarterly* 49 (1976): 45-52; and Stéphanie Condon and Philip Ogden, "Emigration from the French Caribbean: The Origins of an Organized Migration," *International Journal of Urban and Regional Research* 15 (Spring 1991): 505-23.

CHAPTER 9. MUSIC, LE PEN, AND "NEW" BLACK ACTIVISM IN CONTEMPORARY FRANCE, 1974–2005

1. For important authors, see Paul Gilroy, *The Black Atlantic: Modernity and Double Consciousness* (New York: Verso, 1993); Saidiya Hartman, *Lose Your Mother: A Journey along the Atlantic Slave Route* (New York: Farrar, Straus and Giroux, 2007); V. Y. Mudimbe, *The Invention of Africa: Gnosis, Philosophy, and the Order of Knowledge* (Bloomington: University of Indiana Press, 1988); and Joseph Harris, ed., *Global Dimensions of the African Diaspora* (Washington, DC: Howard University Press, 1983).
2. See Molefi Asante, *The Afrocentric Idea* (Philadelphia: Temple University Press, 1987).
3. Here, I use "old" to distinguish between blacks whose ancestors came to the Americas via the Middle Passage from blacks whose families have recently arrived in the Americas or Europe.
4. Edouard Glissant, *Caribbean Discourse: Selected Essays* (Charlottesville: University of Virginia Press, 1996), 18.
5. Frantz Fanon, *Black Skin, White Masks* (New York: Grove Press, 1967). For a historical analysis of colonial hierarchies between African and French Caribbean individuals, particularly during the Third Republic, see Véronique Hélénon, *French Caribbeans in Africa: Diasporic Connections and Colonial Administration, 1880–1939* (New York: Palgrave Macmillan, 2011).
6. Manthia Diawara, "The 1960s in Bamako: Malick Sidibé and James Brown," in *Black Cultural Traffic: Crossroads in Global Performance and Popular Culture*, ed. Harry Elam and Kennell Jackson (Ann Arbor: University of Michigan Press, 2005), 255.
7. Dominique Cyrille, "Imagining an Afro-Creole Nation: Eugène Mona's Music in Martinique of the 1980s," *Latin American Music Review* 27, no. 2 (2006): 149.
8. Eugène Mona, "Ti Milo" (Hibiscus Records, 1975).
9. See Jocelyne Guibault, *Zouk: World Music in the West Indies* (Chicago: University of Chicago Press, 1993); and Brenda Berrian, *Awakening Spaces: French Caribbean Popular Songs, Music, and Culture* (Chicago: University of Chicago Press, 2000).
10. Interview with Mr. Lamine Sal, New York, March 2010.
11. Ibid.
12. Kassav', "An ba chen'n la" (Georges Debs, 1985).
13. Kassav', "Gorée" (Georges Debs, 1989).
14. Idrissa Diop and Ralph Tamar, *Africains et Antillais* (Remark Records, 1994).
15. Unlike the United States where racial minorities are often concentrated in the inner city, in France, especially in the Parisian region, racial minorities tend to reside in the suburbs.
16. See Pierre-Antoine Marti, *Rap 2 France: Les mots d'une rupture identitaire* (Paris: L'Harmattan, 2005); Véronique Hélénon, "Africa on Their Mind: Rap, Blackness, and Citizenship in France," in *The Vinyl Ain't Final: Hip Hop and the Globalization of Black Popular Culture*, ed. Dipannita Basu and Sidney J. Lemelle (London: Pluto Press, 2006), 151–66; and André Prévos, "The Evolution of French Rap Music and Hip Hop Culture in the 1980s and 1990s," *French Review* 69, no. 5 (1996): 713–25.
17. Kery James, "Banlieusards" (France: Warner Music, 2008).
18. One should note that Caribbean views on topics related to immigration and race relations

are not homogeneous. They often reflect one's political affiliation. The majority of French Caribbean people (around 70 percent) tend to embrace the left, usually the Socialist Party. By association, a portion of Caribbean individuals also embrace the anti-African immigration policies that are usually presented by Chirac and Sarkozy's party.

19. See Michael Marrus and Robert Paxton, *Vichy France and the Jews* (Palo Alto, CA: Stanford University Press, 1995).

20. See William Schneider, *Quality and Quantity: The Quest for Biological Regeneration in Twentieth-Century France* (Cambridge: Cambridge University Press, 1990).

21. Ibid.

22. See Erik Bleich, *Race Politics in Britain and France: Ideas and Policymaking since the 1960s* (Cambridge: Cambridge University Press, 2003). This is not true for sub-Saharan Africans. The French never recruited them as labor migrants; they have been trying to keep Africans in their respective countries since the beginning of the sixties.

23. According to the French census in 1946: 1,743,619 foreigners lived in France, and by 1975 the number had increased to 3,442,415. In 1975 only 81,850 sub-Saharan Africans lived in France.

24. From its establishment, the FN has promoted a return to traditional and conservative Catholic values, high tariffs, more independence from the European Union and other international organizations, no immigration from the former colonies, and stricter observance of the cult of domesticity (women should stay at home and take care of their children and husbands). See Claude Askolovitch, *Voyage au bout de la France: Le Front National tel qu'il est* (Paris: Grasset, 1999).

25. See Jonathan Marcus, *The National Front and French Politics: The Irresistible Rise of Jean-Marie Le Pen* (New York: NYU Press, 1995). Also, Herman Lebovics offers an interesting analysis between decolonization and Le Pen's ascendance as an important player in French politics; Lebovics, *Bringing the Empire Back Home: France in the Global Age* (Durham, NC: Duke University Press, 2004).

26. See Shields's impressive study of the far right in France; James Shields, *The Extreme Right in France: From Pétain to Le Pen* (London: Routledge 2007), 187.

27. Ibid.

28. *Le Monde*, May 29, 2002.

29. *Liberation*, April 30, 2007.

30. Jane Freedman, "Women and Immigration: Nationality and Citizenship," in *Women, Immigration and Identities in France*, ed. Jane Freedman and Carrie Tarr (Oxford: Berg, 2000).

31. Abdoulaye Gueye offers a fascinating analysis of Cantet's film. For Gueye, *The Class* perpetuates colonial stereotypes of blackness and whiteness. Blacks, he argues, are physical beings warranting control; whites are intellectuals in managerial positions. In its portrayal of black students, the film masks certain social realities, particularly the importance that France's black communities attribute to education. See Abdoulaye Gueye, "The Color of Unworthiness: Understanding Blacks in France and the French Visual Media through Laurent Cantet's *The Class* (2008)," *Transition* 102, no. 1 (2010): 158-71.

32. Harlem Désir, *SOS désirs* (Paris: Calmann-Lévy, 1987). One should note that the Socialist Party provided much support to Mr. Désir.

33. See Didier Gondola, "Transient Citizens: The Othering and Indigenization of Blacks and Beurs within the French Republic," in *Frenchness and the African Diaspora: Identity and Uprising in*

Contemporary France, ed. Charles Tshimanga, Didier Gondola, and Peter Bloom (Bloomington: Indiana University Press, 2009).

34. *Le Monde*, December 7, 2005.
35. For a good discussion on the racial and political dimensions of secularism in France, see Joan Wallach Scott, *The Politics of the Veil* (Princeton, NJ: Princeton University Press, 2007). See also the important work of Trica Keaton, *Muslim Girls and the Other France: Race, Identity Politics, and Social Exclusion* (Bloomington: University of Indiana Press, 2006).
36. One should note that CRAN's leadership changed in 2011. Mr. Louis-Georges Tin, a Martinican man, is now the current president.
37. Phone interview with Patrick Lozès, January 8, 2010.
38. Ibid.
39. Ibid.
40. One should note that there is a vibrant intellectual current in France that centers racism within the very formation of the nation. For a brief example, see Olivier Le Cour Grandmaison, *La République impériale: Politique et racisme d'Etat* (Paris: Fayard, 2009).
41. Ibid.
42. One should note that initially, from a political perspective, the negritude writers emphasized that blackness and Frenchness were mutually exclusive. However, in the early forties, Césaire and Damas changed their position and supported departmentalization. As Gary Wilder explains, "Césaire's support for departmentalization was a pragmatic response to a given historical conjuncture. . . . For him, the 1946 law was a constitutional act, a founding legal initiative that derived from and would radically alter the form of the imperial nation-state by creating citizenship that built on the imperial history that had bound metropolitan and Antillean populations together within an interdependent entity." See Gary Wilder, "Untimely Vision: Aimé Césaire, Decolonization, Utopia," *Public Culture* 21, no. 1 (2009): 108.
43. Ibid.
44. Amartya Sen, *Development as Freedom* (Oxford: Oxford University Press, 1999), 87.

CONCLUSION

1. Interview with Maryse Condé, New York, March 2010.

Bibliography

PRIMARY SOURCES
Archival Material

- ARCHIVES DE LA CONFÉDÉRATION GÉNÉRALE DU TRAVAIL, PARIS

"Main d'œuvre immigrée." Box Immigrés travailleurs en France. N.d.

"Les travailleurs espagnols dans la métallurgie parisienne." Box A 22g, Immigrés travailleurs en France.

- ARCHIVES DE LA CONFÉDÉRATION FRANÇAISE DÉMOCRATIQUE DU TRAVAIL, PARIS

"Conférence nationale sur les travailleurs immigrés." Box 7 H 28.

- AUMÔNERIE NATIONALE ANTILLES GUYANE, PARIS

Alizé: Bulletin de la Fédération Antillo-Guyanaise des Etudiants Catholiques, December 1965, December 1966–January 1967, May–June 1968.

- L'AGENCE NATIONALE POUR L'INSERTION ET LA PROMOTION DES TRAVAILLEURS D'OUTRE-MER, SAINT-DENIS

Note that all documents have recently been moved to Archives Nationales d'Outre-Mer in Aix-en-Provence.

Bardet, Pierre. "Monographe." N.d.

Bureau pour le Développement des Migrations Intéressant les Départements d'Outre-Mer. *Bulletin d'Information*. Paris 1967.

Bureau pour le Développement des Migrations Intéressant les Départements d'Outre-Mer. "Compte rendu d'activités décembre 1967."

Bureau pour le Développement des Migrations Intéressant les Départements d'Outre-Mer. "Migration en métropole de travailleurs des départements d'outre-mer et de leurs familles," February 1964.

Bureau pour le Développement des Migrations Intéressant les Départements d'Outre-Mer. *Mises au point*. No month, 1972.

Bureau pour le Développement des Migrations Intéressant les Départements d'Outre-Mer. "Rapport d'activité, 1962."

Bureau pour le Développement des Migrations Intéressant les Départements d'Outre-Mer. "Rapport d'activité, 1962: Perspective programme 1963."

Document pédagogique du centre Crouy-sur-Ourq. 1973.

- LE CENTRE DES ARCHIVES CONTEMPORAINES, FONTAINEBLEAU

Africains dans la région parisienne. Box 19810201, art. 6.

Association Etrangère en France. Box 19870799, art. 24.

Direction de la Population et des Migrations. Box 19760133, art. 133.

Direction de la Population et des Migrations. "Main d'œuvre étrangère: Réglementation générale, statistiques." Box 810201, art. 3, 10-12.

"Les problèmes de l'étranger malade." Box 19810201, art. 4.

Préfecture de la Seine. "Enquête sur les travailleurs Africains." Box 19780262, art. 11.

"Ressortissants africains en France." Box 1981020, art. 5.

- ARCHIVES DE LA PRÉFECTURE DE POLICE, PARIS

Afrique Noire: Déplacement de personnes. "L'émigration africaine en France." Direction Centrale des Renseignements Géneraux, May 1971. Box GaA9.

Afrique Noire: Déplacement de personnes. "Enquête sur les foyers de la région parisienne," December 4, 1968. Box GaA9.

"La population antillaise en France." Box Gabr47.

- BIBLIOTHÈQUE DE DOCUMENTATION INTERNATIONALE CONTEMPORAINE, NANTERRE

Association Générale des Etudiants de la Martinique. "Extrait du rapport politique du cinquième congrès national de l'Association Générale des Etudiants de la Martinique," December 1961. Pièce 9899.

Association pour la Formation Technique de Base des Africains et Malgaches. "Travailleurs africains en France." Pièce 9433.

Le Patriote Guadeloupéen. Pièce F 3825.

- THE MOORLAND-SPINGARN RESEARCH CENTER, HOWARD UNIVERSITY

Will Mercer Cook Papers, Series C, Box 157-2, folder 21.

Government and Government Agencies' Publications

Assistance Publique des Hôpitaux de Paris. *Les originaires de l'Outre-mer à l'AP-HP.* Colloque sous le haut patronage du Secrétaire d'État à l'Outre-Mer. Paris, 2002.

Avis et Rapports du Conseil Economique et Social. "Problèmes posés par l'immigration des travailleurs africains en France." *Journal Officiel de la République Française*, July 24, 1964.

Jourdan, M. "Conférence sur l'état sanitaire chez les travailleurs originaires d'Afrique Noire." Paris: Préfecture de la Seine, 1965.

Ministère de la Coopération. *Dix réponses sur l'Afrique: Opinions sur la coopération entre l'Afrique et la France.* Paris, 1963.

Petit, Lucien. *Les travailleurs noirs dans la région parisienne.* Paris: Préfecture de la Seine, 1964.

Newsletters and Bulletins

Amicale Générale des Travailleurs Antillais et Guyanais. *Bulletin d'Information* (1964).

Fédération des Etudiants d'Afrique Noire en France. *Bulletin d'Activité*, no. 1 (1968).

La Voix de l'Emigration (March–April 1966).

"Le role de la femme gabonaise dans la libération nationale." *L'Etudiant du Gabon* (September 1974).

"Le role des travailleurs émigrés dans la lutte de liberation nationale." *Le Patriote Guadeloupéen* (September 1971).

"Rapport du Professeur Brocard." *Revue de Tuberculose et de Pneumologie* (October 9, 1962).

Trait d'Union: Bulletin de l'Association des Étudiants de la Martinique (May 1957).

FILMOGRAPHY
Institut National de l'Audiovisuel, BNF, Paris

Entre les Murs. Laurent Cantet. Sony, 2008.

"Henri Salvador: Inventaire Montparnasse." *L'art et les hommes.* ORTF (January 1, 1963).

Jeunes Africains à Paris. ORTF, September 12, 1963.

L'Afrique des banlieues. Jean Schmidt. ORTF, Collection le Monde en 40 Minutes, 1967.

La Noire de . . . /Black Girl. Ousmane Sembène. Senegal, 1966.

"Ouvriers noirs de Paris." Claude Arnaud, Jean Claude Bringuiernon, and Jean-Luc Leridon. 5 Colonnes à la une de Jacques Krier, 1962.

Paris des négritudes. Jean Schmidt. Atelier 8, 1970.

Travailleurs Africains. Jean-Luc Léridon. ORTF, 1962.

"Une île au soleil." *Cinq Colonnes à la une.* April 6, 1960.

Un Malien d'Ivry. Jean Mailland. ORTF, Série Panorama de Jean Mailland, 1970.

Forum des Images, Paris

Ibrahima. Max Zelenka. Les Ecrans Modernes, 1966.

DISCOGRAPHY

Charlus, "A la Martinique." EMG, 1912.
Idrissa, Diop, and Ralph Tamar. "Africains et Antillais." Remark Records, 1994.
James, Kery. "Banlieusard." Warner Music, 2008.
Kassav', "En ba chen'n la." Georges Debs, 1985.
———. "Gorée." Georges Debs, 1989.
Mona, Eugène. "Ti Milo." Hibiscus Records, 1975.
Salvador, Henri. "Dans mon île." Disque Barclay, 1957.
———. "Faut rigoler." Barclay, 1960.
———."Le travail c'est la santé." Sony, 1965.
———. "Personnalisé." Rigolo, 1967.
Simon, Simone. "Moi tout faire pour te plaire." Paris: Columbia DF 1607 (CL 5043-1), 1934.
Super Combo, *Chalè a Paris*. Debs, 1977.

SECONDARY SOURCES

Absalon, Nora. "Le personnel hospitalier originaire des DOM à l'Assistance Publique de Paris, 1967-1987." Mémoire de maitrise d'histoire contemporaine, Université de Paris I, October 2001.

Adélaide-Merlande, Jacques. *Les origines du mouvement ouvrier en Martinique: 1870-1900*. Paris: Editions Karthala, 2000.

Adi, Hakim, and Marika Sherwood. *Pan-African History: Political Figures from Africa and the Diaspora since 1787*. New York: Routledge, 2003.

Adler, Karen. *Jews and Gender in Liberation France*. Cambridge: Cambridge University Press, 2003.

Aldrich, Robert. *Greater France: A History of French Overseas Expansion*. New York: Palgrave Macmillan, 1996.

Aldrich, V., and John Connell. *France's Overseas Frontier: Départements et Territoires d'Outre-Mer*. New York, 1992.

Alibar, France, and Pierrette Lembeye-Boy. *Le couteau seul: La condition féminine aux Antilles*. Paris: Karthala, 1981.

Anderson, Bridget. *Doing the Dirty Work? The Global Politics of Domestic Labor*. New York: Zed Books 2000.

Anselin, Alain. *L'émigration antillaise en France: La troisième île*. Paris: Karthala, 1990.

Archer-Straw, Petrine. *Negrophilia: Avant-Garde Paris and Black Culture in the 1920s*. London: Thames and Hudson, 2000.

Armand, Nicolas. *Histoire de la Martinique: Des Arawak à 1848*. Paris: L'Harmattan, 1996.

Asante, Molefi. *The Afrocentric Idea*. Philadelphia: Temple University Press, 1987.

Askolovitch, Claude. *Voyage au bout de la France: Le Front National tel qu'il est*. Paris: Grasset, 1999.

Astor, Gerald. *The Right to Fight: A History of African Americans in the Military*. Cambridge, MA: Da Capo Press, 2001.

Ata Aidoo, Ama. *Our Sister Killjoy*. London: Longman, 1977.

Atack, Margaret. *May 68 in French Fiction and Film: Rethinking Society, Rethinking Representation*. Oxford: Oxford University Press, 1999.

Baillard, Danielle, and Germaine Louilot. *Femmes martiniquaises: Mythes et réalités*. Paris: L'Harmattan, 1987.

Banine. *La France étrangère*. Paris: Editions S.O.S, Desclée de Brouwer, 1968.

Barou, Jacques. *Travailleurs africains en France: Rôle des cultures d'origine*. Grenoble: Presses Universitaires de Grenoble, 1977.

Barrow, Christine. *Caribbean Portraits: Essays on Gender Ideologies and Identities*. Kingston, Jamaica: Women INK, 1998.

Bazenguissa-Ganga, Rémy, and Janet MacGaffey. *Congo-Paris: Transnational Traders on the Margins of the Law*. Bloomington: Indiana University Press, 2000.

Beauvue-Fougeyrollas, Claudie. *Les femmes antillaises*. Paris: L'Harmattan, 1985.

Bebel-Gisler, Dany. *La langue créole, force jugulée: Etude socio-linguistique des rapports de force entre le créole et le français aux Antilles*. Paris: L'Harmattan, 1976.

———. *Léonora: L'histoire enfouie de la Guadeloupe*. Paris: Seghers, 1985.

Beriss, David. *Black Skins, French Voices: Caribbean Ethnicity and Activism in Urban France*. Boulder, CO: Westview Press, 2004.

Berlanstein, Lenard, ed. *Rethinking Labor History: Essays on Discourse and Class Analysis*. Urbana: University of Illinois Press, 1993.

Berliner, Brett. *Ambivalent Desire: The Exotic Black Other in Jazz-Age France*. Amherst: University of Massachusetts Press, 2002.

Berrian, Brenda. *Awakening Spaces: French Caribbean Popular Songs, Music, and Culture*. Chicago: University of Chicago Press, 2000.

———. "Chestnut Women: French Caribbean Women Writers and Singers." *Encuentros* 42, no. 42 (2001).

Betts, Raymond. *France and Decolonization, 1900–1960*. New York: Palgrave Macmillan, 1991.

Blakely, Allison. "The Emergence of Afro-Europe: A Preliminary Sketch." In *Black Europe in the African Diaspora*, edited by Darlene Clark Hine, Trica Danielle Keaton, and Stephen Small. Chicago: University of Illinois Press, 2009.

Bleich, Erik. *Race Politics in Britain and France: Ideas in Policymaking since the 1960s*. New York: Cambridge University Press, 2003.

Bogle, Donald. *Toms, Coons, Mulattoes, Mammies, and Bucks: An Interpretive History of Blacks in American Films*. New York: Continuum Press, 2001.

Boittin, Jennifer. *Colonial Metropolis: The Urban Grounds of Anti-Imperialism and Feminism in Interwar Paris*. Lincoln: University of Nebraska Press, 2010.

Bourdieu, Pierre. *Homo academicus*. Paris: Minuit, 1984.

Briggs, Laura. *Reproducing Empire: Race, Sex, Science, and U.S. Imperialism in Puerto Rico*. Berkeley: University of California Press, 2002.

Burton, Richard. *La famille coloniale: La Martinique et la mère patrie, 1789–1992*. Paris: L'Harmattan,

1994.

———. *The Flâneur and His City: Patterns of Life in Paris, 1815-1851*. Durham, England: University of Durham Press, 1994.

———. *French and West Indian: Martinique, Guadeloupe, and French Guiana Today*. Charlottesville: University of Virginia Press, 1995.

Butler, Kim. "Defining Diaspora, Refining a Discourse." *Diaspora: A Journal of Transnational Studies* 10, no. 2 (2001): 189-219.

Camiscioli, Elisa. "Reproducing the 'French Race': Immigration and Pronatalism in Early-Twentieth-Century France." In *Bodies in Contact: Rethinking Colonial Encounters in World History*, edited by Tony Ballantyne and Antoinette Burton. Durham, NC: Duke University Press, 2005.

Carlos, Jacques. "From Savages and Barbarians to Primitives: Africa, Social Typologies, and History in Eighteenth-Century French Philosophy." *History and Theory* 36, no. 2 (1997), 190-215.

Carol, Anne. *Histoire de l'eugenisme en France: Les médecins et la procreation XIXe-XXe siècles*. Paris, 1995.

Castle, Stephen, and Mark Miller. *The Age of Migration*. London: Macmillan Press, 1998.

Cazenave, Odile. *Afrique sur Seine: A New Generation of African Writers in Paris*. Lanham, MD: Lexington Books, 2005.

Césaire, Aimé. *Discourse on Colonialism*. New York: Monthly Review Press, 1972.

Charles, Diane. *Les Grandes Heures de la F.E.A.N.F.* Paris: Chaka, 1990.

Clark, Vévé, and Sara Johnson. *Kaiso! Writings by and about Katherine Dunham*. Madison: University of Wisconsin Press, 2006.

Cock, Jacklyn. *Maids and Madams: Domestic Workers under Apartheid*. London: Women's Press, 1989.

Cohen, Evelyne, and Marie-Françoise Lévy. *La télévision des Trente Glorieuses: Culture et politique*. Paris: CNRS Editions, 2007.

Cohen, William. *The French Encounter with Africans: White Response to Blacks, 1530-1880*. Bloomington: Indiana University Press, 1980.

———. "Legacy of Empire: The Algerian Connection." *Journal of Contemporary History* 15, no. 1 (1980), 97-123.

Condon, Stephanie. "Compromise and Coping Strategies: Gender Issues and Caribbean Migration to France." In *Caribbean Migration: Globalized Identities*, edited by Mary Chamberlain. New York: Routledge, 1998.

Condon, Stephanie, and Philip Ogden. "Afro-Caribbean Migrants in France: Employment, State Policy and the Migration Process." *Transactions of the Institute of British Geographers*, New Series, 16, no. 4 (1991).

Coryell, Schofield. "Africa in Paris." *Africa Today* 8, no. 9 (1961).

Cova, Anne. *Maternité et droits des femmes en France (XIXe-XXe siècles)*. Paris: Anthropos, 1997.

Cross, Gary. *Immigrant Workers in Industrial France: The Making of a New Laboring Class*. Philadelphia: Temple University Press, 1983.

Crusol-Baillard, Danielle, and Germaine Louilot. *Femme martiniquaise: Mythes et réalités*. Paris: N.p., 1987.

Cunha, Maria do Ceu. *Portugais de France: Essai sur une dynamique de double appartenance*. Paris:

L'Harmattan, 1988.

Cyrille, Dominique. "Imagining an Afro-Creole Nation: Eugène Mona's Music in Martinique of the 1980s." *Latin American Music Review* 27, no. 2 (2006).

Davidson, Nicol. "Alioune Diop and the African Renaissance." *African Affairs* 78, no. 310 (1979).

Dedieu, Jean-Philippe. *La parole immigrée: Les migrants africains dans l'espace public en France, 1960-1995*. Paris: Klincksieck, 2012.

Delerm, Robert. "Population noire en France." *Population* 3 (July 1964).

Derrick, Jonathan. "The Dissenters: Anti-Colonialism in France." In *Promoting the Colonial Idea: Propaganda and Visions of Empire in France*, edited by Tony Chafer and Amanda Sackur. New York: Palgrave, 2002.

Désir, Harlem. *SOS désirs*. Paris: Calmann-Lévy, 1987.

Dewitte, Philippe. *Les mouvements nègres en France, 1919-1939*. Paris: L'Harmattan, 1985.

Dia, Oumar. *Yakaré: L'autobiographie d'Oumar*. Paris: François Maspéro, 1982.

Diané, Charles. *Les grandes heures de la FEANF*. Paris: Éditions Chaka, 1990.

Diawara, Manthia. "The 1960s in Bamako: Malick Sidibé and James Brown." In *Black Cultural Traffic: Crossroads in Global Performance and Popular Culture*, edited by Harry Elam and Kennell Jackson. Ann Arbor: University of Michigan Press, 2005.

Diebolt, Evelyne. *Les femmes dans l'action sanitaire, sociale et culturelle, 1901-2001*. Paris: Femmes et associations, 2001.

Dieng, Amady Aly. *Les grand combats de la FEANF*. Paris: L'Harmattan, 2009.

———. *Les premiers pas de la Fédération des étudiants d'Afrique noire en France (FEANF), 1950-1955: De l'Union française à Bandoung*. Paris: L'Harmattan, 2003.

Douay, Georges. *Animation au foyer de jeunes travailleurs de Simandres*. Paris: BUMIDOM, n.d.

Dubois, Laurent. *A Colony of Citizens: Revolution and Slave Emancipation in the French Caribbean, 1787-1804*. Chapel Hill: University of North Carolina Press, 2004.

Duchen, Claire. *Women's Rights and Women's Lives in France, 1944-1968*. New York: Routledge, 1994.

Edwards, Brent Hayes. *The Practice of Diaspora: Literature, Translation, and the Rise of Black Internationalism*. Cambridge, MA: Harvard University Press, 2003.

Ega, Françoise. *Lettre à une Noire: Récit antillais*. Paris: L'Harmattan, 1978.

Ellison, Ralph. *The Invisible Man*. New York: Vintage, 1947.

Enloe, Cynthia. *Bananas, Beaches, and Bases: Making Feminist Sense of International Politics*. Berkeley: University of California Press, 1990.

Ezra, Elizabeth. *The Colonial Unconscious: Race and Culture in Interwar France*. Ithaca, NY: Cornell University Press, 1992.

Fabre, Geneviève, and Robert O'Malley, *History and Memory in African-American Culture*. Oxford: Oxford University Press, 1994.

Fall, Mar. *Les Africains noirs en France: Des tirailleurs Sénégalais au Black*. Paris: L'Harmattan, 1986.

Fanon, Frantz. *Black Skin, White Masks*. New York: Grove Press, 1967.

———. *The Wretched of the Earth*. New York: Grove Press, 2004.

Foredeck, Charles, and David Murphy, eds. *Francophone Postcolonial Studies*. London: Arnold, 2003.

Forth, Christopher, and Bertrand Taithe, *French Masculinities: Histories, Politics, and Culture*.

Hampshire, England: Macmillan, 2007.

Foucault, Michel. "The Subject and Power." *Critical Inquiry* 8, no. 4 (1982).

Fourastié, Jean. *Les Trente Glorieuses*. Paris: Fayard, 1979.

Franklin, Albert. "Le paternalisme contre l'étudiant africain." *Présence Africaine: Les étudiants noirs parlent* 14 (1953).

Freedman, Jane. "Women and Immigration: Nationality and Citizenship." In *Women, Immigration and Identities in France*, edited by Jane Freedman and Carrie Tarr. New York: Oxford, 2000.

Freeman, Gary. "Caribbean Migration to Britain and France: From Assimilation to Selection." In *The Caribbean Exodus*, ed. Barry Levine. New York: Praeger, 1987.

Gadjigo, Samba, Ralph Faulkingham, Thomas Cassirer, and Reinhard Sander, eds. *Ousmane Sembène: Dialogues with Critics and Writers*. Amherst: University of Massachusetts Press, 1993.

Galano, Mireille. "Immigration: Trente ans de combat par le droit." *Plein Droit* (March 2002).

Garrigus, John. "'Thy Coming Fame, Ogé! Is Sure': New Evidence on Ogé's 1790 Revolt and the Beginnings of the Haitian Revolution." In *Assumed Identities: The Meanings of Race in the Atlantic World*, edited by John Garrigus and Chris Morris. College Station: Texas A&M University Press, 2010.

Gastaut, Yvan. "Les bidonvilles, lieux d'exclusion et de marginalité en France durant les Trente Glorieuses." *Cahiers de la Méditerranée* 69 (May 2006).

———. "Figures et présence des immigrés dans les medias." *Confluences Méditerranée* 24.

Gautier, Arlette. *Les sœurs de solitude: La condition féminine dans l'esclavage aux Antilles du XVIIè au XIXè siècle*. Paris: Editions Caribéennes, 1985.

Genova, James. *Colonial Ambivalence, Cultural Authenticity, and the Limitations of Mimicry in French-Ruled West Africa, 1914-1956*. New York: Peter Lang, 2004.

Gesner, Mence. *L'affaire de l'O.J.A.M.* Fort-de-France, Martinique: Editions Désormeaux, 2001.

Gilroy, Paul. *The Black Atlantic: Modernity and Double Consciousness*. New York: Verso, 1993.

Girardet, Raoul. *L'idée coloniale en France de 1871 à 1962*. Paris: Hachette, 2005.

Giraud, Michel. "The Antillese in France: Trends and Prospects." *Ethnic and Racial Studies* 27, no. 4 (2004).

———. *L'école aux Antilles: Langues et échec scolaire*. Paris: Karthala, 1992.

Glissant, Edouard. *Caribbean Discourse*. Charlottesville: University of Virginia Press, 1989.

Goossen, Jean. "The Migration of French West Indian Women to Metropolitan France." *Anthropological Quarterly* 49, no. 1 (1976).

Gregoire, Roger. *Worker-Student Action Committees, France, May 68*. Detroit: Black & Red, 1970.

Grosfoguel, Ramon. "Decolonizing Post-Colonial Studies and Paradigms of Political-Economy: Transmodernity, Decolonial Thinking, and Global Coloniality." *TRANSMODERNITY: Journal of Peripheral Cultural Production of the Luso-Hispanic World* 1, no. 1 (2011).

Guerrand, Roger-Henri. *Hygiene*. Paris: Editions de la Villette, 2001.

Guerrero, Ed. *Framing Blackness: The African American Image in Film*. Philadelphia: Temple University Press, 1993.

Gueye, Abdoulaye. "The Colony Strikes Back: African Protest Movements in Postcolonial France." *Comparative Studies of South Asia, Africa, and the Middle East* 26, no. 2 (2006): 225-42.

———. "The Color of Unworthiness: Understanding Blacks in France and the French Visual Media through Laurent Cantet's *The Class* (2008)." *Transition* 102, no. 1 (2010): 158–71.

Guibault, Jocelyne. *Zouk: World Music in the West Indies*. Chicago: University of Chicago Press, 1993.

Guimont, Fabienne. *Les étudiants africains en France, 1950–1965*. Paris: L'Harmattan, 1997.

Hale, Dana. *Races on Display: French Representations of Colonized Peoples, 1886–1940*. Bloomington: Indiana University Press, 2008.

Hargreaves, Alec. *Immigration, Race, and Ethnicity in Contemporary France*. New York: Routledge, 1995.

———. *Multi-ethnic France: Immigration, Politics, Culture, and Society*. New York: Routledge, 2007.

Harris, Joseph, ed. *Global Dimensions of the African Diaspora*. Washington, DC: Howard University Press, 1983.

Harshe, Rajen. "Guinea under Sekou Toure." *Economic and Political Weekly* 19, no. 15 (April 14, 1984).

Hartman, Saidiya. *Lose Your Mother: A Journey along the Atlantic Slave Route*. New York: Farrar, Straus and Giroux, 2007.

Hassan, Salah. "Inaugural Issues: The Cultural Politics of the Early 'Présence Africaine,' 1947–55." *Research in African Literatures* 30, no. 2 (1999): 194–221.

Haus, Leah. *Unions, Immigration, and Internationalization: New Challenges and Changing Conditions in the United States and France*. New York: Palgrave Macmillan, 2002.

Hayter, Teresa. "French Aid to Africa—Its Scope and Achievements." *International Affairs* 41, no. 2 (1965): 236–51.

Headrick, Rita. *Colonialism, Health, and Illness in French Equatorial Africa, 1885–1935*. Atlanta, GA: African Studies Association Press, 1994.

Hélénon, Véronique. "Africa on Their Mind: Rap, Blackness, and Citizenship in France." In *The Vinyl Ain't Final: Hip Hop and the Globalization of Black Popular Culture*, edited by Dipannita Basu and Sidney J. Lemelle. London: Pluto Press, 2006.

———. *French Caribbeans in Africa: Diasporic Connections and Colonial Administration, 1880–1939*. New York: Palgrave Macmillan, 2011.

Howell, Chris. *Regulating Labor: The State and Industrial Relations Reform in Postwar France*. Princeton, NJ: Princeton University Press, 1992.

Howlett, Jacques. "Présence Africaine, 1947–1958." *Journal of Negro History* 43, no. 2 (1958).

Ikonné, Chidi. "René Maran: A Black Francophone Writer (1887–1960) between Two Worlds." *Research in African Literatures* 5, no. 1 (1974).

Irele, Abiola. *The Negritude Moment: Explorations in Francophone African and Caribbean Literature and Thought*. Trenton, NJ: Africa World Press, 2011.

Ischinger, Barbara. "Negritude: Some Dissident Voices." *Issue: A Journal of Opinion* 4, no. 4 (1974).

Jaccoulet, Marie-Alice. *De solitude à mélodie*. Martinique: Ibis Rouge, 2005.

Jackson, Jeffrey. *Making Jazz French: Music and Modern Life in Interwar Paris*. Durham, NC: Duke University Press, 2003.

James, Winston, and Clive Harris, eds. *Inside Babylon: The Caribbean Diaspora in Britain*. London: Verso, 1993.

Jeanneney, Jean-Noel, and Monique Sauvage. *Télévision, nouvelle mémoire: Les magazines de grands reportages, 1959–1968*. Paris: Editions du Seuil, 1982.

Jennings, Eric. "La dissidence aux Antilles, 1940–1943." *Vingtième Siècle: Revue d'histoire* 68 (2000).

———. "Monuments to Frenchness? The Memory of the Great War and the Politics of Guadeloupe's Identity, 1914–1945." *French Historical Studies* 21 (1998): 561–92.

———. *Vichy in the Tropics: Pétain's National Revolution in Madagascar, Guadeloupe, and Indochina, 1940–1944*. Palo Alto, CA: Stanford University Press, 2001.

Jobs, Richard. *Riding the New Wave: Youth and the Rejuvenation of France after the Second World War*. Stanford, CA: Stanford University Press, 2007.

Jolivet, Marie-José. "La construction d'une mémoire historique à la Martinique: Du schœlchérisme au marronisme." *Cahiers d'études africaines* 27, no. 107–8 (1987).

Jordi, Jean-Jacques. *De l'exode à l'exil: Rapatriés et Pieds-Noirs en France, l'exemple marseillais, 1954–1992*. Paris: L'Harmattan, 1993.

Jules-Rosette, Bennetta. "Conjugating Cultural Realities: Présence Africaine." In *The Surreptitious Speech: Présence Africaine and the Politics of Otherness, 1947–1987*, edited by V. Y. Mudimbe. Chicago: University of Chicago Press, 1992.

Kaupi, Niilo. *French Intellectual Nobility: Institutional and Symbolic Transformations in the Post-Sartrian Era*. Albany, NY: SUNY Press, 1996.

Keaton, Trica. *Muslim Girls and the Other France: Race, Identity Politics, and Social Exclusion*. Bloomington: University of Indiana Press, 2006.

Keaton, Trica, T. Denean Sharpley-Whiting, and Tyler Stovall, eds. *Black France/France Noire: The History and Politics of Blackness*. Durham, NC: Duke University Press, 2012.

Keita, Maghan. *A Political Economy of Healthcare in Senegal*. Leiden, Netherlands: Brill, 2007.

Kelley, Robin D. G. "'Afric's Sons with Banner Red': African-American Communists and the Politics of Culture, 1919–1934." In *Imagining Home: Class, Culture, and Nationalism in the African Diaspora*, edited by Sidney Lemelle and Robin D. G. Kelley. New York: Verso, 1994.

Kergoat, Nadia. "Une secrétaire d'acceuil." Master's thesis, Institut National de Tertiaire Social et de la Formation Continue, 1981.

Kesteloot, Lilian. *Black Writers in French: A Literary History of Negritude*. Washington, DC: Howard University Press, 1991.

Kovats, Edith. *Les blancs créoles de la Martinique: Une minorité dominante*. Paris: L'Harmattan, 2002.

Kuisel, Richard. *Seducing the French: The Dilemma of Americanization*. Berkeley: University of California Press, 1993.

Labache, Lucette. *Les originaires d'outre-mer à l'AP-HP*. Paris: Assistance Publique Hôpitaux de Paris, 2003.

Lachaise, Bernard. "Contestataires et compagnons: Les formes de l'engagement gaulliste." *Vingtième Siècle: Revue d'histoire* 60 (October–December 1998).

Lacrosil, Michèle. *Cajou*. Paris: Gallimard, 1961.

Lara, Oruno. *De l'oubli à l'histoire: Espace et identité caraïbes*. Paris: Maisonneuve et Larose, 1998.

———. *La Guadeloupe dans l'histoire*. Paris: L'Harmattan, 1979.

Larouchez, Roland. *Confessions d'une prostituée à Paris*. Fort-de-France, Martinique: Imprimerie Désormaux, 1975.

Lebovics, Herman. *Bringing the Empire Back Home: France in the Global Age*. Durham, NC: Duke University Press, 2004.

Le Cour Grandmaison, Olivier. *La République impériale: Politique et racisme d'Etat*. Paris: Fayard, 2009.

Leonard, Jill. "Martinican Women and the French State: Race and Gender in the Construction of the Colonial Relation." PhD diss., University of Illinois, 1997.

Lévy, Marie-Françoise. *La télévision des Trente Glorieuses: Culture et politique*. Paris: CNRS Editions, 2007.

Lewis, Shireen. *Race, Culture, and Identity: Francophone West African and Caribbean Literature and Theory from Négritude to Créolité*. Lanham, MD: Lexington Books, 2006.

Lisette, Gabriel. *Le combat du Rassemblement Démocratique Africain*. Paris: Présence Africaine, 1983.

Little, Roger. "From Taboo to Totem: Black Man, White Woman, in Caroline Auguste Fischer and Sophie Doin." *Modern Language Review* 93, no. 4 (1998).

Lovatt, Roland, Christine Whitehead, and Claire Levy-Vroelant. "Foyers in the UK and France—Comparisons and Contrasts." *European Journal of Housing Policy* 6, no. 12 (2006): 151–66.

Loza, Julien Valère. *Les étudiants martiniquais en France: Histoire de leur organisation et de leurs luttes*. Martinique: Editions 2 M, 2003.

Lyons, Amelia. *The Civilizing Mission in the Metropole: Algerian Families and the French Welfare State during Decolonization*. Palo Alto, CA: Stanford University Press, 1993.

Mahamet, Timera. *Les Soninké en France: D'une histoire à l'autre*. Paris: Katharla, 1996.

Mam Lam Fouck, Serge. *Histoire générale de la Guyane française*. Matoury, French Guiana: Ibis Rouge, 2010.

Manicom, Jacqueline. *La graine*. Paris: Presses de la Cité, 1974.

Mann, Gregory. "Immigrants and Arguments in France and West Africa." *Comparative Studies in Society and History* 45, no. 2 (2003): 362–85.

Manville, Marcel. *Les Antilles sans fard*. Paris: L'Harmattan, 1992.

Marcus, Jonathan. *The National Front and French Politics: The Irresistible Rise of Jean-Marie Le Pen*. New York: NYU Press, 1995.

Marie, Claude-Valentin. "Les populations des Dom-Tom en France." *Journal de l'Agence Nationale pour l'Insertion et la Promotion des Travailleurs d'Outre-Mer*," no. 7, supplement. Paris: ANT, 1982.

———. "Les populations des Dom-Tom en métropole." *Ici là-bas*, no. 7 (January 1986).

———. *Les populations des DOM-TOM, nées et originaires, résidant en France métropolitaine*. Paris: INSEE, 1990.

Marseille, Jacques. "Les images de l'Afrique en France (des années 1880 aux années 1930)." *Canadian Journal of African Studies* 22, no. 1 (1988): 121.

Marti, Pierre-Antoine. *Rap 2 France: Les mots d'une rupture identitaire*. Paris: L'Harmattan, 2005.

Massey, David. *Frantz Fanon: A Life*. London: Granta, 2000.

Massey, Douglas. *Worlds in Motion: Understanding International Migration at the End of the Millennium*. Oxford: Clarendon Press, 1998.

Mauvois, Georges. *Louis des Etages, 1873–1925: Itinéraire d'un homme politique martiniquais*. Paris: Karthala, 1990.

Maxwell, Rahsaan. *Ethnic Minority Migrants in Britain and France: Integration Trade-offs*. New York: Cambridge University Press, 2012.

M'Bokolo, Elikia. *Afrique noire: Histoire et civilisations du XIXe siècle à nos jours*. Paris: Hatier, 1992.

McCluskey, Thomas. *Imagining Blackness: Race and Racial Representation in Film Poster Art*. Bloomington: Indiana University Press, 2007.

McCracken, Allison. "'God's Gift to Us Girls': Crooning, Gender, and the Re-Creation of American Popular Song, 1928–1933." *American Music* 17, no. 4 (1999).

McKay, Claude. *Banjo: A Story without a Plot*. New York: Harper & Brothers, 1929.

Mence, Gesner. *L'affaire de l'O.J.A.M.* Fort-de-France, Martinique: Editions Désormeaux, 2001.

Merckling, Odile. *Immigration et marché du travail: Le développement de la flexibilité en France*. Paris: L'Harmattan, 1998.

Mickell, Gwendolyn. *African Feminism: The Politics of Survival in Sub-Saharan Africa*. Philadelphia: University of Pennsylvania Press, 1997.

Mignolo, Walter. *Local Histories/Global Designs: Coloniality, Subaltern Knowledges, and Border Thinking*. Princeton, NJ: Princeton University Press, 2000.

Milia Marie-Luce, Monique. "L'émigration des Puertoricains, des Guadeloupéens, des Martiniquais, et Guyanais de l'après guerre aux années 1960." PhD diss., Ecole des Hautes Etudes en Sciences Sociales, 2002.

Miller, Christopher. *Nationalists and Nomads: Essays on Francophone African Literature and Culture*. Chicago: University of Chicago Press, 1998.

———. *Theories of Africans: Francophone Literature and Anthropology in Africa*. Chicago: University of Chicago Press, 1993.

Mirabel, Bernard. *Négripub: L'image des Noirs dans la publicité depuis un siècle*. Paris: Société des Amis de la Bibliothèque Forney, 1987.

Mirza, Heidi, ed. *Black British Feminism: A Reader*. London: Routledge, 1997.

Moitt, Bernard. "Slave Women and Resistance in the French Caribbean." In *More Than Chattel: Black Women in Slavery in the Americas*, edited by David Barry Gaspar and Darlene Clark Hine. Bloomington: Indiana University Press, 1996.

———. *Women and Slavery in the French Antilles, 1635–1848*. Bloomington: Indiana University Press, 2001.

Morin, Edgar, Claude Lefort, and Cornelius Castoriadis. *Mai 68: La brèche*. Paris: Editions Complexe, 1988.

Mouralis, Bernard. "Présence Africaine: Geography of an Ideology." In *The Surreptitious Speech: Présence Africaine and the Politics of Otherness, 1947–1987*, edited by V. Y. Mudimbe. Chicago: University of Chicago Press, 1992.

Mudimbe, V. Y. *The Invention of Africa: Gnosis, Philosophy, and the Order of Knowledge*. Indianapolis: Indiana University Press, 1988.

———. *The Surreptitious Speech: Présence Africaine and the Politics of Otherness, 1947–1987*. Chicago: University of Chicago Press, 1992.

Murdoch, Adlai. *Creolizing the Metropole: Migrant Caribbean Identities in Literature and Film*. Bloomington: University of Indiana Press, 2012.

N'Diaye, Jean Pierre. *Enquête sur les étudiants noirs en France*. Paris: Editions Réalités Africaines, 1962.

———. *Négriers modernes: Les travailleurs noirs en France*. Paris: Présence Africaine, 1970.

N'Diaye, Pap. *La condition noire: Essai sur une minorité française*. Paris: Calmann-Lévy, 2008.

———. "Pour une histoire des populations noires de France: Préalables théoriques." *Le Mouvement social* 213 (2005).

Nicolas, Armand. *Histoire de la Martinique*. Paris: L'Harmattan, 1996.

Ogden, Philip, and Stéphanie Condon. "Afro-Caribbean Migrants in France: Employment, State Policy and the Migration Process." *Transactions of the Institute of British Geographers*, New Series, 16, no. 4 (1991).

———. "Emigration from the French Caribbean: The Origins of an Organized Migration." *International Journal of Urban and Regional Research* 15, no. 4 (1991).

Okpewho, Isidore, and Nkiru Nzegwu. *The New African Diaspora*. Bloomington: University of Indiana Press, 2009.

Osborn, Emily Lynn. "'Circle of Iron': African Colonial Employees and the Interpretation of Colonial Rule in French West Africa." *Journal of African History* 44, no. 1 (2003).

Pago, Gilbert. *Les femmes et la liquidation du système esclavagiste à la Martinique, 1848-1852*. Guadeloupe: Ibis Rouge, 1998.

Pakenham, Thomas. *The Scramble for Africa: White Man's Conquest of the Dark Continent from 1876 to 1912*. New York: Avon Books, 1992.

Pame, Stella. *Cyrille Bissette: Un martyre de la liberté*. Martinique: Editions Désormeaux, 1999.

Parker, Gabrielle. "'Francophonie' and 'Universalité': Evolution of Two Notions Conjoined." In *Francophone Postcolonial Studies*, edited by Charles Forsdick and David Murphy. London: Arnold, 2003.

Patterson, Tiffany, and Robin D. G. Kelley. "Unfinished Migrations: Reflections on the African Diaspora and the Making of the Modern World." *African Studies Review* 43, no. 1, Special Issue on the Diaspora (2000): 11-45.

Paxton, Robert, and Michael Marrus. *Vichy France and the Jews*. Palo Alto, CA: Stanford University Press, 1995.

Pellier, Jean. *Nécéssité et possibilité de l'émigration pour les habitants de la Martinique et de la Guadeloupe*. N.p.: INSEE, n.d. Available at Archives Nationales d'Outre-Mer in Aix-en-Provence.

Pereira, Victor. "L'Etat portugais et les Portugais en France de 1958 à 1974." *Lusotopie* 2 (2002).

Péron, Yves. "La population des départements français d'outre-mer." *Population* 1 (1966): 99-132.

Pierre, Jemima. *The Predicament of Blackness: Postcolonial Ghana and the Politics of Race*. Chicago: University of Chicago Press, 2013.

Pineau, Gisèle. *L'exil selon Julia*. Paris: Stock, 1996.

Pitti, Laure. "Ouvriers algériens à Renault-Billancourt de la guerre d'Algérie aux grèves d'OS des années 1970." PhD diss., Université de Paris VIII, 2002.

Prévos, André. "The Evolution of French Rap Music and Hip Hop Culture in the 1980s and 1990s." *French Review* 69, no. 5 (1996).

Quijano, Anibal, and Michel Ennis. "Coloniality of Power, Eurocentrism, and Latin America." *Nepantla: Views from South* 1, no. 3 (2000): 533-80.

Rahier, Jean Muteba, Percy C. Hintzen, and Felipe Smith, eds. *Global Circuits of Blackness: Interrogating the African Diaspora*. Urbana: University of Illinois Press, 2010.

Regester, Charlene. "Stepin Fetchit: The Man, the Image, and the African American Press." *Film History* 6, no. 4 (1994).

Rodriguez-Ruivo, Jorge. *Portugais et population d'origine portugaise en France*. Paris: L'Harmattan, 2001.

Rose, Phyllis. *Jazz Cleopatra: Josephine Baker in Her Time*. New York: Doubleday, 1989.

Ross, Kristin. *Fast Cars, Clean Bodies: Decolonization and the Reordering of French Culture*. Cambridge, MA: MIT Press, 1999.

———. *May 68 and Its Afterlives*. Chicago: University of Chicago Press, 2002.

———. "Starting Afresh: Hygiene and Modernization in Postwar France." *October* 67 (Winter 1994).

Rouquie, Genevieve. "Y ça va ou." Mémoire promotion Infac. Paris: BUMIDOM, 1980.

Salvador, Henri. *Attention ma vie*. Paris: Editions Jean-Claude Lattès, 1994.

Samuel, Michel. *Le prolétariat africain noir en France*. Paris: François Maspéro, 1978.

Sander, Reinhard, Samba Gadjigo, Ralph Faulkingham, and Thomas Cassirer, eds. *Ousmane Sembène: Dialogues with Critics and Writers*. Amherst: University of Massachusetts Press, 1993.

Sartre, Jean-Paul. *Colonialism and Neo-Colonialism*. New York: Routledge, 2001.

Sauvage, Monique, and Jean-Noel Jeanneney. *Télévision, nouvelle mémoire: Les magazines de grands reportages, 1959-1968*. Paris: Editions du Seuil, 1982.

Schain, Martin. "Immigration and Trade Unions in France: A Problem and an Opportunity." In *A Century of Organized Labor in France: A Union Movement for the Twenty-First Century?*, edited by Erick Chapman, Mark Kesselman, and Martin Schain. New York: St. Martin's Press, 1998.

Schmidt, Elizabeth. "Top Down or Bottom Up? Nationalist Mobilization Reconsidered, with Special Reference to Guinea (French West Africa)." *American Historical Review* 110, no. 4 (2005).

Schneider, William. *Quality and Quantity: The Quest for Biological Regeneration in Twentieth-Century France*. Cambridge: Cambridge University Press, 1990.

Scott, Joan Wallach. *The Politics of the Veil*. Princeton, NJ: Princeton University Press, 2007.

Sembène, Ousmane. *Black Docker*. London: Heinemann Educational, 1987.

Sen, Amartya. *Development as Freedom*. Oxford: Oxford University Press, 1999.

Senghor, Léopold. *Liberté, negritude et humanisme*. Paris: Seuil, 1964.

Sharpley-Whiting, Tracy Denean. *Black Venus: Sexualized Savages, Primal Fears, and Primitive Narratives in French*. Durham, NC: Duke University Press, 1999.

———. *Negritude Women*. Minneapolis: University of Minnesota Press, 2002.

Sheppard, Todd. *The Invention of Decolonization: The Algerian War and the Remaking of France*. Ithaca, NY: Cornell University Press, 2006.

Sherman, Daniel. *French Primitivism at the Ends of Empire*. Chicago: University of Chicago Press, 2011.

Shields, James. *The Extreme Right in France: From Pétain to Le Pen*. London: Routledge 2007.

Siedman, Michael. *The Imaginary Revolution: Parisian Students and Workers in 1968*. Oxford: Berghahn Books, 2004.

Smeralda-Amon, Juliette. *La racisation des relations intergroupes ou la problématique de la couleur: Le cas de la Martinique*. Paris: L'Harmattan, 2002.

Sot, Michel. *Etudiants africains en France, 1951-2001*. Paris: Karthala, 2002.

Stasiulis, Daiva. *Negotiating Citizenship: Migrant Women in Canada and the Global System.* New York: Palgrave Macmillan, 2003.

Steady, Filomina. *The Black Woman Cross-Culturally.* Cambridge, MA: Schenkman, 1981.

Stoler, Ann. *Carnal Knowledge and Imperial Power: Race and the Intimate in Colonial Rule.* Berkeley: University of California Press, 2002.

Stovall, Tyler. "The Color Line behind the Line: Racial Violence in France during the Great War." *American Historical Review* 103, no. 3 (1998).

———. "National Identity and Shifting Imperial Frontiers: Whiteness and the Exclusion of Colonial Labor after World War One." *Representation* 84 (Autumn 2003).

———. *Paris Noir: African Americans in the City of Light.* Boston: Houghton Mifflin, 1996.

Stovall, Tyler, and Sue Peabody, eds. *The Color of Liberty: Histories of Race in France.* Durham, NC: Duke University Press, 2003.

Sweeney, Carole. *From Fetish to Subject: Race, Modernism, and Primitivism, 1919-1935.* New York: Greenwood Publishing, 2004.

Taguieff, Pierre André. *La force du préjugé: Essai sur le racisme et ses doubles.* Paris: La Découverte, 1988.

Terborg-Penn, Rosalyn, and Andrea Benton Rushing, eds. *Women in Africa and the African Diaspora: A Reader.* Cambridge, MA: Harvard University Press, 1996.

Tester, Keith, ed. *The Flâneur.* New York: Routledge, 1994.

Thomas, Bonnie. "Identity at the Crossroads: An Exploration of French Caribbean Gender Identity." *Caribbean Studies* 32, no. 2 (2004).

Thomas, Dominic. *Africa and France: Postcolonial Cultures, Migration, and Racism.* Bloomington: University of Indiana Press, 2013.

Todorov, Tzvetan. *On Human Diversity: Nationalism, Racism, and Exoticism in French Thought.* Cambridge, MA: Harvard University Press, 1993.

Touraine, Alain. *The May Movement: Revolt and Reform.* New York: Irvington Publishers, 1979.

———. *Le mouvement de mai ou le communisme utopique.* Paris: Editions du Seuil, 1968.

Traoré, Sékou. *Les intellectuels africains face au marxisme.* Paris: L'Harmattan, 1983.

———. *La Fédération des Étudiants d'Afrique Noire en France: (F.E.A.N.F.).* Paris: L'Harmattan, 1985.

Tshimanga, Charles, Didier Gondola, and Peter Bloom, eds. *Frenchness and the African Diaspora: Identity and Uprising in Contemporary France.* Bloomington: Indiana University Press, 2009.

Union Générale des Travailleurs Sénégalais en France. *Le livre des travailleurs africains en France.* Paris: Editions François Maspéro, 1970.

Valère Loza, Julien. *Les étudiants martiniquais en France: Histoire de leur organisation et de leurs luttes.* Martinique: Editions 2M, 2003.

Virgili, Fabrice. *Shorn Women: Gender and Punishment in Liberation France.* New York: Berg Publishers, 2002.

Weil, Patrick. *La France et ses étrangers: L'aventure d'une politique de l'immigration, 1938-1991.* Paris: Calmann-Lévy, 1991.

———. "Histoire et mémoire des discriminations en matière de nationalité française Vingtième Siècle." *Revue d'histoire* 84 (October-December, 2004): 5-22.

White, Edmund. *The Flâneur: A Stroll through the Paradoxes of Paris*. New York: Bloomsbury, 2001.

White, Owen. *Children of the French Empire: Miscegenation and Colonial Society in French West Africa, 1895-1960*. New York: Oxford University Press, 2000.

Wilder, Gary. "Untimely Vision: Aimé Césaire, Decolonization, Utopia." *Public Culture* 21, no. 1 (2009).

Wright, Gordon. *France in Modern Times*. Palo Alto, CA: Stanford University Press, 1995.

Zimra, Clarisse. "Rethinking the Calabash: Writing and History in the Francophone Narrative." In *Out of the Kumbla: Caribbean Women in Literature*, edited by Carole Boyce Davies and Elaine Fido. Totowa, NJ: Africa World Press, 1990.

Index

A

African migrants: Caribbean migrants and, 160–61; causes of migration, 22, 23, 24; French discrimination and, 25, 26; transnational migration, 25, 42, 43, 45, 59, 68, 69, 70, 122, 123, 145. *See also* class differences

African students: activism of, 7, 130–34; Association Générale des Etudiants Africains de Paris and Etudiants, 15; Federation of Students from Black Africa in France (FEANF), 16–19, 130, 132–34; foyer politics and, 14, 15; Rassemblement Démocratique Africain (RDA), 15, 16, 19

African workers, 58–63

Agence Nationale pour l'Insertion et la Promotion des Travailleurs d'Outre-Mer, 177

Alizé, 85

Amicale Générale des Travailleurs Antillais et Guyanais (AGTAG), 137, 138, 149, 152

Ansel, Jacqueline, xviii–xix

anti-Semitism, 28, 167, 168, 170

Asante, Molefi, 160

Association Générale des Etudiants Guadeloupéens (AGEG), 9, 10, 138, 139

Association of Martinican Students (AMS), 9, 10

Association pour la Formation Professionelle des Adultes (AFPA), 107

Association pour la Formation Technique de Base des Africains et Malgaches Résidant en France (AFTAM), 36–39, 48

B

Baker, Josephine, 93, 94

Banine, 57, 58

banlieues: black French youth in, 166, 171; demographics of, 168; poverty and, 172; racism and, 178, 179

békés, 81, 86, 113

Benna, Zyed, 171

black French, 159–60

Brocard, Henri, 30

Bureau pour le Développement des Migrations Intéressant les Départements d'Outre-Mer (BUMIDOM), ix, xviii, 79; helping migrants, 89, 106, 107, 149; and protests, 150–57, 177, 179; and a school for Caribbean women, 80, 82, 84, 85

C

Camara, Gamba, 66, 69

Caribbean men: decolonization and, xix, xx;

case studies of, 109–12, 115; school at Simandres and, 107–8
Caribbean nationalists: history of, 86, 87; political movements in France and, 135–39; representation of women, 87–90
Caribbean political philosophy, 112–14
Caribbean student organizations: AGEG, 9; Association des Etudiants de la Martinique, 9, 10; Comité d'Action des Travailleurs et Etudiants des Territoires sous Domination Coloniale Française, 150
Caribbean women: challenges in the labor market of, 84, 85; decolonization and, xix; fille de salle and, 82, 83, 84, 153; French representation of, 75, 77–79, 90, 92; job placement of, 79, 80, 81; school at Crouy-sur-Ourcq and, 81–84
Césaire, Aimé: Caribbean students and, 12; disillusioned conformism and, 113; First Congress of Black Writers in Paris in 1956 and, 5; influence of, xxi, 1; Maryse Condé and, 9; and patriarchy, 155; in 1960s Paris, 153, 154; role in *Présence Africaine*, 3, 4
class differences: African migrants and, 46–49; Caribbean migrants and, 8–10, 149–51
colonialism: the French and, xxi, 12, 21–23, 42, 43; Grosfoguel's definition of, xvi
Comité d'Action Sociale en Faveur des Originaires des Départements d'Outre-Mer en Métropole (CASODOM), 126–28, 129
community organizations: characteristics of African, 126; French trade unions and, 125; UGTSF and, 129; influence of CASODOM on, 127, 128
Condé, Maryse: on the Caribbean community, 144; experience as a student, 6, 9, 51; on race relations in France, 178, 179
Conseil Représentatif des Associations Noirs (CRAN): goals, 172, 173; negritude and, 174; new black political activism and, 175, 179; and secularism, 171
Coryell, Schofield, 17–18
Cosney, Marie-Joseph, 136

D

Dacosta (African migrant), 43, 49–53
Damas, Léon, xxi, 1, 5, 114, 161, 174

Dancenis, 127, 154, 177
Davidson, Nicol, 6, 7
Debré, Michel, 22
decolonization: conceptual framework of, xvi, xvii, xviii. *See also* African workers; Caribbean men; Caribbean women
de Gaulle, Charles, 77, 113, 147, 168
Delgrès Day, 10, 11, 12
Désir, Harlem, 170
Desvarieux, Jacob, 164
Dia, Oumar, xiii, xvii
Dieng, Amady Aly, 16
Diop, Alioune: black internationalism and, 2, 3, 7; First International Congress of Black Writers and Artists and, 5, 6; *Présence Africaine* and, 2–5, 13, 14, 19
Diop, Christiane, 6, 43, 46, 47, 48, 49
Diop, Idrissa, 164
Direction Centrale des Renseignements Généraux (DCRG), 72
disillusioned conformists, 113, 114, 116, 144, 146
documentaries: French, 41, 42; *Ibrahima*, 55; *Jeunes Africains à Paris*, 47; *L'Afrique des banlieues*, 45, 46, 47; *Ouvriers noirs de Paris*, 43, 44, 45, 54, 56
Dubois, W. E. B., 46, 98

E

Entre les Murs, 169–70
évolués, 22, 38, 42, 46, 53

F

Fanon, Frantz: on African behavior, 161; on colonial societies, xxi, 87; on colonization language, 54, 55; on domestic violence, 90; influence of, xii, 86, 138; intellectual production on, 1, 13; political goals of, 73; participation in the Front Antillo-Guyanais, 137; unawareness of patriarchy, 155
far right politics: Le Pen and, 168–70; *poujadisme*, 167; Sarkozy on racial minorities, 169, 170, 171
femme matador, 90–91
Foucault, Michel, xx–xxi
foyers Africains, 64, 65, 66, 67–73
Frank (Caribbean worker), 108, 109, 112, 116
Franklin, Albert, 14

French primitivism, 45
French trade unions: African migrants and, 119–24; Caribbean migrants and, 124–25
Front Antillo-Guyanais, 87, 136, 137, 142, 143, 152

G
Gissoko (African worker), 46
Glissant, Edouard, 136, 137, 142–44, 160
grand enfants, 14, 84, 105
Groupe d'Organization Nationale pour la Guadeloupe (GONG), 87, 138, 149
Grosfoguel, Ramon, xvi–xvii
Guacide (Caribbean worker), 115

I
indigènes, 22, 42, 43, 46, 53, 57, 64, 66, 180

J
James, Kery, 166
Jean (retired Caribbean officer), 108, 112, 114, 116
Joachim, Paulin, 46, 47, 49, 90
job flight, 63
Joseph (Caribbean health-care provider), 108, 110, 112, 114, 116
Jourdan, M., 21, 30, 32

K
Kassav', 162, 164, 175
Khlidou (African delegate), 120–21

L
Lafon (African migrant), 48
Larouchez, Roland, 88–89
Le Pen, Jean Marie, 159, 168–70
Lépine (doctor), 29, 30
Le Secours Catholique, 39, 48
L'Etudiant d'Afrique Noire, 16, 18, 130
Lozès, Patrick, 171–74, 176
Lumumba, Patrice, 18

M
Manville, Marcel, 87, 136, 137, 177
Martin, Janine, 153, 154
May '68, events of: African experiences of, 144–47; Caribbean experiences of, 147–55; national memory of, 141–42

métissage, 47
Michalon, Georges Lassare, xix, xx, 125, 151, 153, 154, 177
mizik tradisionel, 161–62
Mona, Eugène, 161–62, 175
Moreland, Mantan, 98, 99

N
N'Diaye, William, 59, 61, 71, 72, 91, 129, 146
N'Dongo, Sally, 122
negritude, 12, 161, 174, 176
neocolonialism, 19, 130, 131, 147, 175
Niger, Paul, 87, 136

O
Office National d'Immigration, 23, 24, 25, 26
Organisation de la Jeunesse Anticolonialiste de la Martinique (OJAM), 86–87

P
Pan-Africanism: African students and, 15–18; black-French sociopolitical activism and, 160; Caribbean students and, 11; CRAN and, 171, 173, 174, 179; Front Antillo-Guyanais and, 136–37; *Présence Africaine* and, 4, 5; rap music and, 175; UGTSF and, 129
petit nègre, 52, 53, 54, 55, 180
Pieds-Noirs, 65, 80, 120
Pierre (retired Caribbean soldier), 108, 110–11, 112, 113, 116
postcolonial civilizing missions, 23, 39; NGOs and, 36–38; the press and, 33–36
pragmatic conformists, 113–14, 148
public health officials, 27–32

R
racial eugenics, 28, 29, 31, 32
rap music, 166–67
Renault, ix, 59, 60, 61
Robin (director of public health in France), 30, 32

S
Sal, Lamine, 163–64
Salvador, Henri, 93–98, 101–4, 105, 108, 114, 115
Sartre, Jean-Paul, xxi
schœlcherisme, 113
Sembène, Ousmane: *Black Girl*, 49; on

Marseille, 23, 24; on transnational politics, 119, 120

Senghor, Léopold, xxi, 1, 5, 8, 174; accessibility of, writings, 161; African organizations in Paris and, 134

St. Luce, Yvette, 127

Super Combo, 115

T

Tamar, Ralph, 164–66

transnational politics: African students and, 12, 16, 118, 129, 131, 132; Caribbean students and, 118, 138, 152

Traoré, Bouna, 171

Trente Glorieuses, xvi, 24, 115, 121, 125

U

Union des Travailleurs Mauritaniens en France, 126, 127, 134, 178

Union Générale des Travailleurs Sénégalais en France (UGTSF), 122, 126, 128, 129, 133, 134, 178

W

Wright, Richard, 3, 4, 5

Z

zouk music, 161–63